Single Infertile Female

Leah Campbell

Adventures in Love, Life, and Infertility…

Disclaimer: I am not a doctor. This is my personal story, based on my personal experiences. The opinions expressed and medical decisions made are mine and mine alone. You should always consult with a medical practitioner you trust when it comes to making your own medical decisions.

Single Infertile Female

Copyright © 2013 by Leah Campbell

All rights reserved. This book or any portion thereof may not be reproduced or used in any manner whatsoever without the express written permission of the publisher, except for the use of brief quotations in a book review.

ISBN-13: 978-1483911335
ISBN-10: 1483911330

Printed in the United States of America

First Printing, 2013

Cover design ©Sarah Hansen of Okay Creations
Photography ©Robin Haws of Studio Eleven Photography, Skidmore, TX

singleinfertilefemale.com

Acknowledgements

There are only two things I have ever really wanted to be in life – an author and a mother. I have my friend Jenner to thank for pushing me to pursue that first dream. While in the midst of yet another quarter life crisis, she was the one who asked me why it was I had been so afraid of taking this leap. When I told her I wasn't sure I had a story worth telling, she called me crazy and demanded I write this one.

This book would not have come to be without her. And now that I know what I am actually capable of, I can finally see this as my future.

A dream that before now, I had always assumed would remain just that – a dream.

In my head I have already written the next five books, and I know who each of those books should be dedicated to. But waiting to give those people "thanks", assumes there will for sure be a next book. Without yet knowing where this one will go, it feels safer to acknowledge as many people as I can now. Just in case.

So thank you to my grandmother, for always being my biggest supporter in everything I do.

To my dad, for, well… being my dad. And for taking over the role of mother, cheerleader, mentor, and friend along the way as well. He is hands down the most incredible man I know, and the person I look to every time I want to become a better version of myself.

To Justin, my best friend for as long as I can remember. The boy who I cut out of this book, if only because telling our story would have made it a tome too large to carry. I would not be the same person without you, and I am thankful each and every day for your presence in my life. A man who gets me, loves me, and somehow always knows how to make me smile.

To Lindsay and Stephanie, for standing by my side and being the best surrogate partners a girl could hope for. Women who held my hand and let me cry, even when they may not have always been able to understand.

And to Lindsey and Dawn, for coming along and showing me that I was not alone. For being the amazing friends I would have wanted in my life, even without this connection we share.

To Dr. Cook, of Vital Health Institute in San Jose, California, for literally giving me my life back.

And to Josie – my love, my heart, my everything. The answer to that second dream, who came along just when I had stopped allowing myself to hope she ever would. Every tear shed along the way was worth it, and every heartache endured one I would experience again – because every step along the way has brought me to you, and there is no place else in this world I would rather be.

Part 1: The Beginning

(Or: Settling Down and Spiraling Out)

Part 2: The Infertility Chronicles

(Or: Adventures in Baby Making)

Part 3: Rebounding

(Or: About a Boy)

Part 1: The Beginning

(Or: Settling Down and Spiraling Out)

"Hard is trying to rebuild yourself, piece by piece, with no instruction book, and no clue as to where all the important bits are supposed to go." – Nick Hornby, *A Long Way Down*

Chapter 1

I have always been a wanderer; a restless girl looking for the next great adventure or opportunity to start over. I suppose that is to be expected based solely upon the chaotic and broken environment in which I was raised. My childhood was a modern tale of abandonment and loss, with my mother out of the picture and my father doing the best he could. We each have our stories to tell, pasts that shaped the person we have now become. My past taught me to embrace my independence and protect my heart at all costs. I discovered early on that when all else fails, running away continues to be a viable option.

I did not look at it as running, of course. I simply learned that I grew bored when life became stagnant. A piece of my heart constantly craved new challenges and opportunities to prove myself worthy. That was how I found myself, one early June morning, packing the few belongings that had survived a moving sale into the back of my CR-V. I was saying goodbye to roommates—who over the years had become family—and I was heading north. To Alaska. By myself.

At 25 years old, I had just graduated college with a degree in psychology; a choice of study that reflected my constant need to understand myself and those around me. It was the fourth major

I had declared, at the third school I had enrolled in. I graduated with enough credits to have a few degrees, had they all only followed a similar path of study. This was the restlessness with which I lived my life.

I had been living in San Diego for three years, working at a popular bar right by the water. Most of my nights were spent either serving drinks or downing them myself. I rode my beach cruiser everywhere, spent days with my toes in the sand, and was always caught up in the breathlessness of falling for whatever man had most recently caught my eye. None of them ever lasted long, because in an effort to protect my heart and the independence I so fiercely valued, I never allowed any of them to get too close. Still, I had built a good life for myself, brick by brick. The list of things I had to complain about was small.

I was constantly surrounded by friends, men and women aged 20 to 40 all living the same life I was. Drinking, partying, surfing, piling roommates into homes they otherwise could not afford, and trading partners like children playing games. We were all avoiding growing up, living in this college bubble we had created for ourselves. Pacific Beach California was the place Peter Pan dreams were made of.

It was as I was flipping through my university's newspaper one day, that I came across an ad for egg donors. I knew a friend who had done this, and I had always been intrigued by the idea. Low on cash (as most college students are), I called the number listed. I went on to donate my eggs to two different families during my last year of school. It was an opportunity to make extra money, but it was also a chance to help women who had come up against circumstances that were completely out of their control in the pursuit of motherhood. I could not relate to their plight, but my heart went out to them.

That was the start of my yearning for more out of life. The partying, beach going, and casual dating – it had all been fun, but helping women so ready to build their families made me begin to wonder when I would be ready to build my own. So when a friend from college, now living in Alaska, got knocked up by a guy she had only been dating for a few months; I was already primed to make a leap.

It was just that if you had told me my leap would be so far and so north, I probably would not have believed you at the time. Growing up in Arizona and now living in Southern California, my exposure to snow had been limited. I was a girl who reached for a sweater any time the temperature dipped below 70. I could not fathom why anyone would ever *choose* to live in an icy climate.

But when my friend's son was born in January, I immediately got on a flight. Despite how unsure I was of the cold, I was determined to be there to meet her little boy. I rolled off that plane wrapped in so many layers that those around me had likely started to contemplate whether or not I would suffocate beneath the weight of wool.

And then something unexpected happened. Over the next 10 days, I surprised myself. I slowly removed those layers, acclimating to the cold and almost even beginning to enjoy it. I had never lived anywhere with seasons. Seeing the trees and mountains encapsulated by snow gave me a glimpse into a life so much more quaint and picturesque than my own. A life I had started to believe I might want.

When I came back for another visit the following summer, I was hooked. I had fallen in love with Alaska. Not just with the scenery, but also with the way of life. The quiet pace that made my time in San Diego now seem frenzied and uncomfortable. Most of all, it was seeing my friend with her baby. She was building a family that was so different from anything I had ever known. I suddenly realized that *this* was what my life had been missing.

I had always wanted kids and had always known I was meant to be a mother. But I had waited. I had been smart. My own childhood had left me with plenty of damage I knew I needed to work through. So over the years, that was exactly what I did. I worked on myself. I healed. I traveled. I grew. My time spent living in California had transformed me. I built my own life, separate from the hurts of my past. I let go of the anger and self-destructive behavior of my youth. I figured out who I was and what it was I wanted, all while diligently taking my birth control like the responsible young lady I was. I was waiting for the right time, the right place, and the right man. But I was sure that one day, my life as a mommy would bring me more joy than anything else could ever promise to.

I was also sure I was never going to find that life in San Diego. I had dated enough to have seen a theme. The men there were all fun to have around, but most weren't the type I wanted to entertain for long. Mentioning babies in that Peter Pan town typically resulted in a stampede out the nearest exit.

It seemed different in Alaska though. Th*e people* seemed different. It was the kind of place I could see myself building a family; the last stop on a journey to whatever was meant to come next. A journey that started that June morning, as I headed north out of San Diego.

Ready for my life to begin.

Chapter 2

Anxious to get to my new home, I drove long past the point of exhaustion and made the trip in just over four days. I slept in my car and survived on trail mix, apples, and five-hour energy shots. It was a miracle when I made it in one piece.

I would never forget the days I spent on the road headed for Alaska though. I saw bison and bears and scenery so beautiful I knew that no pictures could ever do it justice. I stopped at middle-of-nowhere gas stations that sold guns and knives in the display cases. I contemplated seemingly empty hotels that directed customers to enter rooms with no locks and pay in the morning. I cursed myself over the two days my phone was out of service, thinking for the first time that perhaps my dad had been right; perhaps making this trip on my own *had not* been the safest idea ever. But when I finally neared Anchorage, I was filled with a sense of accomplishment. I had driven to Alaska, by myself, in four days.

It took two months before I found work. I had enough saved up that I was able to be picky and wait for the right opportunity. Never before had I held down a "grown-up" job, but I knew that was what I wanted now. No more nights, weekends, or holidays spent dealing with drunks and surviving off tips. I was ready for a 9-to-5 and all the boring implications it would hold. After all, I had moved here to settle down—because somewhere along the way, settling down had become the next great adventure.

When I was finally offered the perfect position, I knew I had been right to take my time. It was a job with a big corporation where I would be wearing slacks and heels every day; a job with amazing benefits and pay that surpassed anything I had ever earned before. I was pretty sure I had just lucked myself into a future as a career woman, and I marveled at how the pieces of the puzzle were falling into place. I had no idea that the same day I landed the perfect job, would also be the day I met the first man I would ever really love.

I spied Michael at a BBQ I had reluctantly attended with the few people I now knew in town. While I appreciated the invite and opportunity to make new friends, I was also tired and eager to cross a few items off my to-do list before the start of my new career. Knowing I did not plan on staying long, I had not bothered with makeup and had barely managed to throw my hair under a baseball cap before leaving. As soon as he appeared though, I stopped paying attention to the time. He had dark hair, a trimmed beard and captivating green eyes. I was drawn to him immediately, somehow instantly knowing that he was meant to be *something* to me.

There was a little boy running around the yard with friends, and the resemblance between the two of them was uncanny. Rather than being scared about the fact that he clearly had children, I was intrigued. I had never considered dating a man with kids before, but it signified to me that he was at the place in his life I *wanted* to be. It did not take much asking around to find out that he was divorced and had been for a while. He was single and I was interested.

That night, I focused on catching his eye, only to fail miserably at any attempt I made to get him to look my way. At first it seemed as though he was sure I was looking at someone else (anyone else), convinced it could not possibly be him I was fixated upon. I later learned that there was an almost 9-year age difference between the two of us. He had been getting married and having children when I had just been starting high school. It never occurred to him that my glances were meant to gain his attention.

I could not deny that initial physical attraction though, and his shy smile only worked to captivate me more. So I continued looking his way until it seemed that he finally got it. But just as he was initiating a conversation, the friends I had arrived with decided they were ready to leave. I caught his eye once more on my way out and smiled, sure that even if it was months before our paths crossed again, there was going to be something between us.

Thankfully, I did not have to wait months. Three days later he called, even though we had barely spoken 10 words to each other at that BBQ and he had never asked for my number. I quickly learned that one of the benefits (and drawbacks) of living in Anchorage was that everyone knew everyone. He had been able to track down my information through the few degrees of separation that stood between us. Now that he had me on the phone, he made small talk for all of 60 seconds before saying, "Well, I just thought after meeting you the other night that it would be nice to get to know you more. So now you have my number too. The ball is in your court. If you're ever interested in getting together sometime, give me a call."

He quickly hung up. I sat there, incredulous. I had been approached, hit on, and picked up by many men in my life. None had *ever* so promptly dropped the ball into my lap this way. I honestly was not sure what to do with it. It took me three days before I called him back. Three days of contemplating before I convinced myself it was worth the effort. And when he answered the phone, the first words out of his mouth were, "It's a good thing you called. I was about to give up on you." All I could do was laugh. I knew even then that I had never dated anyone like him before.

From that point on, our relationship catapulted forward. We spoke every day, getting to know each other with an ease I had never otherwise experienced. For our first date, we met at the state fair with a larger group of mutual friends. It was already dark when we attempted to find each other in the crowd. The fireworks were about to begin. We were on the phone, each trying to describe to the other where we were exactly. I was convinced there were too many people to maneuver through and that this was a hopeless endeavor, but then he told me to turn around. I did so slowly, not sure exactly where I was supposed to be looking. And then I saw him, about 10 feet away, with the phone still to his ear. He smiled and hung up, so I did too. The sight of him forced my heart to lodge up into my throat. The wave of butterflies hit me with such ferocity that I was barely able to walk his way. I could not remember having ever felt so strongly for anyone I had just met.

We continued talking every day, as I learned about his marriage and the scars he still carried with him from its demise. He also spoke dotingly about his children, Morgan and Tyler, who held unquestionably large pieces of his heart. I discovered what a devoted father he was, and what a dorky man he could be. I was falling for that dorky man, and without my even realizing it was what I so often called him, "dork" stuck and become our pet name for each other.

We went on three dates where he did not kiss me once. He paid every time, picked me up and dropped me off, and played the role of a perfect gentleman; never making a move. I knew he was interested, but I had never known a man to take things so slow with me. In San Diego I had considered myself lucky if I could get through most first dates without having to fight to keep my pants on. With Michael, though, I didn't know if he was ever going to attempt to cross those lines. It was infuriating and mesmerizing all at once.

And then one day, only a few weeks in, he said he wanted me to meet his kids. We still had not yet kissed. It seemed insane to get them involved so soon. But somehow, I knew that this was real. And because of that, I agreed.

The four of us went out for ice cream, and any concerns I harbored quickly faded away. Morgan and I connected immediately, bonded by the fact that she was so similar to how I had been at her age. Tough and funny. Sarcastic and fearless. She was me, just 13 years younger. Tyler I could not read as well at first. He was polite, but quiet. Shy to the point where I could not tell if he liked me or just wanted me gone. It was not until we were saying goodbye at the end of the night that he said, "Nice to meet you. Dad will call you tonight. Like he does *every* night." He said it with his sister's sarcasm, and I could hear him rolling his eyes. But he was flashing me a smile, filled with pride over pulling me in on their teasing. Already, I knew I loved these kids.

So when Michael asked if I would join them at their lake cabin that weekend for Labor Day, I could not resist. Even though we still had not kissed, let alone spent the night together. And even though it meant three days with just him and his children at a location far enough away for escape to be difficult if things went south. I said "yes"—without even thinking twice.

♌

We had only just arrived at the cabin when he finally kissed me for the first time. I was running around with the kids while he unpacked the truck. Morgan wanted me to jump in the lake with her and Tyler wanted me to race on jet skis with him. They were both vying for my attention, and I was soaking it up. I went inside to throw on a swimsuit while they waited for me by the dock, and on my way back out stopped in the kitchen where Michael was unloading groceries. I placed my hand on his back and asked if he was sure he did not need my help with anything. He seemed ecstatic with how quickly his kids were taking to me though, and urged me back outside with them.

As I turned to make my way to the door, he grabbed my hand unexpectedly. I spun around to face him, caught off guard when he hooked an arm around my waist and drew me in, placing his lips upon mine. I had not seen it coming, and my knees almost gave out beneath me as butterflies erupted from within. It was a soft kiss, short but so sweet, and when he pulled away we were both smiling. "I've been wanting to do that," he said. "I've been wondering when you would," I replied breathlessly. It took everything inside of me to extricate myself from his embrace and return to Morgan and Tyler—still patiently waiting for me outside.

We kept the rest of the weekend PG, playing with the kids during the day, taking trips around the lake on the boat and building campfires as the sun began to set. Hiking and exploring and enjoying Alaska for all it was worth; pulling out board games only when the rain began to fall. But at night, once Morgan and Tyler were tucked in, Michael and I stayed up talking and drinking wine, getting to know each other and making out like teenagers. With the kids sleeping in the other room, we never crossed any lines. But I was falling, hard and fast. This was it. This was the life I had been waiting for.

That weekend away solidified us as a couple. It was the first time I realized I was falling in love. When we returned home from that trip, we fell seamlessly into each other's routines, rarely spending a day apart. I began going to Tyler's hockey games and spending nights helping Morgan with her hair. He started spending time with my friends and taking me on dates where he insisted on holding my hand. We spent his birthday holed up at his cabin—just the two of us—finding very few reasons to put on our clothes

Everything felt right, and before long we were talking about forever. He was mentioning marriage. I was bringing up babies. Neither of us was suggesting making those leaps any time soon, but we both knew they were in our future, that we were the real deal and that this relationship was for keeps. Never before had I felt so safe with anyone. For the first time in my adult life, I trusted another person with my whole heart. I could see it every time he looked at me ... he was not going anywhere, he would never hurt me, and he would do anything to make me happy.

And we *were* happy. We were in love, quickly becoming a family. Everything seemed perfect.

Until nothing was at all.

Chapter 3

We had only been together for a few months when I realized that my period was late. I was not on birth control when we met. There had been so many drugs involved in my egg donations less than a year before that I had wanted to give my body a break from the hormones. It was something Michael and I discussed from the start, and we were always careful as a result. As committed as we were to each other, neither of us wanted to be dealing with an unplanned pregnancy. So when my period failed to arrive, I had a hard time hiding the panic.

Initially I tried to convince myself it was nothing to worry about. I had never been regular before, so it was hard to even be sure how late I was exactly. But I finally said something to him after a month had gone by, unable to carry the weight of that burden myself. He handled the news stoically, promising to take care of me whether or not I was carrying his child. I knew this was not what he wanted though. As much as he loved me, this was too soon for both of us.

We got up the next morning together, in silence as I took a pregnancy test. When only one line appeared, we both felt the relief wash over us. He joked he had simply scared my period away with our phenomenally good sex. I laughed, and we fell into bed; resuming what had gotten us into this situation in the first place.

The relief did not last, however. Two weeks later, when I still had not started, I finally made an appointment at a local clinic. I was convinced that despite the results of my home tests, I *had* to be pregnant. It was the only thing that made any sense. When the in-office test came back negative, I assured the doctor that this was not normal and that my period had never disappeared for so long. I attempted to explain to him my gut feeling that if I was not pregnant, then something was wrong. But he did not take me seriously, impatiently reminding me that I had just moved 3000 miles. According to him, the stress from uprooting my life was the real culprit to blame for my missing period.

What I could not get him to understand was that the absence of my period was the *only* thing I was stressed about. Moving had been nothing. It was the kind of change I was built for. I had been through far more stressful situations in the past without ever having had my body go so haywire on me. If I was not pregnant, something was wrong. But I could not allow myself to *believe* that something was wrong. Not when less than a year before, everything had been so perfect. I had donated my eggs and listened to doctor after doctor tell me how impeccably healthy I was. I could not comprehend something now being amiss. So instead I became convinced that I was pregnant and that for some strange reason, the tests just were not detecting it yet.

I began testing myself at home, multiple times a week. I was peeing on sticks even after the stress over my absent period had caused us to stop sleeping together almost entirely. This thing, whatever it was, was creating tension between us. I knew that if I was pregnant he would do the right thing. We loved each other, which meant he would want to get married and start a life together. But I did not want it that way. I did not want us getting married and starting that life simply because we felt we had to. I had seen too many friends make the same mistake and go on to regret it—miserable in marriages they longed to escape. I did not want that for us. I did not want it for me.

I started to notice the things about him I did not like. I began to tell myself they were the things I was not sure I wanted in my future partner. He had plenty of baggage from his divorce, including abandonment issues that rivaled my own. We would fight, and he would immediately ask if I was breaking up with him. Then he would wonder aloud if I should be saying goodbye to the kids, which only ever served to feel like a threat. It was as if he was using them to coerce me into staying, or into letting go of whatever it was I was angry about. He refused to talk to me about the issues at hand though, seeming to fear talking would only lead to the end.

Having no real relationship experience myself, I was no better. I would get frustrated and shut down, giving him the silent treatment for hours on end. Then I would simply pretend that nothing had happened, even though I continued to carry the weight from every fight with me. I had never in my life taken on challenges with someone by my side. I only knew how to face the difficult times by myself. I had worked so hard at becoming "strong"; I had no idea now how to rely on another person. So the more stressed I became about whatever it was that was going on inside of me, the more I pushed him away.

When my period finally returned almost three months late, the pain was so bad it brought me to my knees and forced vomiting I could not control. My cycles had never been pleasant, but this was a different level entirely. I was rendered incapable of functioning for days until it passed, knowing only that I had been right—something was wrong.

As soon as I was lucid enough to return to the land of the living, I made an appointment to see that doctor again. He explained to me (quite condescendingly) that what I had experienced was completely normal for some women. I could not believe that though. The level of pain I had suffered through could not have been normal. I pushed for him to look for something more; an explanation of some kind. I begged him to listen to what I was saying and consider the possibility that perhaps I knew my body well enough to know that something was off. Reluctantly, he agreed to do an ultrasound.

Once I was lying on that table, everything changed in a matter of minutes. He looked at my insides without saying much, before finally asking when my last ultrasound had been. I told him it had been with my previous egg donation, now a year before. He asked if I had ever been told I had cysts. Surprised, I said "no," and explained that everything had been perfect before each of my donations. "Hmmmmm …" he finally replied. "I'm not sure I believe that. I'd like to see those pictures. Your ovaries look like hell."

I was stunned. Not just by his cold bluntness, but also by the ramifications of his words. During each of my egg donations, I had been assured of my fertility and told that when the time was right, conceiving would come naturally. Was he now saying that was no longer the case?

He explained that my ovaries were covered in cysts, but that they were not the same size or consistency he would typically have expected to see. Speaking more to the pictures than to me, he mentioned the possibility of ovarian cancer. As I fought to understand, he said that if it were not for my age and lack of familial history, he would be pushing for surgery right away.

Instead, he felt we should give it a month or two and then look again. In the meantime, he asked me to have the records from both of my egg donations sent to his office.

I was numb; sick to my stomach and unable to shift my focus away from that word.

Cancer.

No longer sure of my future fertility or my life, I was already shutting down as I walked out to my car. Every part of me went into survival mode. I thought of Michael and the kids, suddenly painfully aware of what this would mean to them. I had no idea how to ask him to help me with this; no clue how to lean on him, and no time to figure it out.

I sent a text saying we needed to talk. When he called me that night, I ended our relationship. I did not give him an explanation beyond the simple fact that it was not going to work. And because of his past and the baggage he was already carrying, he did not fight me. It was almost as though he had been waiting all along for me to figure out he was not what I wanted.

The next day I waited until I knew he was at work before going to his place and letting myself in. He and Tyler were leaving for a hockey trip out of state later that week, and days before he had asked me to print up their itinerary and directions to a few locations near their hotel. He was not great on the computer, and I could not bring myself to let them go without that stack of papers to guide them. But I also knew I could not face him. Not if I wanted him to truly believe I was done. And I needed him to believe that, because I was not so sure I could hold strong if he attempted to change my mind.

I left the directions on the kitchen table, and then I consciously walked out of his life. I was cold and calculating about the whole thing, shielding myself from the fallout of what was about to come as best I knew how: by shutting out anyone who stood even a chance of becoming collateral damage.

Chapter 4

I trudged through the next few months like a soldier in battle, never allowing myself to succumb to the fear. Instead, I did exactly as I was told. I put all my trust into a doctor I barely knew, one who had already made it clear he did not have the same faith in me or my ability to assess what was going on with my body. But what else could I do? He was the one with the medical degree. Surely that must have meant he knew better than I did.

He conducted two more ultrasounds, each within a few months of the other. Both showed continued growth, my abdomen becoming so overtaken by cysts that I swore I could feel them from the outside. The pain was increasing. Not just with my periods (which had returned with regularity and were now accompanied by progressively intense agony), but also in my day-to-day life. My lower back was constantly aching, and my stomach often felt too knotted for eating. There were times when I would get up quickly only to feel as though something inside of me was tearing—a sharp stab to my lower pelvic region that frequently elicited unintended vocal reactions on my part.

And yet still this doctor spoke to me as if I did not matter, acting as though the symptoms I was describing were nowhere near as interesting as the pictures he was able to see from my ultrasounds. Month after month he remained uncertain about my condition. He threw the "cancer" word around like it meant nothing, but then just as flippantly would suggest it might still resolve itself if we continued waiting. When I pushed (needing explanations, answers, and relief) he said he could do exploratory surgery, but that he could not make any guarantees he would be able to save my ovaries. He wanted me to agree to the possibility of a hysterectomy prior to the procedure.

I had no confidence that this man was in any way invested in preserving my fertility. He seemed to view me as a burden more than anything else. But it took seven months from when I first saw him for me to grow the courage to seek a second opinion. Never before had I dared to question the expertise of a medical practitioner in charge of my care. Then again, never before had I been truly sick. It took the threat of a hysterectomy for me to determine I needed to see someone else. I knew only that I did not want this man responsible for the state of my insides.

On the recommendation of a friend, I called and made an appointment at another local clinic with a Dr. Olson. As soon as I met her, I knew that I had made the right decision. She was patient and understanding, quick to explain things to me and to pay attention to what I was telling her. When she did an ultrasound of her own she agreed that these were not typical cysts, but she also did not seem to believe it was cancer either. Still, she wanted to move forward with surgery in order to be sure. She expressed particular concern over my right ovary, saying she was worried it might be difficult to save due to how overrun by cysts it had become. But she seemed committed to trying.

Surgery was scheduled for a month out, only we never made it to that point. About a week later, I woke up in excruciating pain. I was throwing up and incapable of moving. My temperature spiked. A friend drove me to the emergency room, where they concluded a cyst had burst. The doctor explained it was fairly common, but when my fever still had not gone down over 24 hours later, she decided that waiting was no longer prudent. I went into surgery only a few days after, terrified.

The entire procedure lasted less than two hours. The first frantic words out of my mouth as I came-to in the recovery room were, "Do I still have my ovaries?" She smiled warmly and assured me she had saved them both, but it was not until the next day that she was able to fully explain to me what had been discovered. It was then that I was diagnosed with endometriosis.

Dr. Olson explained that endometriosis is a disease where the uterine tissue implants itself outside of the uterus. Wherever those implants grow, there is bleeding with every period. While the uterus is designed for that bleeding and shedding away of old tissue, the rest of the body is not. The result is scar tissue, adhesions, and pain. She said that a large number of women deal with endometriosis, all in varying degrees; some with mild cases that only contribute to slightly more difficult periods, and others with more advanced cases that involve the endometrial tissue traveling to organs outside of the reproductive area. She further explained that endometriosis is known to be one of the leading causes of infertility.

I tried to take her words in. I had heard of endometriosis before, but my knowledge of it was limited. No one had ever mentioned it as a possible cause for my problems. I learned later that was because my presentation was not typical. Endometriosis is not something you can usually see on an ultrasound. Laparoscopic surgery is the only way to obtain a true diagnosis. Those cysts I had were actually endometriomas —pockets of this uterine tissue all packed together. They are not totally uncommon, but they are not usually seen as abundant as I had them, either.

The doctor said she had never seen a case as extensive as mine. She had removed one of my tubes during the surgery (it was too scarred down and damaged to be viable) as well as my appendix (endometriosis had eaten away at it). She wanted me to start on birth control right away as a means of treatment, but was convinced I would still be able to have children. She even believed my remaining tube would one day allow me to conceive naturally. Her confidence was all I needed to hear at that point. I did not have cancer, and I had not lost my ability to conceive.

I could still have the future I had always pictured.

Now that the mystery was solved, my attention returned to the aspects of life I had otherwise been distracted from. I missed Michael. I had missed him almost as soon as I left him. But it took feeling secure in my own health again before I was able to admit that to myself; before I was able to admit it to him.

I reached out, asking if we could meet for drinks and talk. Initially he agreed, but at the last minute backed out, saying simply that he was not open to getting bitten twice. I knew his ex-wife had played this game with him, leaving and coming back multiple times before the eventual end. He had allowed it because of the kids, but going through that had made him less likely to forgive me now. Even when I ended things, I had known this. I wanted to believe I could fix everything though, that I could fix us. So I kept trying.

Weeks passed and we were having only one-way conversations; the kind where I called and left messages, never hearing back from him in return. I kept those voicemails brief, without ever fully explaining what I had been through in the previous months. It all felt too personal to divulge in a message. So instead, I apologized over and over again, begging for just an hour of his time. I thought that if I could get him face-to-face, then I could make him understand. It was becoming almost stalker-esque on my part. But I was convinced that if I kept trying, he would eventually see how sorry I was. I trusted in his feelings for me enough to believe that in time, he would give me another chance.

When my calls continued to go unanswered, I decided to show up at his house and force him to talk. I had been so sure that seeing me would do the trick, until I saw his face and realized for the first time how much damage I truly had done. He was kind and polite, inviting me in and hearing what I had to say. But the look in his eyes kept me from revealing all. I could read the hurt all over his face, and suddenly I felt selfish for making excuses. Nothing I had been going through made what I did to him alright. He had loved me, and I had left. Telling my sad story now felt wrong. It felt manipulative. I hung my head in shame, simply apologizing once more and pleading for forgiveness. It was obvious that seeing me shook his resolve slightly, and I could tell by the way he looked at me that those feelings were still there. But he was not giving in to what he felt. Instead, he remained firm on the fact that I had hurt him and that no matter how much he loved me, he could not give me the opportunity to do so again. I felt defeated by the time I left, sure for the first time that there would be no going back.

So when he called a few days later saying he wanted us to take a shot at being friends, it caught me off guard. I was not sure what a friendship between us would look like exactly, but I was willing to take whatever he could give. We began speaking a few times a week, polite conversations about work and the weather at first, but eventually delving into deeper topics. I bought a condo and he was the one I called about renovations. We talked about paint colors and the old fixtures that all needed to be replaced. We *built* a friendship. And a few months later when a mutual friend was married, we went home from the reception together. He was drunk and I was sober, so I told him it was not a good idea when he kissed me and asked that I spend the night. I wanted to fix this, but I did not want him waking in the morning and regretting my presence there. I told him I loved him, and then I got in my car and drove myself home.

We began dating after that. It was not like it had been before though. We did not slide seamlessly into each other's lives, and he made a point of keeping me separate from his children. I understood it, but I ached for the day when we would be able to get back on the track I had derailed us from. I accepted what he was willing to give, all the while yearning for more.

As focused as I was on him, I could not ignore it when the pain in my abdomen returned. It came on slowly at first, but it was not long before I felt it every day. I knew exactly what was going on before I could even get an appointment with Dr. Olson. This was a pain I had only ever experienced with endometriosis. By touching my stomach, I could once more feel the distortion on my right side that I knew was caused by those cysts. I knew.

I did not talk to him about any of this though. He knew the barest of details about what I had been through, but I was still opposed to bringing him in on this part of my life. I did not know how to lean on him; how to ask for his help. I was so invested in making things appear as normal as possible between us, that I did not want to bring this piece into it.

As soon as I was able to get into my doctor, she performed an ultrasound and discovered multiple new cysts. They were larger than seemed possible in such a short period of time. It had been only four months; she could not explain how everything had returned so quickly. Our only option at this point was another surgery. It was scheduled for two months later, the first non-emergency opening she had. And once more I was left waiting and seeing.

Repairing my relationship with Michael had become such a priority of mine that I did not allow myself to worry as I had in the days leading up to the previous surgery. *He* was my main concern now, and a perfect distraction from any of the apprehension I otherwise would have felt. In October we spent his birthday together for the second year in a row. I told him then that I loved him, and that I needed him; that I would do anything to restore our broken relationship to what it once had been, if only he would let me.

He was gearing up to leave for the winter, having landed a job in Seattle for a few months that he could not turn down. We agreed we would not try to figure out the state of our relationship until he returned. Maybe the distance would be a good thing, giving me time to heal and reassess after surgery number two, before turning my focus back to him once more.

Saying goodbye was bittersweet, but I was confident the year ahead held good things for us. With time, he would forgive me completely. We would build the life that had been meant for us all along. Endometriosis would be just a blip on the radar; something I managed like millions of other women. I would be fine.

And so would we.

Chapter 5

I went to see Michael in Seattle just a few weeks after he left. As we ate dinner my first night in town, he gave me a grin and said he was going to call his mother. I knew she had been pulling for the two of us to make this work, and I could practically hear her shrieking with excitement on the other end of the phone as he told her I was there. He smiled too at her reaction, seemingly proud to be sharing this news.

We had an amazing night, cuddled up together in a hotel room as if we had never been apart. The next day we drove around Washington, checking out the town and wasting our time shopping and playing at a go-cart facility. We laughed, held hands, and talked without discomfort or anger. It finally felt like we were finding our way back to "us" again. When it was time to say goodbye, I wrapped my arms around his neck and kissed him first. I whispered in his ear that I loved him, and that he was not allowed to forget that fact. I got on a plane back to Anchorage feeling more confident about where we stood than I had in a long time.

He called to wish me luck the night before surgery. I had shared some of the details with him, while remaining careful to keep from sharing too much. Hearing the worry in his voice though, I began to trust in the fact that I could lean on him. I was elated to see us making these steps toward healing; a happiness that clouded any fear I had over what was to come the following day.

This time I had faith in my doctor. I went in hopeful and with a sense of humor. I had been through this before. I knew what to expect. My anesthesiologist was gorgeous. So when I woke post-surgery to see him standing over me as the catheter was being removed, the first hazy words out of my mouth were, "Oh no! Hot doctor just saw my vagina!" They were words that were far less panicked than those which had bubbled up out of me upon waking from that first surgery. I went home happy and high, with no real reservations about what the results would be.

Michael's mom and sister came to visit me that night. They had flowers and handmade cards from the kids. Still feeling loopy, happy tears sprung quickly to my eyes. I was starting to realize that there was something to be said for allowing people to be there for me. He called that night and I gushed about the visit from his family, thanking him for telling them to come. He laughed at the nonsense I was spouting under the influence of narcotics, but I was happy. I felt safe, in us and in my health.

That all came crashing down the next day, when the doctor called to give me my surgery report. She said that in just a few short months, I had the amount of endometriosis growth and damage she would have expected to see in a patient who had not been doing *anything* for treatment over the course of two to three years. She was no longer hopeful about my future fertility. My left ovary had been completely scarred into my pelvic wall and my right had been severely damaged by cysts. Dr. Olson explained my remaining tube was so scarred that even if I could get pregnant on my own (an occurrence she now gave less than 10 percent odds), the risks of ectopic pregnancy would be astronomical. The disease had also spread to my bladder, my bowel, and all of the surrounding tissues. She had not been able to remove all the endometriosis; there had simply been too much to combat.

She wanted to immediately start me on a drug called Lupron, in an effort to slow the growth. She also suggested I consult with a fertility clinic, saying I should weigh my options before I no longer had any to consider. I was crushed, thoughts racing. The tears were flowing before we ever made it off the phone.

And the first call I made was to the only man I had ever loved.

I was sobbing by the time he answered, the drugs I was on obliterating my inhibitions. I could barely breathe. And I could also barely speak. The tube that had been down my throat the day before had done enough damage on the way out that my voice was no longer my own. Instead, it was a raspy and broken imitation with hardly any volume to give.

During a 15-minute conversation, it seemed likely that all he was able to gather was my repeating over and over again "I … can't … have … babies …" I was a wreck. He had never before known me to be like this. Ever.

He called his mom when we finally hung up; a woman who had endured a hysterectomy at my age. She immediately called to check on me, but there was nothing she could do. Nothing she could say to calm me. I was spiraling out of control under the influence of drugs and grief.

I had always wanted babies and had always known I would be a mom. This was not supposed to happen to me. That was all I kept thinking. This was not how it was supposed to be.

In the days that followed, I did not hear from Michael again. I kept waiting for him to call, expecting he would see the significance in the fact that *he* had been the one I reached out to when my world was falling apart, but he never did. He just disappeared, seemingly incapable of handling whatever this had now become. It was a situation I likely would have been more concerned about, had it not been for this new and far more pressing issue. I could not worry about him now, or why he had suddenly vanished when I needed him the most. I was not going to beg for his comfort. After no more than a week, I became resigned instead to facing this alone.

It was only at my follow-up appointment the following week—with my head now clear of the narcotic high—that I was able to gather the information I needed. The outlook was still bleak. Dr. Olson was worried a hysterectomy was in my near future and that with a case as aggressive as mine, waiting it out would be a mistake. She gave me my first injection of Lupron that day, along with a referral to a fertility clinic in Seattle—the closest option for women facing infertility in Alaska. I had no idea what I was supposed to do next.

I immediately turned to the internet for answers, my plan being only to formulate a plan. I wanted to believe that in knowing my next steps, I would find hope again. I was accosted by blogs filled with stories of "miracle" babies that were all incredibly uplifting, but I could not find a single page dedicated to someone dealing with this on her own. I knew there was a whole different set of challenges to facing infertility as a single woman. If I had been part of a couple, I would already have been looking into doing whatever needed to be done to get pregnant. But being single, the answers were not so clear.

I had wanted children my entire life, but I had also grown up wishing every day for a family that was whole. Could I really bring a baby into this world knowing that he or she would not have a father from day one? Then again, if I did not try, would I spend the rest of my life feeling empty and unfulfilled?

I knew that adoption would always be a possibility, but at least once I wanted the full experience for myself. I wanted to grow large, I wanted to feel that baby kicking inside of me, and I wanted to breastfeed. I had moved to Alaska because I had decided I was ready for this stage of my life. Looking at my friends—who were all in varying stages of pregnancy or already with families of their own—I wanted it more than I had ever wanted anything else. I had just never felt rushed before.

Until now.

Part 2: The Infertility Chronicles

(Or: Adventures in Baby Making)

"Courage is the discovery that you may not win, and trying when you know you can lose." – Tom Krause

Chapter 6

The first time someone casually labels you "infertile," it feels as though they have just sucker punched you across the jaw. I remember that first distinctly. I was at work, taking a break to call Dr. Olson's office about some information I needed for the fertility clinic referral. While I had the nurse on the phone, I asked her a fairly generic question about the process. She paused for a moment before replying, "You know what, dear? I don't know the answer to that. I don't usually work with our infertility patients. Give me a second though and I'll go ask."

By the time she came back on the line, I was huddled under my desk trying desperately to muffle the sound of my own sobs. It was not as if I did not know that I now qualified as infertile. There had been in-depth conversations with my doctor about this, and I obviously understood why I was being referred to fertility clinics in the first place. It was just that this was the first time someone had used that term to refer to me directly. And she had done it in such a nonchalant and conversational manner, as if it was the most normal thing in the world to say. My guard had been down and I had not been prepared for the instantaneous realization that the word "infertile" now defined me—and would for the rest of my life. I could choose what that meant, and I could choose how to react to it, but no matter how stoic I remained or how much information I sought out and retained, there was no changing this fact now. I was infertile. The sheer weight of what that label stood for was crippling.

At what point had this become my life?

♌

I was sure I was drowning that first month. The tidal wave of grief, fear, and disbelief was threatening to pull me under before it even had a chance to fully hit. I could not breathe, could not function, and could not settle myself into the reality of this situation.

It was just too much and it had happened too quickly. I was losing the only thing I ever truly wanted. Even worse, I could not find the words to explain this hurt to the people in my life. I feared they would never understand. Opening up was a concept entirely foreign to the fiercely independent girl I had always been.

Then came the afternoon when I simply topped trying to explain. I was going through the list of options with one of my closest friends, struggling to find an answer I had not yet seen. But before I could finish my train of thought she stopped me and said, "I don't understand what the big deal is. If it were me, I would just plan on adopting. Why are you even worrying about this right now?" As these words came out of her mouth, she sat there rubbing her hands over a swelling pregnant belly. Her first-born—the happiest piece of her life—was running around our feet. Both pregnancies had been conceived essentially by accident.

And with these words, she completely dismissed the part of me that yearned to experience the same miracle she had so easily been granted. She turned this issue that was rocking my world into something so simple, as if she could not comprehend why I was still talking about it.

It was not the fact that she did not understand that hurt me the most. I did not *expect* her to understand, any more than I could fully understand the dilemmas in her life. But it was the lack of compassion and concern for what this meant to my future that truly jolted me. I did not believe for even one second that her reaction would have been so blasé had she been in my shoes, but that did not matter. It did not change the fact that now, in this moment, she seemed to think I was not justified in my hurt and confusion.

I began shutting down after that. I stopped talking about what I was feeling almost entirely, terrified that those around me were convinced I was being a drama queen. I could no longer vocalize the hurt, anguish, and inability to understand or choose. Something inside of me broke.

Seeing this disconnect, my friend Stephanie encouraged me to start a blog. Not talking about it was causing me to retreat further into my own despair, but she knew putting words on paper had always been a positive outlet for me. She thought that if I could just start writing, I might be able to work through this.

I had been reading infertility blogs for over a month, becoming strangely connected to these women baring their souls on the internet. It was difficult for me to wrap my head around the fact that there were real people on the other side of my computer, but I knew that they were the only ones in my life who seemed capable of understanding.

So I started a blog, quickly naming it "Single Infertile Female" with a laugh over how this diagnosis had transformed me into a less-stable version of myself. I was doing this for me, embracing the only way I knew how to work through my feelings on infertility and the choices which had been placed at my feet. I thought that maybe this space on the internet I had claimed as my own would serve as a way for the people in my life to remain updated, saving me from ever having to actually talk about it again.

But I never believed anyone else would be reading. Until one day a few weeks in, when I received my first comment from a stranger. I was not sure how she had found me, but she explained that she had been captivated by my story and was enthralled by words that described feelings she herself had experienced. She said she wanted me to know that she would be rooting for me no matter where this journey led. Suddenly, it seemed like someone understood.

Stephanie had been right. Blogging opened a door for me. And for the very first time, I began to believe that maybe I was not entirely alone in this.

Chapter 7

While I tried desperately to figure out the rest of my life, Dr. Olson prescribed quarterly injections of Lupron. She had warned me of the side effects, but it was only after I was reduced to throwing up in the trash can beneath my desk at work that I began doing my own research.

I learned that Lupron worked by shutting down a woman's estrogen and putting her into medically induced menopause. I already knew that endometriosis was seen as an estrogen-dependent disease, so it made sense that cutting off estrogen could halt the disease from spreading. What I had not been prepared for was what that would mean for the rest of my body. As I read, I learned about the drastic bone density loss attributed to Lupron, and I came across the very clear warnings against taking it for longer than a year. There were myriad other side effects noted online, and sifting through the real-life horror stories that other women had posted, I could not help but become concerned.

The nausea was just the start for me. I had been told it would be at least a week before side effects began, but within 24 hours I experienced my stomach rising to my throat for the first time. I was retching in the trash can before I had a chance to stop it. That was when I knew I was in trouble. As the weeks passed, I learned to breathe through the bouts of nausea. But it was always there, threatening to attack when I least expected it.

Then there were the hot flashes. I left the house every day bundled for brisk winter weather, but it was never long before the heat was rising up the back of my neck. As I tore off layers, I was fully aware of the watchful eyes attempting to assess my mental state. A few minutes would pass and I would suddenly be freezing, drenched to the bone in my own sweat as the temperatures outside lingered near zero degrees.

The night sweats were even worse. My sheets were soaked through nearly every morning. I began to worry that I was destined to be alone, a fear that was only exacerbated by the spotting which started a week after that first shot. With continuous bleeding that never stopped, I was sure I would never be with a man again.

Then there was the exhaustion. I was 26 years old and going to bed at 9 p.m. on weekends. My past of all-nighters and living up my single existence to the fullest had disappeared. I was too tired to be that girl anymore.

But it was my irritability that caught me the most off guard. I was on edge all the time, simply waiting for someone to say the wrong thing so that I could explode. I now regularly had to resist the use of the c-word (yes, *that* c-word), even though it had never before been a common utterance in my vocabulary. Suddenly everyone was a cunt. I began thinking it in daggers towards the people who annoyed me, sure that they could feel it. Gone was the calm and rational adult version of myself, overtaken by a teenage rendering constantly on the verge of detonation. I felt like I had no control over my emotions anymore. I was incapable of rising above, forced into opting instead for counting backwards from ten, thinking naughty words, and reminding myself to breathe daily (if not hourly).

This drug was a bitch. And now, apparently, so was I …

♌

At my first post-op appointment, Dr. Olson gave me a referral to Seattle Reproductive Medicine (SRM). I immediately arranged a phone consultation with them, hoping for answers I had not been able to find myself. When that consultation arrived though, the reproductive endocrinologist (RE) on the other end of the line simply explained what I already knew: my time was running out.

The way she saw it, I had three options:

1.) Embark upon In Vitro Fertilization (IVF) now, as a single woman
2.) Have my eggs harvested and frozen
3.) Do nothing and cross my fingers, hoping for more time

As far as I was concerned, choice number 3 was not even worth acknowledging. I was all for wishful thinking, but I was not going to rely on *hope* while watching my chances of motherhood fade away.

That left IVF or egg freezing. I researched the differences between the two, learning that the practice of egg freezing had not been around for very long, and the procedures involved were far from perfect. While the end costs were the same, the success rate using frozen eggs was much lower than what I could hope for with a fresh embryo IVF transfer.

Knowing this going into the consult, I was leaning toward IVF. Egg freezing was still experimental, and I hated that I would have no idea whether those eggs were viable until I decided to take them out of the deep freeze and use them. By then, if they were not, it would be too late to do anything else. In theory it was a good idea (because I was single and it would buy me time), but it also felt like a huge gamble. At least with IVF, I would know right away.

The downside to IVF, of course, was that I would be doing it on my own. And if I did meet someone who I eventually fell in love with, it would likely be past the point when I could give him a biological child. I knew this, and it was something I was struggling with even before the RE brought it up. But when she did, I suddenly grew defensive. "What if you meet the man you want to marry in 2 years, and all you have is a baby that's not his and a bunch of embryos that aren't his either?" she asked. "You have to think about what he would want."

It hit me like a ton of bricks. What he would want? I did not even know that "he" existed at this point, so how the hell was I supposed to know what "he" would want? This decision already felt like so much pressure to make. Did she really want me to take "him" into consideration as well? What if "he" never showed up, and then I had just wasted all of my opportunities because I was too busy considering what "he" may want? I had to fight the urge to tell this woman that if "he" wanted a say so badly, then maybe "he" should not have been taking "his" sweet ass time showing up in my life. I was fairly sure the Lupron had nothing to do with my irritability this time around.

Throughout the conversation, she continued to push egg freezing, and I continued to grow frustrated. Not because I was entirely against it (I still had not made up my mind), but because I felt like my status as a single woman was influencing the way she was informing me of my choices. I did not want to be made to feel like I did not deserve the same options a married woman would have been given, simply because I had not run off and gotten myself hitched directly out of college.

I knew that if happily ever after happened for me, it would happen in the right way and for the right reasons—regardless of whether or not I was a single mother. But right now I just wanted to be given the facts and then allowed to make my own choices based on what I knew I could handle. This woman did not know me. She had no idea what I was capable of when I wanted something, and she did not understand what a leap it was to assume that I would one day have that elusive "he" she was referring to. Or what a risk it would be for me to wait for "him" now. I thought I had found my "he" once already, but I hadn't heard from "him" since the night I had reached out needing "him." Was I really supposed to base my decisions now on what the next "he" to come along might want?

When we got off the phone though, I allowed her to play devil's advocate in my head. Suddenly my thoughts shifted completely and I was overcome by the worry of not being *enough*. I refused to take into consideration my future maybe-baby daddy, but it was impossible not to consider my future baby. Weighing the needs of this currently non-existent child against my own felt daunting. My mother had not been a part of my life. When I was 13 years old, she had simply stepped away—handing the reigns over to my father. She had detached herself emotionally long before then, but that was the point when she really did just give up. My mom was not a bad person. She was just so ... selfish. She had been so concerned with *her* needs, *her* life, and *her* wants that she often forgot to see everyone else around her (my brother and I included). She recklessly hurt people, and she refused to care about what anyone else needed from her.

I had never believed that I was anything like my mother. But now, up against these choices, I began to worry. What if I was more like her than I cared to admit? I had always vowed that when I became a parent I would put my children's needs first. If I was being honest with myself, I knew that I really did believe the best-case scenario for most kids was to have a mother *and* a father. But I also truly believed that having a child was the best-case scenario for *me*.

Was I being incredibly selfish to take what was best for me over what was best for my baby? I knew I would be a good mother. I knew I could provide more love and compassion on my own than many couples could provide as a team. I knew this deep down in my heart.

But I could not help but wonder… Had my mom also once believed that she would be a good mother, before she had me?

Chapter 8

I flew home to Arizona for the holidays that year, craving sunshine and warmth almost as much as time with the people who knew and loved me best. I hoped a change of scenery would allow me to decompress and make the choices I had been so afraid to make.

After only a few hours in town, I received an unexpected e-mail from the agency where I had once donated my eggs. One of their coordinators was writing to update me on the first family who had received those eggs, saying they had conceived and given birth to twins—a boy and a girl. They were now looking to expand their family further, and wanted to know if I would consider donating to them again.

Almost immediately I was hit with that familiar pang of jealousy I had started to experience when faced with any woman blessed with children. This pang was even worse because of the hand I had played in helping to create those babies. In an irrational moment I was not exactly proud of, I felt I was *owed* a baby of my own after having helped to give two to someone else.

I had always maintained that I felt no claim on those children, and that was still true. Their mother had carried them, nurtured them with her body, given birth to them, and guided them every second of their lives up to now. But when I donated, it had never occurred to me that one day I would be facing infertility myself. Now that I was, it was suddenly difficult to be confronted head on with the fact that there were children out there who might be like the ones I could have had.

Additionally, there was the tiniest part of me that blamed my problems on those donations. I did not regret donating exactly (I knew now more than ever how much it must have meant to those families), but the timing of everything felt so suspect to me. I began to believe that endometriosis had always been an underlying condition and that it had simply been exacerbated by putting my body through that process (and on those drugs) not once, but twice. Every time I was reminded of how that decision I made back *then* had begun to affect me *now*, it was difficult to swallow.

Beyond all that, there was a draw I still felt to help this family. I had always been compassionate toward the couples I donated to, but I had never fully understood how painful their journey was. Now that I could relate to it so intimately, I felt tied to them. There was nothing in the world I would have loved more than to help them complete the large family they (and I) longed for. But obviously I knew that now I could not. I was no longer the same donor I had been. My ovaries had suffered a great deal of damage in those two surgeries, and I had been told that women with severe endometriosis typically had the egg quality of women 10 years older. My time was running out. I was no longer in a position to help anyone else.

I waited 24 hours to respond to the coordinator, mostly because I was not sure how to respond. I finally penned a characteristically long e-mail detailing my last year and urging her to please pass this information on to the family so that they could be on the lookout with their own daughter. I ended the e-mail by stating that as much as I wished I could help, I simply was not in the position to do so at this time.

Even as I hit "send," I did so with regret. I wanted to help, but I had now become the one who needed the help. There was nothing I could do for them. We both wanted a baby, and neither one of us was capable of achieving that goal on our own. We were suddenly on the same side.

Only they had each other and their children.

And I just had me.

♌

Contemplating this new request helped me wrap my head around what it was I wanted and what the consequences of waiting could mean. I was fairly sure I had made my decision by the end of that trip, but I was not quite ready to say it out loud. My dad was the one who saved me from having to say it at all.

He was driving me to the airport when he broke the silence by proclaiming, "I don't know why you're making this such a drawn-out process. We all know what you're going to end up doing."

I eyed him suspiciously before replying, "Oh yeah? And what is that?"

He took his eyes off the road to meet mine. "You're going to have a baby." He said it so matter-of-factly that for a second, I almost believed this was a normal path to pursue.

"Do you understand how scary that is, Dad?" I needed to play devil's advocate in this moment, both with him and myself. "What if I mess it up? What if I'm not enough to do this on my own? What if I ruin everything?"

He paused for a second before replying, "Are you kidding me, Leah? You are one of the most strong-willed people I have ever met. If you set your mind to this, not only will you do it, but you will do it better than anyone ever would have thought you could. You are going to make this work, and you are going to be an amazing mother. It is what you were always meant to be." The tears were running down my cheeks before he ever finished speaking.

I could not figure out how he had so much faith in me. Our relationship had been rocky over the previous 10 years, but we had always been close. I had confided in him more during the past months than anyone else, so he knew what a mess I was. Yet he still thought I could do this, and that I could do it well. He believed in me, which made me want to believe in myself.

By the time my plane landed in Anchorage, I had decided. I was going to be a mother. No matter what it took.

Chapter 9

I spent that New Year's Eve home by myself formulating a plan of action. I needed to know how I was going to make this work, not just financially but also physically. I overhauled my diet and exercise plans, determined to be as healthy as possible. Then I created a strict budget, knowing I would have to adhere to it exactly if I was ever going to be able to afford the $15,000-plus that IVF would cost. I was ready though, resolved in my decision and committed to making this work. I would continue on Lupron for the recommended year of treatment and then I would travel to Seattle for IVF. I was going to be a mom, even if I had to do it on my own.

In the back of my mind though, I still had hope that Prince Charming would show up on his white horse and save me from all of this at the last possible moment. I did not *want* to do it by myself. I knew I could, but deep down I wanted to believe I would get my own romantic comedy ending.

It was that hope that led me to put aside my pride one evening and contact Michael. I had not spoken to him since that panicked night two months before. His mom and sisters had become huge sources of support for me, and they often swore he was calling them asking how I was doing. But he certainly was not calling me himself.

It broke my heart, because I had truly believed we were getting back on track. Reaching out to him first when I was hurting had been an automatic reaction of mine, something that carried significance to it I was not even sure he fully comprehended. He had pulled away and disappeared as soon as I needed him though, igniting within me abandonment issues that had roots settled deep within childhood. I had responded in the only way I knew how to at that point; by closing myself off and pretending I did not care.

What I learned as those weeks of silence passed was that letting go of someone you love is not as easy as I had wanted to believe it could be. So one night when I could not get him out of my head, I sent a text message. I had intended simply to open the door between us once more, and at first it seemed to have worked. He responded in a teasing manner and we were quickly joking with one another, as though there was nothing there between us to cause any pain. But then hurt feelings on both sides found their way into our conversation. It turned out that I had overestimated my ability to establish peace, and we fell quickly into a childish texting war that eventually ended with my saying:

> You're a dick and I hope you get Chlamydia.

It was not one of my finer moments. He sent a few more messages after that, but I ignored them all. I was angry at myself for trying to forgive and angry at him for proving to me that I never should have. I blamed the Lupron. I had never been this irrational before, had I?

I woke up the next morning still upset. I could not figure out how everything had gone downhill so fast when all I had wanted to do was repair the rift between us. He called that afternoon and I stared at my phone for a moment, debating whether or not to ignore it. I finally answered, only because I wanted to hear what explanation he could possibly have for some of the cruel things he had texted the night before. There may also have been a part of me feeling like I had a few explanations of my own to give.

But before I had a chance to speak, he was chastising me for my anger. He said he had simply done to me exactly what I had done to him, now over a year before. He even called it "pulling a Leah."

He was justifying, comparing the two situations and punishing me in the process. Upset, I asked how he could still keep going back to that point after everything we had been through since. I further questioned how he could care about me so little that he would not even call to see how I was doing in the midst of circumstances he knew were tearing me apart. He explained that he had been checking on me through his mom and sisters, but I could not seem to make him understand that I had wanted *him*. I had needed *him*.

I fought back the tears as I tried my best to explain it all, noting how much his absence had hurt me and how many nights I had spent crying while waiting for his call. I told him how difficult things had been, and how much I had needed to know that he cared. But the more upset I grew, the more withdrawn he became. He repeated over and over again that he did not know how to respond, until finally he said that Morgan was calling on the other line and asked if he could call me back.

When we got off the phone, I knew that I would not hear from him again. Even when we had been together, he had never been especially great at heavy conversations. Then it had been because he was always afraid I was going to leave. Now, I knew it was because I already had.

Chapter 10

Life no longer afforded me the time to dwell on Michael and the demise of our relationship. Within days, I was presented with another distraction. The egg donor agency was calling once more, this time with a proposition I had never imagined. They explained that when the original recipients of my eggs had heard about my situation, they immediately called the coordinator to express their gratitude over all I had already given them. They described to her their perfect 1½-year-old twins before going on to explain that they felt as though they now owed me the same happiness.

It was at this point when they brought up the idea of splitting a cycle between us, offering to sign an agreement stating that they would cover all the costs and that my getting pregnant would be the main priority. They were willing to guarantee that no matter what, I would get a set number of eggs. If some were then left over for them, great. Either way, they just wanted to help me achieve the same dream I had once given them.

I listened to the voice on the other end of the phone, completely overwhelmed by what was being said. The coordinator explained that she would never typically advocate for a situation like this, but that in knowing the three of us, she believed we could make it work. I could tell she was crying as she shared this information with me, and then I realized that I was, too. She pledged to give her services for free, as well as those of any others she could find willing to help throughout the agency. She just wanted to see us all come out the other end with what we needed, explaining that she could not help but feel as though this family and I were meant to be in each other's lives.

I was in such a state of shock, I was not even sure how I felt about this offer. I asked if I could have the weekend to think it over, explaining that I needed time to digest. As the idea began to settle in though, I realized how excited the possibilities made me. I started to feel like maybe this family was supposed to be in my life, and I began envisioning a future with us as friends. I was not sure why exactly—everything about this entire scenario had always been anonymous, and no one had suggested it would be any different now. Yet suddenly I pictured us cycling together and being equally invested in the outcomes of each other's pregnancies. I saw a future where we would be forever connected, where there would be two people standing by my side who really *got* what I was going through. Two people who wanted it as badly as I did.

Of course, the financial help would have been beneficial, but what I liked more was the idea of this camaraderie. I wanted to do this with them. I wanted to help them build their family and to have them rooting for me as I built mine. I wanted to meet their children, not in the sense of claiming them, but in the sense of possibly getting a glimpse into what my own children would one day be like. I wanted to know them, and I thought that if I did this (if we did this together); we might all come out the other end as family.

I called the agency the following Monday and explained my stipulations: The cycle would still have to wait until I finished

Lupron in November so that I could be at the healthiest possible place for conception. Also, I wanted their doctor to have the opportunity to review my medical records. I did not want them agreeing to any of this until they fully understood how damaged my insides now were.

They came back quickly and agreed to everything. Over the next several weeks, excitement and doubts battled in my head. As much as I loved this idea, there was a voice taunting me with all the negative possibilities.

As soon as I got the chance, I spoke to my RE about these new plans. She advised me strongly against it, explaining that eggs do not equal embryos and that embryos do not equal babies. She pointed to my own experience and the fact that while in total I had donated 28 eggs to two different families, only two of those had eventually become babies. She asked me how I would feel if the eggs that were produced from my cycle were split, but then none of the ones I had gotten for myself developed into embryos. Then she asked me the question that I had been too afraid to ask myself: How would I cope if I did this and they got pregnant but I did not?

When I first donated, I was asked how I would feel if somewhere down the line I faced infertility myself. I had been adamant then that I would never regret my decision, no matter what the future held. I was thankful to find I still felt that way, even after my diagnosis. But if I did this now, and they got pregnant and I did not? If I *never* got pregnant after they did? I was not sure I would forgive myself for sharing with them once more what I may have actually needed to achieve my own dream. And suddenly, I knew I could not split this cycle.

I wrote an e-mail to the coordinator, asking for her thoughts. She explained that while she loved the idea of us all cycling together as well, it was more important for me to have a child, no matter what needed to occur to make that happen. She did ask me to make a decision one way or another soon though, so that the family was not left waiting for me if it was not going to happen.

After hearing from her, I began to compose another e-mail. It was the e-mail I eventually sent to the donor agency for the couple who wanted this as much as I did:

> I am not entirely sure where to begin this letter, and most of me hates that I am writing it at all. When I initially heard of your offer to do a shared cycle, I was over the moon and overwhelmed with emotion. I fell in love with the idea of it, and with the idea of us both walking away with babies in the end. I fell in love with this picture of "Happily Ever After" for all involved. In my discussions with my RE, however, and in my own knowledge about how this process works, I have been consumed by doubts, worrying about how many successful embryos I may be able to produce with a full cycle, let alone with a split cycle. In focusing on those numbers, I am so sorry, but I think I have to tell you that I cannot share a cycle. I don't have it in me to share. I am too afraid of not having enough for myself.
>
> I think I initially got caught up in the idea of doing this as a split cycle because I loved the thought of having someone experience it all with me. I know that sounds silly, since everything about this situation has been anonymous from the start, but as much as I am aware that I am capable of doing this on my own, I also feel very alone in the process. I read about women who rave about having doting husbands by their side through their infertility struggles, and I find myself wishing someone was holding my hand along the way. I am strong and independent and capable. I can do this on my own, but some days I wish I didn't have to. The idea of having two people as invested in a cycle as I am was more tempting to me than I could ever hope to explain.

I want to apologize for leaving you hanging, and for not coming to this conclusion sooner. I feel as though I have wasted your time, and I am so sorry for that. I really and truly did love the idea of doing this as a split cycle, but I just don't think I can take that risk right now. I want to be a mom more than anything in this world, and I would be a *good* mom. As much as I would love to help you expand your family (and as much as I love the idea of your two children having the large family I always dreamed of when I was growing up), I just can't take the risk of sharing and then finding out that I don't have enough. In this case I don't think I would ever forgive myself if everything didn't turn out perfectly. I am not typically a selfish person, and I am so sorry that I can't get past that feeling now, but ... I can't.

I hope you understand and can forgive me for allowing this to draw out as long as it has. If I weren't in the position I am in now, I would donate to you again in a heartbeat. I wish you all the luck in the world in finding a new donor and in conceiving again. I have nothing but love in my heart for you and your children and I think of your family often. Thank you again for all that you have offered to do and for all the kind words you sent.

I wish for you nothing but happiness.

Chapter 11

As soon as I hit "send" on that e-mail, I knew I truly was doing this on my own. Which meant I needed a sperm donor. Never one to miss a silver lining, my grandmother was quick to point out that at least getting pregnant this way would mean I would not have to worry about any of those "STD things." I laughed before starting in on the piles of paperwork associated with this endeavor.

When I came to a page titled *Consent to Accept Donated Sperm*, for half a second I caught myself thinking, "What am I doing? Is this really what I want? Some nameless, faceless daddy for my child?" I had to stop and remind that voice of all the reasons why I had made this decision, and all the ways in which it had been the right decision for *me*. Still, there were moments when I could not avoid thinking, "How is this my life?" It seemed like everything had changed so quickly and drastically. I was still struggling to right myself.

Not to mention, I had never before realized how expensive sperm was. A vial alone was going to cost me almost $600, before shipping. I started joking that if I had known how much that stuff could go for, I would have begun stockpiling it years before. For the cost of this ooey-gooey substance I had wiped off my own stomach countless times in the past (discarding it like the bodily waste I saw it to be), I could have bought myself three new pairs of coveted leather boots.

Then there was the $200 I had to spend speaking to a social worker just to be granted approval for purchasing the sperm. I was having a difficult time hiding my own bitterness over that piece of the puzzle. I kind of just wanted to say, "Listen: Do you have any idea how much sperm I have had my hands on? You can either agree to let me pay for the stuff, or I can go out and find some of my own to bring in. But either way, someone's sperm is going to be introduced to my eggs. You might as well save us both some time and just sign off on me being an acceptable candidate."

I really hated that I needed to jump through even more hoops to get this show on the road, when so many women got pregnant every single day without anyone paying attention to what they were doing. But this was the reality I had been dealt. If convincing a social worker that I was fit to be a mother was what I needed to do, so be it.

The day of that consult, I realized I had made a far bigger deal out of it than I should have. Going into that conversation, I had somehow convinced myself this woman's job was to talk me out of moving forward with IVF or to judge me as being unfit. Because of this, my guard was up before our consultation even began. In reality, the session turned out to be exactly what I should have logically known it would be from the start: an informative discussion during which she simply wanted to ensure I knew what I was getting into. All the bitterness I had felt going into this had been completely unwarranted.

Throughout the course of that hour it seemed as though we talked about *everything*: my history with endometriosis, my feelings about those past egg donations, my familial issues, and what it was that had led me to pursue single motherhood in the first place. She was not judgmental, but she did ask me questions that made me think, including what I planned on telling my child when asked why he or she did not have a father.

I caught my breath when she said it, but after a few moments I answered as honestly as I could. I told her that one of the main reasons I had struggled with this decision as much as I had in the beginning was because of the fact that I had longed for a "complete" family throughout most of my childhood. When my mother disappeared from my life (first mentally and then physically) I felt that hole for a long time. It took years to fill it and stop missing the presence of a mother figure, and even then I still found myself wishing for a "whole" family. The thought of putting a child in a similar situation was one of my biggest reservations with this entire thing. I explained that I did not yet know what my answer would be, and that my only hope was that if I kept moving forward and loved my child with everything I had to give, it would come to me eventually.

I expected a scolding and for her to tell me that I needed to figure it out. But she did not do that. Instead, she concluded that having an answer right now would be almost impossible. She said she was glad I had answered honestly. Then she explained that I needed to remember I had actually *lost* my mother, in a way that had left me with feelings of rejection, grief, and hurt. She pointed out that my child would not have that same loss and rejection I had experienced over an absent parent. It would not be nearly as traumatic as it had been for me, because it would be the reality he or she knew from the start. I had not even thought of that, but I realized almost immediately the social worker was right; this was not the same thing.

When the hour was up she told me she thought I was an amazing woman and that I would be a wonderful mother. It took everything in me to keep the tears at bay. This lady was trained to detect crazy (and I was pretty sure that I occasionally sprayed crazy like a skunk), but she still thought I was going to be good at this,

Everything inside of me wanted to believe her.

Chapter 12

Two weeks before my second shot of Lupron, I began hurting again. It was a distinct pain that I recognized immediately, a gnawing and unrelenting ache I had only ever before experienced as a result of endometriosis.

I did not allow myself to think about it. I did not say a word to anyone. I was tired of all my conversations being about my current medical status, and I did not want to make this lingering thought in my head real by vocalizing it. In ignoring the ache, I reasoned my way into oblivion. I tried to tell myself that being on the strongest drug available and only two months out from surgery, it simply was not possible. But as the pain increased, that voice in my head became insistent. The obvious was growing harder to ignore.

The whole point of this drug had been to buy me time. Still, I could not stop wondering "what if?" What if I was one of those rare women for whom it simply did not work? I had already been told that my reproductive abilities might not survive another surgery. What if, after all the turmoil I went through to make this decision, it was already too late?

I did not want to be right about this. I wanted to be crazy. I wanted the explanation for my pain to be some kind of psychosomatic manifestation of mental illness. I wanted to find out that this disease had in fact turned me into a complete hypochondriac. Anything, as long as it meant that it was not a return of endometriosis causing this pain. Because there was just no way I could be one of the small (almost undetectable) percentage of women for whom Lupron did not work. There was no way those endometriomas on my ovaries could have returned full force in just two months.

When the appointment for my next Lupron shot finally arrived, I cried in the car on the way there. I was not sure where the tears came from. I thought I had done such a good job of being strong, but then it was time to leave and I was breaking down. I spent the whole drive wiping at my eyes and thinking about all those "what-ifs." I was worried past the point of reason about losing my chance.

This was how I knew that I was ready to be a mother: because the idea of *not* being a mother made me feel like I could not breathe.

As Dr. Olson began my exam, I finally heard myself admitting the pain I had been experiencing. I could tell she was concerned but unwilling to jump on the crazy train as quickly as I had. She reasoned that perhaps the previous shot wearing off was to blame for my increased levels of pain now. After administering the follow-up injection, she suggested we give the Lupron two weeks. If I was still experiencing pain after that, she told me to come in for an ultrasound.

Before I left, she reminded me that this shot marked my being a quarter of the way through with this round of Lupron. I was three months closer to the start of my baby-making journey. Even though she did not say it explicitly, I knew it was her way of telling me to keep my eye on the prize. I could handle this. I could handle anything, just so long as I was still going to be a mommy in the end.

♌

Every day that passed, I succumbed further to the pain. Meanwhile, the Lupron side effects were only getting worse. My hair had started to fall out and my skin was covered in acne. Not just on my face, but also on my chest and back. I was a mess, and there were days when it seemed as though this treatment was worse than the disease.

I needed to feel like I was doing something, like I was playing an active role in my health rather than just taking a shot in the ass and counting on it to be my savior. I had begun doing my own research on alternative treatments, a path I was starting to hope would offer me at least a sense of control. One day, when I felt as though I couldn't take the pain and hot flashes any longer, I did an internet search and found a clinic in town that combined western and eastern therapies. The website made it look like the television show "Private Practice," and the more I read, the more excited I became.

On the day of my first appointment, I arrived equipped with my last years' worth of medical records. When I was called back, I sat in the office quietly while a nurse practitioner reviewed my history. After a few minutes, she asked all the same questions I had already answered for every new health care provider I had come in contact with over the last 12 months. It had gotten to the point where I felt like I could answer these questions in my sleep. I realized that there was hardly any emotion left as I explained the timeline of the previous year.

Once I finished giving her the rundown, she suggested I see a naturopath within their clinic who specialized in infertility. She also wrote a referral to their in-house acupuncturist, assuring me it would help with the nausea and exhaustion I had been experiencing on Lupron.

And then she gave me a tall red bucket. It was for a 24-hour urine collection test meant to give her a better idea of my current hormone levels. As I sat there staring at this thing, the running commentary in my brain looked something like this: "That is never going to fit in the toilet. I am going to have to put it in the shower and kind of squat over it could make that work." I was pondering the logistics when she mentioned, "You'll just need to get a small container to urinate in, and then you can transfer it to the jug." That made a lot more sense.

I was still nervous about this though. Collecting my urine for 24 hours straight had me questioning my desire to explore alternative treatments. Even as the doubts were running through my brain, she began talking about supplements. Quickly, my one vitamin a day habit transformed into handfuls of pills. I was going to need an old lady pill minder just to keep track of them all. I secretly wondered if they would even make a difference. I was willing to bet most of them would wind up in that pee bucket in the end, but I knew I had to try. Because when somebody offers you a solution that might help in a situation where you feel helpless, there is comfort in embracing it.

I was still hoping for my miracle, for the magical cure that would make this all go away. I wanted to find the piece of the puzzle that would allow me to return to my carefree life, as if the last year had been nothing more than a bad dream, easily erased and happily forgotten. If collecting my own urine in a bucket could possibly give me that, I would never pee in the toilet again.

Chapter 13

I spent most of my nights writing on the blog and responding to e-mails. I had never before been an anti-social girl, but as the pain increased and the reality of infertility set in, my own mental and physical exhaustion became harder to ignore. The relationships formed with the women I met on the other side of my computer screen were simply the easiest to sustain.

It was as I was editing a new post one night that my phone began to ring. I glanced down to see who was calling, only to be jolted by Michael's name flashing across the screen. After our previous fallout, I had not expected to hear from him again. I stared at that ringing phone for what felt like forever before eventually tossing it across the bed, as if it was a lethal weapon I was desperate to distance myself from.

As much as seeing his name made my pulse race, I was not sure I wanted to hear what he had to say. It had only been a few weeks since we had last spoken, and I was not prepared to have the same argument all over again. I assumed he would leave a message and I could decide whether or not it was a conversation worth having from there. Only he left no such message. I toyed with the idea of calling him back to see what he wanted, but I eventually decided against it. If he wanted to talk, he would call again.

A week later I received a text message. It was nothing more than a generic:

Hey you! How's life?

Again I stared at it, trying to decide what to do, before once more choosing to ignore it. I still had no idea what it was he wanted and, given our last conversation, I was hoping for more of an apology. I had needed to fight back the tears while explaining to him all the ways in which he had hurt me, and I had offered up plenty of "I'm sorrys" for all the ways in which I had hurt him. I needed more from him now. I could not just pretend like the past had never happened.

It was only a few days later when I received another text:

Ouch!! Not even friends?

It interrupted my otherwise relaxed evening. Again I stared. Again my heart started beating much too quickly. But again I realized that it was nothing more than him fishing to see if he could guilt me into responding. He knew I had never been great at ignoring, perhaps because I had always hated being ignored myself. With this though, I had no idea what to say. How many times could the same words fall on deaf ears? We had been having the same fight over and over again; I did not want to have it anymore. I did not want to keep begging him to forgive me only to wind up disappointed in the end. One way or another, we had to break free of this cycle.

I loved him, and there were nights when all I could think about was how much I needed him. That was especially true now, when it seemed as though he was trying to sneak his way back into my life. But I knew I had to keep moving forward. I did not deserve to be punished anymore. So I ignored his messages, waiting until the day when he would give me some reason to believe I should not. I was not counting on that reason though.

I was not counting on him.

Chapter 14

My first acupuncture appointment could not have come at a better time. The pain I started experiencing weeks before had not yet dissipated, and now on top of that I was dealing with the increased side effects caused by a new round of Lupron. I needed relief and was hoping that perhaps this alternative therapy could offer me that.

Tina, the acupuncturist I had been referred to, was an itty-bitty thing who fluttered around like a giant ball of energy. She enthusiastically chatted away while still somehow conveying unending compassion and concern. I immediately knew I liked her.

The two hours I spent on her table flew by as she inadvertently played the dual roles of both my acupuncturist and therapist. We talked about everything, touching on topics I had avoided discussing out loud since the day I realized that most people were not capable of understanding. Something she was doing with those needles opened me up, and I was suddenly speaking freely.

I had gone into this concerned it would hurt, but I was surprised to find that I barely felt most of the needle pricks. Those that did cause me to wince in pain were correlated to issues I was having. It was amazing how quickly I could feel the connection.

When the session was over, we talked about what I could expect from acupuncture. Tina explained that at this point, the damage which had already been done was likely irreversible. She was quick to point out that acupuncture alone would not be a "cure" for endometriosis, but she was confident she could end the nausea, headaches, night sweats, breakouts, and fatigue I was experiencing regularly while on Lupron. After just two hours with her, I trusted in that. I began to believe I could regain some of the pieces of myself I had lost to this disease.

I ventured back to the clinic a few days later for a follow-up on my 24-hour urine test. Something about collecting my own urine in a bucket and storing it in my refrigerator had made me question the direction my life had taken, but I was anxious to review the results.

After we both sat down, the nurse practitioner showed me a piece of paper listing all the different hormones in the body. My results were located next to each category, with the "normal" range of results listed next to that. Out of the 20 hormones listed, only two of mine fell within that normal range.

As expected, the estrogens were barely detectable—Lupron was doing its job in that aspect. Of course, I still had to fight back a sense of bitterness when she explained that she had seen post-menopausal women with better estrogen levels than I had. Nothing about that felt right.

She then took the results back, highlighted a single row, and returned them in front of me. It was the row for testosterone. My level was 111 and the normal range for women was listed as

4 to 18. "So it turns out," I said, my filter completely shutting off upon receiving this news, "that I'm actually a man."

She grinned and replied that it was not quite so drastic, but it could explain some of the other issues I was experiencing. Without any estrogen to even things out, it made sense I suddenly had the skin of a teenage boy and an upper lip I was waxing more than ever before. It was one more humiliating aspect of this drug that had left me feeling less attractive every single day. I was growing convinced that the only real purpose of Lupron was to keep me single and alone. This disease stripped me of my ability to bear children, and this drug had turned me into a man.

There really was no more dignity left.

A few nights later I was lying in bed, unable to focus on anything besides the tenderness in my stomach. It had been two weeks since my last Lupron shot, but the pain did not seem to be going away. I initially refused to allow myself any feelings about what this meant, still not wanting to acknowledge how much I was hurting. Yet as the days passed, my ability to ignore it diminished to the point that I finally picked up the phone and scheduled an ultrasound. I requested something the following week, hoping for a slightly longer reprieve from reality. I replied truthfully when asked what was going on, and the nurse on the other end of the line immediately bumped the whole schedule around to fit me in the following morning. The urgency and extra level of care they were affording me made it nearly impossible to continue pretending this pain meant nothing.

Once more I was approaching this appointment as though I did not care. I was so over the whole thing that I almost refused to worry about it. I was expecting new growth. The Lupron clearly was not doing its job, but what could I do about that now? What did it matter *now*?

When I arrived for my appointment, I walked into the ultrasound room with a smile on my face. I exchanged small talk with the technician and continued grinning even as I shared my concerns, determined not to let my fears show through. I reacted with such confidence that I knew what was going on, it must have caused her to let her guard down. She made no attempt to hide her surprise once the exam began.

There were signs of new growth almost immediately. Typically, endometriosis cannot be seen on an ultrasound and can only ever officially be diagnosed with laparoscopic surgery. Once endometriosis has been confirmed though, there are certain signs doctors can look for. In my case, there had been a history of those chocolate cysts, called endometriomas. As the tech was looking at my ovaries, she told me that she had never before seen anyone have new endometriomas grow while on Lupron. She then pointed at the screen to the new endometriomas on each of my ovaries. It seemed as though she was more upset than I was.

I remained calm, submitting to blood draws and urine cultures before sitting down with Dr. Olson and asking her what I should do. She had no answers, explaining that she had never treated a patient whom Lupron had not worked for. She had heard of cases where this happened, but had never witnessed it herself. The only thing she could think was that it might be best to simply skip the last two rounds of Lupron and move straight to

IVF. She suggested we forward my ultrasound results to the reproductive endocrinologist I had been consulting with and ask for her opinion.

I left defeated. As I walked out those doors, I finally felt something: hurt, angry, and let down. A long list of "Why me?" thoughts flooded my brain as my eyes began to fill with tears. After e-mailing the ultrasound results to the RE, I waited anxiously for her reply. I just wanted to figure this out. I was tired of being faced with impossible decisions. Finally, she e-mailed me back:

Are you ready to get pregnant? :)

Suddenly, I saw the silver lining. If this was not working, it meant no more Lupron. There would be no more feeling sick, no more lack of energy, and no more waiting. Everything was going to work out. I would just be getting my baby sooner.

♌

I went home that night determined to pick a sperm donor—only I immediately grew frustrated. I had not counted on there being so much information to dig through. I was not entirely sure where to start. The multiple banks and varied options at each quickly became more overwhelming than I had anticipated.

Just as I was about to shut the computer down in exasperation, I received an e-mail I had all but stopped waiting for. It was from the family who had asked me to donate my eggs to them once more, a response to the e-mail I had sent them a few weeks prior. I was unable to concentrate on anything else as I read their words to me.

> Dear Leah,
>
> There is so much I want to say to you, but let me begin by saying thank you for our beautiful children. The gift you gave, when you gave of yourself, is beyond words. I can tell by the babies we have that you are a spectacularly special lady. I dearly want to tell you how much you mean to us; how often I think of you and your wonderful spirit. Please know that we are thrilled to pieces with our little girl and little boy. They are the joys of our life and the most amazing little beings that we could ever imagine. Aside from their beautiful little souls, they are supremely gorgeous as well. People routinely remark on how beautiful and calm they are. Recently, during an outing to the grocery store, they captivated a large number of people at the checkout, smiling and waving and attracting all kinds of attention. Afterward, one man remarked that he found them extraordinarily captivating and that he noticed they caught the eye of everyone around them. He finished by saying they had a special gift, one that would serve them well in life.
>
> If you wonder who these little babies are, I can tell you that our little boy is outgoing and social. When we take our morning walk, he loves to stop at the neighborhood school and watch the kids at play—and he can't wait to join them! He enjoys climbing and loves to show you how fast he can run and how strong he is. Our little girl is feminine and pretty. She loves to be with me and is usually at my side. Ask her for a kiss and she will take your face in her hands and give you one!
>
> I understand that you will soon be embarking on your own journey to become a mother. I truly hope that you are successful. I also understand that you have some health issues you are dealing with. I'm sorry for any concerns that this may cause you. But I can only believe that the good you put into the world will come back to you many times and that you will be successful. Perhaps you will let us know. I would like that very much.

> Let me close by letting you know that our little ones are deeply loved and that they are surrounded by people who cherish them; that we will do everything in our part to make their lives happy, successful and enjoyable. Please also know that I am reminded of your love and kindness every day when I hear my babies laugh, when they look at me and smile and when they hug and kiss me. I promise you that we will love and care for these darling babies for all of our lives.
>
> Signed,
>
> Two adoring parents

The tears were streaming down my face as I allowed myself to read it again, a mixture of emotions I couldn't even describe taking over. I was growing frustrated, and in that frustration I questioned whether I really had it in me to travel this road alone. The message from these parents helped remind me what I was fighting for. One day, I would know the love they described for their babies as I held my own. Every step that brought me closer to that was worth it.

Chapter 15

My 27th birthday arrived without much thought on my part. With everything else going on, I had not been able to find the excitement I typically reserved for this day. My friends Lindsay and Stephanie were determined to get me out though, arguing that I needed one night away from infertility, IVF, and sperm donors. We drank and ate for over three hours, laughing and talking more than I had in months. I realized that night how little time I had been spending with the people I cared about. I had always been a social girl with a strong group of friends, but over the previous year I had lost so much of the person I was. Between the pain, drugs, and stress, I was always tired.

These two girls had stood by me though, my constant cheerleaders on a journey that had been anything but easy. They were selfless in their desire to support me, even when I was quick to recognize I had not been nearly as good a friend in return. That night they accomplished the impossible by getting me to separate myself from everything else that had been going on in my life. We drank more than necessary, latched on to random men to flirt with, and laughed hard and loud until our stomachs hurt. By the end of the evening, we all needed a cab home.

It was past 3 a.m. when I crawled drunk and alone into bed, my phone clutched dangerously in my hand. Michael had continued calling and texting occasionally, but there had still been no apology or indication of what it was he truly wanted. So even though it was not easy, I had endured in denying his attempts at contact—until that night, when alcohol managed to put a quick end to the willpower I had been so proud of. I drunkenly typed a response to his previously ignored texts:

> **There isn't a whole lot I wouldn't give for you to be the guy I thought you were...**

As far as drunken texts were concerned, I was actually quite pleased with myself. There were no misspelled words and it was hardly an overly dramatic diatribe. It was just real. Raw. Perfect. I fell asleep shortly after hitting send, waking early the next morning to his response:

> **You are alive!**

Now facing the sobering reality of a hangover, my defenses were up. Immediately I was angry at myself for breaking the silence, knowing that it never would have happened had I not been drunk. Even after my carefree night out though, I had been thinking of *him*. I had wanted *him*. I had missed *him*. That was why drunk me texted, because she knew that sober me never would. Still, I could not shake this overwhelming desire to now protect myself from my own mistakes. So before I could overthink any of it, I snarked back:

> **Apparently drinking makes me remember the numbers I've deleted for my own good.**

He replied almost immediately:

> **You're funny!**

That was it. Except I knew he would call. As both Lindsay and Stephanie rallied on his behalf (worried I had been too harsh), I remained fairly confident that I would be hearing from him that night. I could not explain how I knew, but I knew. And at 9:15, my heart stopped when the phone rang.

As soon as I picked up, the first words out of his mouth were, "Look who's answering the phone to talk to me!" Before I could control myself, those defenses that had been momentarily surrendered shot right back up. "You know what?" I said. "You made it pretty clear how little you cared about me, so I don't really understand why you think I should want to talk to you at all."

I was primed for a fight, prepared for his defenses to go up as well, and for this to turn ugly fast. Even though it was not what I wanted, I could not see how it would go any other way. But then, he did something amazing. Something totally unexpected and ... perfect.

"Stop," he said. "Stop being angry. I don't want to fight with you. I'm not going to fight with you. This is going to be a friendly conversation."

And I stopped. I calmed down. I put ugly, angry, defensive me away, and we talked. Like two old friends who did not have nearly as much emotional baggage as we had between us. We just talked, catching up on the events of the previous few months and seeming to lay aside old wounds as well as we were capable of doing.

The way he was speaking to me was exceedingly different from how we had talked over the previous year. He went out of his way (without my asking) to explain that there had been no new women in his life for a while. In the past he would have let me

83

believe there had been others, just to hurt me and make it clear he was still a free man who could do whatever he wanted. During this conversation though, he was very careful of my feelings.

Before we hung up, we discussed the events that had led us to this point. I told him I could not be punished anymore for how our relationship had ended. I apologized once more for hurting him, but said that he needed to understand how badly he had hurt me as well. We talked about the hurt we had caused *each other*, and then agreed that we *both* needed to move past that. He suggested we stop trying to figure the future out, and just *be* for a while. Suddenly, that did not seem like such a difficult thing to do.

When we got off the phone, I was not sure what was going to happen from there. I honestly was not sure *anything* was going to happen from there. It had been a good conversation, and there was no doubt we were two people who deeply cared for each other. But we were also two people who had each been damaged and broken in our own ways. Still, I wanted to believe that at the very least we would find a way to be friends. The rest, if there ever could be a rest, would happen in its own time. For once, I was content with allowing the future to figure itself out.

Giving us an opportunity to just ... be.

Chapter 16

While I was allowing myself to live in the now, I still needed to find a sperm donor. It was an endeavor which turned out to be more difficult than anticipated. I had never believed genetics counted for much, but now that I had all these options to choose from for a baby daddy who would never actually be there, genetics were suddenly everything.

It was like sifting through dating websites looking for the perfect match. Only I was not looking for the man of my dreams, at least not in the traditional sense. I knew I would never meet the man I chose, but I realized I was seeking out qualities I typically found attractive. I was looking for a future husband in those profiles, hoping that if I could guess what that man would be like and select a donor who shared his traits, he would seamlessly be able to step into the role of "daddy" without anyone being the wiser once he finally decided to show up.

Obviously I knew that was not how it worked, but I could not help looking at these men as if they were potential suitors rather than prospective baby daddies. I had never pictured myself sitting in front of a computer judging men based on the traits they could pass on to my future progeny. It was uncomfortable and hilarious and confusing all at once.

Eventually, I narrowed down the pool of donors to three men. They were all over 6 feet tall, had dark hair, olive skin, and green eyes. I definitely had a type, and these men were it. From there though, I was stuck. There were things about all three that I liked and things about all three I did not.

Donor number 1 was my "safe" donor. Based on blood type and test results alone, he was the perfect match for me. There was nothing about his profile that gave me any reservations. Of course, there was also nothing there that I felt absolutely drawn to either.

Donor number 2 was not quite so safe. In fact, he was described more than once by the staff that interviewed him as having a "rock star" quality. There were a lot of things about him I loved. He seemed incredibly intelligent, and he was obviously the best looking of the bunch according to staff evaluations. Throughout his profile though, he came off as cocky and arrogant—traits I had always despised. Beyond that, he had apparently decided to become a sperm donor after watching his sister struggle with infertility. It did not say anywhere what issues she had dealt with, but it made me nervous – what if she had endometriosis? I did not want to pass that on to my child from both ends of the genetic spectrum.

Donor number 3 was the guy who resided somewhere in the middle of these two extremes. Based on his profile, he reminded me of that cute kid in the high school band who you never notice, but the day you finally do, he kind of blows you away. Everyone at the bank raved about how sweet he was. They said he was passionate about music and often brought the staff mix CDs—two things I adored. The one drawback I had with him was how much his profile reminded me of my little brother. This was a resemblance that I was not sure I was totally comfortable with, because as much as I loved my brother; I did not want to be conceiving his clone.

All three donors were so different, each with their own pros and cons. I felt lost on how to make this decision. I was describing my dilemma one night to Lindsay and Stephanie, when for some reason we started laughing about putting the whole thing to a vote on the blog. At first it was nothing more than a joke, but then the idea began to form into reality.

By this point I had been blogging for a few months. The general reaction to my writing had been very positive, and it seemed as though every week more people were reading and commenting on my journey. These strangers from around the world had embraced me and were quickly becoming my most vocal cheerleaders. The same people were checking in every single day for updates, offering advice, and lifting me up even as I struggled. I had never imagined this kind of reaction when I started blogging, but there was no denying the fact that an online community of support surrounded me.

Putting it to a vote on the blog seemed like the perfect way to make this decision; both because it would bring forth hundreds of varying views and opinions for me to consider and because it would serve as a way to lighten the mood. I liked the idea of taking an otherwise stressful and atypical situation and turning it into something I could laugh about. Stripping some of the seriousness away suddenly made the decision feel more manageable.

By the end of the week, I had placed the profiles online. I was determined to make this fun, completely unaware of the can of worms I had just opened.

Within days of posting the donor profiles online, my pre-IVF labs were scheduled. I was oddly gleeful, as it felt like the first step towards making this process real.

Then I received a phone call that changed my perspective a bit. The day of the appointment my doctor's office called to make sure I knew this visit would not be covered by insurance. For a second, I faltered on my words. I did know that my insurance would not cover anything related to fertility treatments, but I had not put two and two together just yet. I kept thinking about IVF in terms of the big sum I had been quoted at the beginning of this process, without thinking about the fact that I would still need to pay for every doctor's appointment leading up to that point as well.

I thanked the voice on the other end of the line for the reminder and asked how much I should expect to pay. She hesitantly told me that this one visit would run a little over $700. I momentarily lost my ability to breathe. "OK." I winced. "I'll move some things around and will have it for you." I hung up the phone feeling deflated.

I had gone into this endeavor with so many different fears and reservations that I had not fully acknowledged the *financial* toll yet. To those around me, it probably seemed as though money was not an issue. It was definitely a factor though. But I refused to allow money to be *the* factor that kept me from having a child. I had a good job and I made a decent salary. I lived a sufficiently middle-class lifestyle and had always been able to provide myself with some luxuries. In preparing for IVF, I had simply needed to acknowledge how limited those luxuries would now be. I was not rich, and money was a factor, but I was confident I could make this work.

Early on I had decided to finance my treatments. I reasoned that most people financed the cost of their cars and then rarely ever kept those for more than a few years. Why should it be acceptable to finance a car, but not make that same investment in one's family? When I thought about it like that, financing had become the logical choice.

The only problem with financing was that I had come to think of all these costs as being under that one umbrella. I kept focusing on the main number I had been quoted and forgetting about all the "little" costs along the way. There would be at least two more appointments like the one I was about to have that day, each with a big tab of its own. My sperm sample was going to be almost $1000 by the time shipping costs were included, and the hormones I would need to buy promised to run up to $2000. Contemplating numbers like that—and the big-ticket number in the end—made me ill. I worried about whether or not I would be able to afford this and how far into debt I would have to go before I reached the end. Even more, I knew that IVF was only a drop in the bucket when it came to the actual costs of raising a child. It was terrifying. But by now, I could not imagine any other way.

♌

While the debate was waging online over who my sperm donor should be, I was secretly hoping I would not have to choose a donor. Michael was back in Washington, but we were speaking more frequently. We still had not seen each other or discussed the future possibilities of our relationship, but at least we were talking.

One night, while going over the decisions I had made while we were apart, I cracked a joke about how much it was going to cost. I told him he could save me a few hundred dollars if he just took one for the team and dropped a sample of his man juice off at my clinic before leaving Seattle. I was expecting a laugh and quick brush-off, but instead he threw me for a loop. He asked what would happen if I gave birth to what would genetically be his child, and he then started to develop feelings for me again.

It was in this moment that my long-standing history of being socially awkward reared its ugly head. I had always lacked a filter when caught off guard, typically saying the first inappropriate thing that came to mind. So without thinking, I immediately replied, "We would have a legal agreement to protect against that."

As soon as the words escaped my lips, I wanted them back. I had still been stuck in the joke of his being nothing more than a donor. When he switched gears on me and alluded to it being something more, I froze. I mentioned a legal agreement only because I knew that was what would have been in place if he were just a donor with no intention of being the father. I had been too scared to tell him what it was I really wanted: that I would have given just about anything for him to be the one walking by my side on this journey.

He laughed when I stuck rigidly to the joke, knowing full well how uncomfortable I could get under pressure, and then the conversation awkwardly moved on to something else. We did not touch on the idea of his being the baby daddy again.

I spent days pondering that conversation and trying to figure out the pros and cons of owning up to what I really wanted. I wondered if perhaps he, too, was trying to determine his place in all of this. I began to realize that if all I had to lose was a little bit of pride, it was a small price to pay for the possibility of everything working out in the end. So a few days later, I sent him a text message:

> **I've got my sperm choices narrowed down to three guys—if you want to be in the running, you should let me know now.**

Within minutes, he responded back:

> **Call me later dork.**

I felt a tiny twinge of hope. He had not said "no." That had to mean something, right?

We had a serious conversation that night where I laid it all on the line, completely forgetting the promise I had made to us both about keeping things pressure free. I explained that I still loved him, and that I wanted him to be the father of this baby just as much as I wanted to be a permanent fixture in his and his children's lives. I said that despite everything we had been through, he was still the person I saw myself spending my life with.

He had always known how important being a mom was to me. Whether or not he was open to children in the future was something we had explored fairly early on, because for me it was a deal breaker if he was not. He had always maintained he could see himself one day having more and that he liked the idea of creating a family with me. So this was not a completely illogical discussion for us to now be having, except for the fact that we were not currently together and that my biological clock had since become a ticking time bomb.

There was a lot going on in his life, stress surrounding money and work and his kids. We discussed it all, and I knew how much pressure he was already under. I knew that in reality, the last thing he needed was me saying, "Do you want to have a baby with me? You have to decide now or never!" But I could not stop myself. I needed to know where he stood (where *we* stood) before I moved any further in this process.

He surprised me with how well he took everything, but he still seemed so unsure. He explained that while he could not tell me this *was not* what he wanted, he also did not know what going down this path would mean. Not wanting to put any more pressure on him than I already had, I told him that he now knew what I wanted and that the ball was in his court—a little joke we still shared from the very first time he had called. I said I would be fine if he never came around and that I would continue forward on this journey with or without him. But before we hung up, I told him again that what I really wanted more than anything was for us to build this life together. We got off the phone, and I waited for him to call and say he wanted the same.

Except he never did.

I continued looking at the donor profiles and struggling with the decision. It felt impossible. It was not the way I wanted it to be. There was a man in my life I loved—a man I believed loved me back. I wanted him to be by my side for this. I was strong. I knew I would be just fine if I had to do this alone. In my perfect world though, I would have already had a baby daddy, not just a sperm donor. In my perfect world, I would have him.

I knew that this was hard for him as well. I was expecting him to come to a decision in a week, when it had taken me months to make the same decision myself. I knew how much pressure that was. But in my heart, I believed this man and I could have a wonderful life together, if we could just figure out how to make it all work. I did not think I was asking for a lot.

I just wanted it all.

Chapter 17

Something unexpected was happening online while I was busy focusing on my relationship drama. It turned out that soliciting sperm donor votes had drawn a fair amount of attention to my little slice of the internet. Suddenly, reporters were requesting interviews and my blog stats were skyrocketing. I was completely overwhelmed.

I had very intentionally kept my blog anonymous, using it solely as a platform for exploring my personal feelings about infertility. The idea of opening that up to an even wider audience made me nervous. But then I thought of all I had learned about this disease or, rather, all I had not learned. No one truly understood what caused endometriosis, why the severity of illness could vary so greatly from woman to woman, or how to effectively treat it across the board for everyone with a confirmed case. From what I understood, there was not a whole lot of research being done to answer those questions either. The longer I had been talking about endometriosis, the more I realized how limited the general public's understanding of this disease was—and the medical world's understanding of it was not much better.

Now that the opportunity was being placed at my feet, I suddenly *wanted* to talk about it. I wanted to highlight what this disease was and what it had taken from me and from thousands of other women just like me. I had not started my blog with the intention of becoming an advocate, but now that I had the chance to be just that, I felt as if I had to try.

The first interview was with a publication based out of Colorado. We completed it over the phone and the writer seemed kind and open-minded toward the choices I was making. The article turned out very positive and I was pleased, maybe even a little proud. Within hours of it appearing both online and in print however, I made the mistake of looking at the comments people were making about the story.

Some were funny, if not slightly uncomfortable, to read. One guy called me a SIFILF, which took about 30 minutes for me to figure out. I blogged as Single Infertile Female (SIF), and once I put two and two together, I just felt dirty. But I was even more surprised with how many of the comments were simply cruel:

- *Hope she dies during childbirth*
- *Christ. Bitch needs to spare the world her moronic genes. Her kid will likely end up as another Darwin award winner anyway.*
- *Ok, so she can't have a child naturally because of her endometriosis. She is (admittedly) impatient, and wants a baby ASAP. She is effectively looking to become a single mother. It looks to me like she wants what she shouldn't have. I'm thinking she should take the "endo" as a hint -- she's not meant to reproduce.*

There were so many along those lines. Comment after comment that left me feeling ill. I had not realized how lucky I had been with my blog. The vast majority of feedback I received there had always been positive and warm. But now these people who had never met me were judging me, even hating me.

I had to fight the urge to respond. There was part of me that wanted desperately for these people to understand. I thought that if I just explained it to them further, maybe they would. But how do you respond to someone who wishes death upon you, even though they have never met you?

The blog had become my therapy. Connecting with women who understood (women who had been there) was how I had gotten through to this point. Writing about this journey was the only way I explored those feelings I otherwise kept bottled up inside, and it felt good that I was also letting other women know they were not alone. Was I doing something wrong though? I had always been open with my life. I kept no secrets from my close circle of friends, and I wrote with my heart on my sleeve as well. Had that somehow been a mistake?

When I received a call from a local news station a few days later asking if I would be willing to do an on-screen interview for Mother's Day, I hesitated. The idea of any more media attention turned my stomach. Did I really want to break out of my bubble and invite in even more criticism?

I was just about to call the station and turn down the interview when I received an e-mail from a girl who had been struggling with endometriosis herself. It was warm and heartfelt and full of gratitude as she explained what reading my story had meant to her. It was the reminder I needed of the good that could come from being open about this part of my life. Just like that, I changed my mind. I knew that I was not doing anything wrong. In fact, I was doing everything right. I would be a phenomenal mother, and I was strong enough to share my story so that others could have a face to put to this disease. If I was given an opportunity to raise awareness for infertility and endometriosis, I was going to take it. I was going to be a voice. Even if it meant some stranger on the internet saying I was a moron.

The day the cameras showed up at my house for filming, Stephanie and Lindsay came for moral support. Upon arrival, the reporter decided she wanted to interview them as well. Seeing how positive they were on camera about me and my journey reminded me that *these* were the people who mattered. The opinions of my friends and family were the only ones that counted. And they were supporting me completely.

It was still difficult for me to understand the interest in my story though. I had come to realize that women were making these same decisions every day, with more than 90 million women globally suffering from endometriosis. And while it was one of the most common causes of infertility, it certainly was not the only one. I was not the only woman confronted with the possibility of losing her chance. I had made the choices that were right for me. I had prayed and cried and consulted with the people who meant the most to me. It was not an easy decision, but it was the right one. And now I was just another mommy-to-be. There was nothing unique or special about my story. It was just … my story.

The whole thing gained attention solely because of that silly poll I put up on my blog. I had never intended for it to draw that kind of response. It had just been my way of attempting to make light of an otherwise stressful situation.

After everything was said and done, I did not even pick the donor who won the majority of the votes. People had fallen for donor number 3's apparent charm, and I would have been good with that if it was not for the fact that everyone who actually knew me was leaning toward donor number 1. For a variety of reasons, they all seemed to think he was the one I should choose. The more I talked to those who knew me best, the more I was leaning towards him as well.

So in the end, I went with my "safe" choice rather than the one who had actually received the majority of the votes. The reality of the situation was that I had never planned on letting an online vote make such an important decision for me anyway. And I had certainly never planned on it being the catalyst behind my 15 minutes of fame. None of that mattered anymore though, because my decision was finally made. A few days after that interview aired on the nightly news, I placed my order. I spent $600 for one tiny vial of sperm and $170 just to ship it a few hundred miles to my clinic in Seattle.

It was certainly the most money I had ever invested in bodily fluids.

♌

With my sperm purchased, life started to return to normal once more. The desperation and pressure I had felt over the previous weeks finally faded away and I was able to look at my relationship with Michael realistically again. One night while getting ready for bed, I sent him a text message:

Can we just forget the last two weeks ever happened?

He called me shortly after I hit send. It was a brief exchange, but it was all it took for things between us to smooth over. He seemed willing to forget I had gone a little overboard in trying to convince him to be all in, and he began calling again every few days after that. Our conversations were now filled with small talk though, as if we were both afraid of creating another chasm. I was willing to take whatever I could get, but it was still hard to be talking like acquaintances rather than two people who had once loved each other.

During this time his dad was admitted to the hospital for what was supposed to be a fairly routine surgery, only there were complications. He was forced to stay in the hospital for a week before undergoing a more in-depth procedure. Since Michael was still out of town for work, I spent a lot of time at the hospital with his family. They had all been huge sources of support for me over the previous months, and his mom was fond of reminding me that I would be family to them regardless of what Michael and I were to each other. So every time one of them picked up the phone and asked me to come, I dropped everything and went. Michael and I touched base every other night or so as his dad's hospital stay progressed, and he seemed to appreciate the fact that I was there.

The Saturday before he was set to come home, he called me twice for no particular reason. Something I could not quite put my finger on shifted during those conversations, and it seemed as though the wall between us might be coming down. That night he went out with his buddies, eventually calling me four times long after I had already fallen asleep. I never heard the phone ringing, but I could not erase the smile from my face when I saw those missed calls in the morning. I knew they were drunk dials, but I liked knowing I had been on his mind. I wanted to believe that perhaps we were edging toward a reprieve from handling each other with kid gloves.

We were less than a week away from him coming home for good. For the first time in almost six months, I knew that I was actually going to get to see his face. There was still something between us. I was not sure how strong it was, or if we would ever be able to find our way, but I knew there was still something there.

And I knew he knew it too.

♌

Within days of Michael arriving back in town, we made plans to get together for drinks. From the second he picked me up, there was an awkwardness between us. It was as if we could not remember how to behave anymore when sharing the same space. Once we sat down at a local bar and started in on margaritas though, we quickly found our joint comfort zones again.

Mostly we just caught up, bantering back and forth as though no time had passed. We each steered clear of serious subjects, and my impending baby-making never entered the realm of conversation. It was obvious we were feeling each other out, attempting to determine where we now fit in the other's life. There we were in this bar where we had actually gone on our very first date: two people who had once loved each other and who maybe could again, but who just were not there yet. In the moment, I was content with that. It seemed like enough, so long as we had not lost one another completely.

When he took me home, he parked his truck instead of dropping me at my door. It did not occur to either of us that it was now past one in the morning as we ventured together up to my condo. We were both flirty, but nothing took place beyond that flirtation. We did not even kiss. At one point, as we sat there talking on my couch, he boldly questioned whether or not we were going to go there. I held firm though, and told him that I could not continue to walk that line with him. I explained that we were either going to be friends or we were going to be together, but we were not going to be friends who sometimes fell into bed together.

Of course I wanted his hands to wander and his lips to find mine, but I knew that I was right in this. I could not put my heart on the line again without guarantees. I needed more, from him and from us. I was not giving up yet though.

♌

As that last round of Lupron wore off, we were waiting for my period to start before setting my IVF cycle dates. After reading about women on Lupron who took months to get back to normal, I was beginning to panic when my period did not show as expected. My RE ordered a blood panel to check on my hormone levels, and we were both surprised to find that they were perfectly in line with where they needed to be. She declared we no longer needed to wait for my period; I was cleared to start my cycle now.

In a moment, I went from worry to excited anticipation. I suddenly had a calendar in front of me with official transfer dates in mid-July. For the first time, I allowed myself to believe this was actually going to happen. That calendar earned a prominent place on my refrigerator to serve as a reminder of just that, and the confirmation of dates magically freed me up for something else.

Michael's sister was getting married in the beginning of July out of state. I had always considered her a close friend, and she and his entire family had been encouraging me to come, even going so far as to offer a place for me to stay while there. I wanted more than anything to attend, but I could not initially justify buying a plane ticket with everything else going on—especially since I had no idea when I needed to be in Seattle for my egg retrieval. But then the dates lined up perfectly. It just so happened that my first appointment in Seattle was scheduled only a few days after the ceremony. When I started playing around with the tickets, I found an incredible deal that would allow me to fly first to the wedding and then to Seattle for only $100 more.

I called the cycle coordinator to see how she felt about my traveling just a few days prior to arriving at SRM, but I was not exactly optimistic. By that point I knew I would be giving myself daily injections which would require close monitoring. I was fairly sure she would shoot down this idea. Instead, she quickly arranged for me to have monitoring appointments at the local clinic where I would be, assuring me it was no big deal. Just like that, I was able to confirm my RSVP.

I knew that Michael's mom and sisters were hoping this wedding would serve as the catalyst for our reunion. They had said as much on the many occasions when they urged me to come. And while I was excited simply to be celebrating with this family I loved, I could not ignore the side of me that was also harboring hope for our future. There was something about weddings that seemed to promise romance, and with everything falling into place the way it had, I wanted to believe it was all meant to be.

That perhaps, he and I would find our way back to each other after all.

Chapter 18

I had always been a big believer in signs. I thought numbers repeating themselves or good things happening out of the blue were gifts from the universe meant to indicate I was on the right path. The dates lining up for me to be able to go to this wedding already had me thinking I might just get it all, but then something even greater happened.

With my cycle date approaching, I had been researching online pharmacies to purchase my medications from. I was hoping to find the best possible deal, knowing that the drugs I would need were not going to be cheap. I called my coordinator one day with a few questions about the various options, but before I even finished my train of thought she was telling me to hold off on this endeavor. She said she knew of a couple in Alaska that was getting ready to donate their leftover medications, and she wanted to see if she could claim them for me first.

I had a hard time wrapping my head around anyone making such a generous donation. This was not a paltry sum we were talking about. It was $2,000 to $3,000 worth of drugs. But I held off anyway, thinking that it was too good to be true while still allowing myself the tiniest glimmer of hope. It turned out my hope was not entirely unfounded, because just a day later I received an e-mail telling me that almost all of my cycle meds had been donated. They would be waiting for me to pick up at my appointment the following Friday, just a few days before my cycle start date.

I was in disbelief. An entire cycle's worth of drugs had just fallen into my lap. Someone in my small town just so happened to have the meds to donate at the exact same time I found myself needing them. These drugs were not over in Seattle or across the coast in New York. They belonged to people who were patients at *my* doctor's office. It was too incredible to be a coincidence. I wanted to believe it was a sign that I had made the right decisions in this, and that I would be a mother soon.

After my excitement wore off, I realized that in order for someone to be in a position to donate these meds, they must first have had a cycle canceled. That was the only conclusion I could come to anyway. My heart went out to this woman I had never before met. I knew immediately that I wanted to do something to let her to know how much this gift meant to me.

I wrote my coordinator asking if there was anything she could tell me about the couple that had donated the medications. She responded back saying she knew them well and that they were wonderful people. Apparently they had been lucky enough to have infertility insurance coverage, so they had purchased two cycles worth of medications at once just in case. When they realized they would no longer need that second cycle, they had decided to donate the remainder of the drugs.

She would not confirm it, but I gathered they must have achieved pregnancy their first cycle. With that knowledge, I immediately started looking at infertility necklaces online, eventually happening upon a beautiful one that carried a charm which said "miracle." I secretly coveted it for myself, but worried about jinxing my own cycle by prematurely making that purchase. Buying one for the woman who had donated this medication though, felt right.

When the necklace arrived I went to the store and bought the most heartfelt thank you card I could find before penning my own note about what their gift meant to me. I had the gift and card in hand when I went in that Friday for my suppression check—the appointment meant to ensure I did not have any cysts that would prevent me from moving forward with IVF. I was bubbling over with excitement as I handed the necklace to a nurse who had a far greater gift waiting for me in return: a bag full of medications that I did not have to pay a single cent for.

My suppression check that day went perfectly. I was told to begin the injections that evening. I was confident about giving myself shots because I had done it already before. Twice. Ironically, donating my eggs had prepared me well for infertility. I felt like an expert when it came to measuring out syringes and plunging needles full of hormones into my stomach. I was not thrown by the bruises and side effects. As my belly swelled with bloat and my emotions grew increasingly raw, I knew that this was all normal. I was ready for it.

The universe was giving me all the right signs. This cycle was meant to happen. I was on the right path.

And I was going to be a mommy.

Chapter 19

Michael and I continued talking with regularity and spending time together as friends. Friends who kissed occasionally, but nothing more. I still was not sure where we stood, but at least we were trying. He knew what I was doing and where I was in this cycle. He knew about the needles and hormones and impending baby making, and he was still spending time with me. I had to believe that counted for something.

Life was moving quickly, and before I knew it his sister's wedding arrived. When the day came for me to get on a plane, I had a bag full of clothes meant to sustain me not only for the four days I would be with Michael's family, but also through the yet unknown period of time I would be spending in Seattle. So much about my trip still depended on how I responded to the drugs. My egg retrieval date would be set with only a few days' notice, based entirely on how long it took my eggs to mature. From there, a transfer date would not be set until the embryo quality could be determined. I left work telling them I had no idea when exactly I would be returning. For the side of me that tended to be a control freak, having so much up in the air was difficult.

Then there was the anxiousness I felt over flying with all those medications. I could not risk putting any of it into my checked baggage, so needles, syringes, and vials of various liquid hormones were all sealed tightly into my carry-on. I was sure that TSA was going to have a blast with me, and I was terrified of how awkward that conversation would inevitably play out.

"Ma'am, can you please explain why you have all these needles in your bag?" I imagined the agent questioning.

"I'm trying to have a baby," I would say. "By myself. With a sperm donor."

Awkward. By any and all standards, it promised to be awkward.

After all that worry though, they never said a thing. On the day of departure, TSA waved me and my needles right on through without even requesting a prescription. On the one hand, I was grateful to avoid that uncomfortable confrontation. But on the other, I wondered how anyone could claim security in airports was going too far, when here I was walking right on a plane with a bag full of needles and drugs that no one had even batted an eye at.

Arriving in Colorado, I was immediately swooped up at the airport by Michael's sister. She was clearly excited to see me and began rattling off all the plans we had for the days to come. I was instantly grateful to be there with people who felt like family. We took tours of a local brewery and spent time lounging in the sun and gorging on all the food we could never find in Alaska. Michael remained distant but playful. When introducing me to his grandmother for the first time, he did so by saying, "Grandma, this is Leah. The girl who broke my heart." A wide grin spread across his face as he said it, but I glared at him just the same. I knew how close he was to his grandmother, and this was hardly the first impression I wanted to be making.

Still, our interactions were few and far between. He explained he did not want to give his kids the wrong impression about where the two of us stood. I understood that. But it stung to have him suddenly keeping his distance from me after the closeness we had been regaining over the previous weeks. I kept hoping that when it came time for the actual wedding, some of his barriers would break down.

The day before the big event, the wedding party headed off together for the rehearsal. I tagged along and took pictures for his mom as everyone practiced their parts. I was the only non-family member there who was not in the wedding, but as everyone kept reassuring me ... I *was* family. I belonged there, with them. Something about that felt safe.

Michael was one of the groomsmen. As he practiced his walk toward the altar, I could feel him watching me take pictures. He was staring, a grin on his face that told me he had something sarcastic fighting to escape from his mouth. I wanted so badly to hear that he was glad I was there or that he thought I looked beautiful. I wanted to hear that he missed me and was ready to fully forgive. Instead, I heard him say, "This could've been you," as he walked past me. He let the laughter he had been holding on to escape. It took everything in me not to tackle him.

He said it in jest, but in my hormone-induced haze I was having a difficult time not taking everything personally. Our relationship had always been fun and playful. It was based on a mutual ability to give each other a hard time. If anything, he had always been the one more capable of opening up and making his deeper feelings known. So I could not fault him now, with people around, for maintaining a joking demeanor and not letting anything else break through. But I also could not help feeling especially sensitive, hopped up on hormones that would make any sane woman unhinge. I wanted him to hold me, to comfort me, and to care. I wanted him to be my partner, not the guy who could not let the past go.

♌

The morning of the wedding, I was scheduled for my monitoring appointment. I needed to get up early and travel to the local clinic for a blood draw and follicle check before the afternoon festivities began. It was going to be the first glimpse at how I was responding to the hormones. I was a bundle of nerves in anticipation of the outcome.

This anxiety deepened with the discomfort I felt sitting in the waiting room. The appointment was in the early morning after we had all been out late the night before for the rehearsal dinner. I managed to arrive at the clinic in sweat pants, an overgrown sweatshirt, and a baseball cap. I knew immediately that I did not fit in.

The waiting room was extravagantly designed and filled with couples dressed to the nines, all sitting in varying stages of worry and distress. These couples wanted the same thing I wanted with every fiber of their being. They wanted it so badly that they could not help but sit in that waiting room as though it was the most serious thing they had ever done.

Meanwhile, there I was—completely scrubbed out, sucking down coffee as if I needed it to survive, and lacking that partner by my side. I felt awkward, uncomfortable, and out of place, like I was not serious enough, classy enough, or married enough to belong there. Maybe I imagined the looks the other couples were throwing my way, but I was sure they were questioning what I was doing there. I think we were all beginning to wonder if it was even possible I was one of them at all.

I knew I was being crazy, but all I kept thinking about was that song from Sesame Street.

One of these things is not like the others. One of these things just doesn't belong.

I wanted to belong. *And I did not want to.* I wanted to fit in. *And I did not want to have to.* Sitting in that waiting room made me feel small and lost.

When my name was called, I walked back to the room and listened as a tech explained the internal ultrasound. It was a tool that closely resembled a dildo with a condom conveniently attached. I had already endured far too many experiences with this piece of equipment and referred to it affectionately as the vagisound.

Immediately after we began, I could see my own follicles and knew that was a positive sign. The tech pointed to the 11 follicles I had just starting out. She told me to wait for a phone call about my blood results, but that based on what she had seen, I was off to a good start. I was giddy with excitement as I returned to the hotel and threw myself into getting ready.

But then I received the call just as we were preparing to leave for the ceremony. My blood work had come back; my estrogen levels were exceptionally low. These low levels meant that everything was now at a standstill. While I should have been starting a new round of meds that night, I was instead being placed in a holding pattern. I was told to continue taking the same drugs I had been taking up to this point, with the hope that my estrogens would eventually rise and those perfect follicles I had seen earlier in the day would actually mature into something I could use.

I did my best to pull it together for the wedding, even though everything inside of me ached. The news that I did not seem to be responding to the hormones punched me in the gut so hard I was not sure I would be able to get back up. But I did. I put on my dress and makeup. I did my hair and threw on some uncomfortable shoes. I slapped a smile on my face and pretended as though everything was fine, because this one night was not about me and my insides.

I would have blood drawn again in just a few days, once I landed in Seattle. Until then, I would have to wait, riding on the hope that I was simply responding slowly and that my estrogen would catch up soon. It was all I could do not to think about what it would mean if that did not happen.

♌

I went to the wedding determined not to let anyone know what was going on. I danced and I laughed and I did my best to pretend that I was not terrified of the heartbreak the coming weeks could bring.

Even in that though, I was clinging to the hope that Michael would somehow miraculously know how much I needed him. I wanted to believe he would step up to catch me before I fell. During the ceremony, as the pastor recited the well-known "Love is patient, love is kind" verse, I caught him staring at me. We held eye contact throughout the verse as I wondered what he was thinking. Was he finally remembering what it was we once had? Was it possible he could still be the man who had said not too long before that he would marry me one day?

He and I had a few interactions throughout the night, but it was as the evening was winding down that I got my real answer. The DJ announced the final slow song and I managed to grab onto Michael just as he was exiting the dance floor. We had been to weddings together in the past and had danced with each other on more than one occasion. This should have come naturally to us. We should have fallen into each other's arms with ease. Only we did not. It was as if there was an invisible barrier between us, forcing our physical separation. I kept trying to get closer, attempting to maintain intimacy as we had so many times before. He kept pulling away from me, keeping the kind of distance reminiscent of a junior high dance.

I finally said something, questioning why he was dancing with me like I was his pre-teen cousin. His response was that he did not want anyone getting the wrong impression about what we were. He said it with a straight face, not wanting to hurt me in any way, as if it was simply something I should have known and understood.

And with that, something inside of me broke. After a weekend of getting the cold shoulder from him, I was done. I finally realized that his change toward me since we arrived had everything to do with his not wanting people to think he cared about me. There was nothing I could really do with that.

Morgan wandered past us as I felt the tears rushing to my eyes. I grabbed her and told her to dance with her dad. As soon as I could manage, I slipped away by myself. I was trying my best not to let all the emotions hit at once. When I heard him calling my name outside the reception hall, I knew I could not handle seeing him. I was already raw and hurting over the state of my insides. I was not up for a tête-à-tête about how he still was unable to let me in. I pretended I did not hear him and made a beeline for the car.

Moments after I shut the door, I began to cry over everything. My insides hurt and my heart was breaking. I was crying over my failing body and a cycle that I wanted to go according to plan. I was crying over all the false hope I had carried for this weekend. And I was crying over a man I had promised myself I would never cry over again.

I had been holding out hope for so long because he never said he did *not* still love me. Yet I knew none of that meant anything if he didn't want his family thinking we were falling back together. After all, this was a man who had introduced me to his family before we even kissed. A man who had decided he wanted to marry me before we were two months into our relationship. He had loved me deeply once, and he had worn that adoration on his sleeve. He was now clearly a man who did not love me anymore, even if he was not yet able to admit that fully to himself or to me.

So I cried, both because I was hurting over this change for the worse in my cycle and because the man I needed to hold me and help me through this hurt would not be doing that. I cried, because I knew that we had to be over. I did not want to love someone who did not love me back.

As I opened my eyes the next morning, I knew that I could not endure another day of Michael treating me differently because he was afraid of what others might think. I was still a wreck and could not figure out how to calm myself. The crying continued without warning or reason. I tried to blame the hormones because this onslaught of never ending tears was so unlike me.

But in reality, I knew that my heart was broken and that I could not be around him any longer with this open wound in my chest.

I picked up the phone and called a friend who lived nearby. I asked if she would mind taking me to the airport. It was far too early for my actual flight, but I knew I needed to put some distance between Michael and myself. I said my goodbyes to his family and tried to keep my tears at bay, but it was clear to all involved that I was on the verge of an emotional meltdown. I placed the blame on the drugs and felt silently grateful as they pretended to believe me. Over and over as they hugged me and whispered, "I love you," they repeated that I was family—no matter what. They said they would be there for me when I returned from Seattle, ready to rejoice over my baby-to-be.

I did not say goodbye to Michael. As I walked out of the hotel with my bag in hand, I heard him calling my name from behind. Once more I pretended to be unaware of his voice, and headed straight for my friend's waiting car without looking back. I could not handle him seeing my tears – I was not willing to let him witness the hurt in my eyes. There had been no fight or blowup, no angry words spoken or tension to explain the hurt. There had been no true catalyst for my breakdown, just a moment in time where all I could do was acknowledge the truth.

And the truth was: we were over.

It was time for me to let him go, and focus on becoming a mother.

Chapter 20

I woke up that first morning in Seattle knowing that no matter what, I would make it through this. I went to my initial appointment at SRM and sat in the lobby, waiting to hear my fate. I had never spoken to the doctor I would be meeting with that day, as the doctor who had conducted my phone consults up to this point was on vacation.

It did not matter though. It turned out this new doctor was incredible—kind and warm and understanding of my anxiety. After completing the exam, he sat down and talked me through everything. He explained that he was not overly concerned about my cycle and that it seemed as though I was simply slow in getting started. He still had faith that this would work out just fine, and his faith was all I needed in that moment.

I left the office feeling more at ease and hopeful for good news regarding my blood work. I drove around downtown Seattle, attempting to distract myself as I waited for that call. It was odd to be there by myself, doing something so huge with no one who loved me by my side. I had always been independent and had traveled plenty on my own in the past, but this was different.

When my phone rang that afternoon, my adrenaline began pumping. I answered anxiously and listened quietly as the voice on the other end of the line said my estrogen levels had more than doubled since my appointment just a few days before. My hormones still were not exactly where they should have been, but at least they were steadily rising. This meant I could now move on to the next round of medications, adding an antagonist shot to keep from ovulating unexpectedly. Everything was back on track.

Over the next week I went in for appointments almost every other day. I was still responding slower than expected, but with every ultrasound I saw my follicles growing. They were my babies-to-be waiting for their chance at life. I could not help but see the magic in that.

I spent my days after appointments exploring Seattle, going shopping when I had the energy and lounging around my hotel room watching movies when I did not. I focused on eating healthy and getting enough sleep. I was taking care of myself as best I knew how and staving off loneliness with regular phone calls to those I loved. Under normal circumstances, this would have been the most relaxed vacation I had ever been on. Except, of course, it was not a vacation and it was anything but relaxed.

Finally, about a week after we originally thought I would be ready, I received the call that my levels were where they needed to be and my follicles were the appropriate size. I was told to take my last shot that evening. My egg retrieval was scheduled for two days later.

I was shaky as I hung up. This was it. The moment had finally arrived. In a week's time, I would have my baby inside of me. There was just one problem: This final shot was a big one, and I would somehow need to plunge it into my backside. I had become a pro at sticking myself in the fatty tissue surrounding my gut, but getting a much larger needle directly into the muscle of my ass was going to be another story entirely. I was actually a little scared.

I started practicing almost as soon as I got the call, putting a chair in front of the mirror in my room and arranging myself all backwards cowgirl on it while attempting to figure out how I would actually sink this needle into the not-so-willing skin of my behind. The only conclusion I could come to was that this was not going to be easy. I was mildly annoyed that this part of baby making had not been covered in health class all those years before.

Everything from here on out was very time-specific. I was expected to give myself this final shot exactly 36 hours before my egg retrieval was scheduled. About 10 minutes before I was meant to do the injection, I set out to mix the medication. Before I could start though, I realized I had left the instructions in my car. I threw on some shoes and quickly ran down to the parking garage, thinking I still had plenty of time.

When I got back to the room though, I was dismayed to find my room key no longer working. Trying not to panic, I ran down to the front desk, only to be greeted by a sign that said, "Currently away. Will be back momentarily." In the entire time I had been staying in this hotel, I had never once seen that sign. I was irritated to find it there now, when it was actually important for me to get into my room.

All I could do was wait. And wait. And wait. By the time the concierge arrived back to the desk and fixed my key, it was now 7:25. I had been scheduled to take my shot at 7:15. I was already 10 minutes late.

I ran up to my room and hastily mixed the medication, drawing it up into the largest needle I had ever held in my hands before plunging it directly into my backside without hesitation. There was no time to think about it. I had to act, trying my very best to ignore how much it hurt.

Once it was over though, I was proud of myself. Most women had husbands to help them with this part, but I had done it on my own. Without any assistance, I sunk a giant needle into my ass.

No one would ever be able to say I had not fought for this baby.

Chapter 21

I drove to the clinic the morning of my egg retrieval with a mix of apprehension and excitement pulsing through my veins. Technically, I had been through this part twice before. I knew what to expect from this procedure, so there was no anxiety over the half hour I would be put to sleep or the discomfort I would feel after it was over. In the past though, I had never been this emotionally invested.

Suddenly, the number of eggs retrieved carried an importance for me it had not the first two times around. During each of my donations, 14 eggs were retrieved. I knew based on the ultrasounds leading up to this point that there were not even 14 eggs available to retrieve now, but I was hoping for 10. Even by conservative standards, I assumed that 10 eggs would yield at least five embryos. I wanted to be able to transfer one and have four to freeze for some point in the future.

Right before I was put under, the doctor performing the procedure (another new doctor who I had never before met until this day) came to speak to me. He explained that given my age, he would have hoped to see better blood and ultrasound results over the previous weeks. He was less than optimistic about how I had been responding, and he wanted me to keep my expectations realistic for what was to come.

Hearing that right before surgery threatened to put a damper on my mood, but I slapped a smile on my face and reminded him that this was why we were here. If I had not gone from perfect to far from it so fast, I would not have been sitting in front of him now. Then I told him that my ovaries were just being a little bitchy and he would need to show them who was boss. That got him smiling. He reminded me that all we needed was one viable egg to make a baby, and then he wheeled me off into the surgical room.

Thirty minutes later I woke in recovery and was told that 10 eggs had been retrieved: seven from my left ovary and three from my right. The nurse said that all 10 were not completely mature and would not likely fertilize, but I did not care. I had gotten the number I had been hoping for. I chose to hold on to that moving forward.

Once I was able to return to the hotel, it was back to the waiting game. I had been told to expect a call the following morning letting me know how many eggs had fertilized, and then every morning thereafter with an update on how many had survived another 24 hours. My transfer date would be in three or five days, depending on the quality of the embryos that made it. I learned that day five transfers were preferable because the best embryos could be evaluated and selected. Transfers were completed on day three only when the number and quality of the embryos was low, with the hope that they would fare better inside the mother than they would in the lab.

I could not think about any of that though. All I could focus on was the fact that my 10 eggs had already been united with the donor sperm I had purchased. Those babies-to-be were already in a dish somewhere growing to their fullest potential. They were already mine, and I already loved them.

♌

I did not receive a call from the embryologist until the following afternoon. She started the conversation with pleasantries, inquiring about my recovery and various post-retrieval symptoms. She had to have known that all I wanted was for her to tell me how many of my little embryos had made it through the night, but for a grueling 60 seconds she continued on as though there were better things to talk about.

Finally, she proceeded to give me the report. Of the 10 eggs initially retrieved, only eight had been deemed mature enough to fertilize. They were each graded fair, on a scale of poor-fair-good. I winced at the memory of the good grade my eggs had received only a few years prior. My age should have all but guaranteed me good eggs now as well, but it seemed as though the promise of my youth was only continuing to let everyone down.

She then informed me that my donor sperm (which had cost more than anyone should ever spend on bodily fluids) had also been graded fair. When I expressed my disappointment over this fact, she explained that it was not uncommon. Sperm banks did not make a habit of testing each sample, and the freezing process was known to diminish quality. I was blown away by this new bit of information.

All eight mature eggs had fertilized without issue, but two ceased to split any further after only a few hours. Another three continued the fertilization process, but did so abnormally. That left me with only three embryos at the time of this call, and they would still have to survive the next few days.

Sensing my disappointment, the embryologist reminded me that I could still have a successful pregnancy. "Your age is on your side," she told me. I was starting to feel as though everyone should stop talking about my age as an indicator of anything. Every doctor up to this point had believed my age would be the key to success, and yet here I was: a slow responder with fair-quality eggs and only three embryos left 24 hours after retrieval.

I was heartbroken. Within moments of her mentioning my age, I was rendered incapable of fighting back the tears any longer. It was embarrassing, but I could not force myself to stop. I felt like seven of my babies had died. I knew that was not really how it worked, but the loss still felt so real. She kept asking if I had any questions, but I was simply trying to fight back the ache I felt inside.

As soon as I composed myself, she explained that my embryo transfer would now officially occur on day 3. I would get a call with quality reports on all of the embryos the following day and we would decide which ones to transfer then. I was reduced to the helplessness of waiting, simply trying to hold it together until the next report.

When the phone rang the following afternoon, the nurse on the other end of the line was more understanding of my mental state. She jumped right into the specifics, explaining that all three of my embryos were still there. Still growing. Still thriving. Still mine.

There was not much more she could tell me beyond that. She said they were hoping to have a better idea of grading for me the following day, right before my transfer. As of that call though, there were still three embryos waiting for me to be their mommy. The only thing left to decide now was how many to transfer and how many to freeze.

The emotional side of me wanted to transfer all 3. Chances of survival were known to go down with freezing, and I suddenly wanted *all* of my babies to have the best possible hope. I obviously knew that transferring three was not an option though. I was single with a limited income. There was no way I could handle triplets on my own if all three made it. Even handling twins on my own would have been a stretch.

I was leaning toward transferring only one for myriad reasons, the silliest of all being that I did not like the idea of one of my embryos being sent off to the deep freeze by itself. I knew it was crazy to think this way, but already I wanted to protect these babies. I did not want one in there alone. I just wanted them to be safe, comfortable, and happy, even though they were still technically nothing more than a cluster of cells. They were a cluster of cells that owned my heart.

♌

As I sat in the lobby of the clinic the following morning, my anxious excitement trumped the peaceful calm I had hoped to go into this procedure with. This was the day I was going to get pregnant, and I was bubbling over with elation because of it. Sleep had been near impossible the night before, with the anticipation of what was to come waking me every few hours. It did not matter though. All I cared about was getting my baby inside of me.

I followed the instructions that morning precisely, eating and drinking as normal before voiding (the term for urination that peppered my medical orders, making me laugh every time I saw it). I then drank 24 ounces of water and did not void again. I checked out of the hotel and drove to the clinic, oddly aware of the fact that no one was congratulating me on my impending pregnancy. Didn't these strangers around me know what was about to happen?

When I arrived at the clinic, I stripped down and exposed my very full bladder to the ultrasound tech. She immediately deemed it too full and sent me off to the bathroom with permission to void, but only enough to fill a small paper cup. One cup of voiding, and then back on the table.

The embryologist came and spoke to me then, carrying with her the most beautiful picture I had ever seen. It was my baby-to-be, from that very morning. She told me that all three embryos were still thriving and exhibiting good quality. It was her suggestion that I only transfer one and freeze the remaining two in a few days' time. I had already been leaning toward this and was tired of making decisions on my own, so I agreed with ease.

Once she left, another doctor who I had never before met came in to greet me. There was something disconcerting about how SRM seamlessly passed me from doctor to doctor, as though I was merely on the conveyor belt of their baby-making factory rather than a patient with real needs and concerns. Since my arrival, I had been greeted by a different face at every appointment.

Yet in the moment it did not seem to matter. This was the doctor who was officially going to get me pregnant. I watched on the screen as he flashed a picture of my embryo over from the lab, and I focused all of my love and attention on that little speck as it was placed into a catheter and handed off to the man who was about to knock me up. The insertion was painless as he directed that small tube inside of me. It took less than 30 seconds total. I continued to watch as the screen switched over to a view of my uterus, where I was able to witness the catheter releasing that embie of mine. I saw it find its way, and I knew this baby was meant for me.

After the procedure, I was left on the table to recline with my feet in the air for 10 minutes. I prayed, became lost in my thoughts, and talked to that little embie inside of me. I promised that I would be a good mommy and that I would sacrifice all if necessary. I warmly explained that I would love it with everything I had to give. I swore that it would always know how wanted and adored it was, if it would only just find its way into this world.

When the timer sounded letting me know it was now safe to move, I gingerly stepped off the table. I dressed and then made my way to the bathroom where I was finally allowed to void for real. I was anxious throughout the entire process (against my better logic) that my little embie might just fall out. I knew this was not possible of course. In fact, I had heard over and over again from the various doctors on this journey that this baby would either stick or it would not, but that nothing I did at this point would change the outcome. Still, I could not help but find myself waddling with my legs pressed tightly together as I walked my way out of the clinic. I could not bring myself to button my pants either, for fear that my embie would get squished and assume it was not welcome.

I made my way to the airport for my flight home knowing that now it would simply be a waiting game. My blood draw to see if this embie of mine had stuck around was almost two weeks away. Until then, I would be in limbo, assessing my symptoms and hoping for the best.

Chapter 22

It was not long after getting home that I realized I had become "that" woman. I was overanalyzing every flutter and movement from within my midsection; attempting to determine whether or not there was an actual baby in there long before my scheduled blood test.

For every gurgle and gas bubble, I questioned what was going on with my insides, wondering whether or not my embryo was still floating around waiting for the perfect moment to attach. I Googled every symptom I could find, monitoring and scrutinizing in an attempt to convince myself I was experiencing each and every one. I diagnosed morning sickness, rather than blaming my nausea on the hormones I was still taking. I read about pregnant women exhibiting cold symptoms, and suddenly I could not breathe. When a friend told me that her nipples had noticeably changed very early on in her pregnancy, I began studying my own with a pornographic intensity. I was obsessed.

After a few days, I received a call from SRM informing me that both of my remaining embies made it to the day six blast stage and had been frozen that morning. I was comforted by this news, and hopeful that this little one inside was still thriving as well. That baby of mine was all I could think about. The two-week wait was barbaric.

I realized around day eight that I was starting to twitch. I was not built for this kind of uncertainty. I had already decided that I could not wait for the blood draw, even though my doctor strongly recommended it. I had this picture in my head of how I was supposed to find out I was pregnant, and it did not involve a phone call. I was supposed to be standing over a pee stick, jumping up and down with elation in the privacy of my own home, not hovering over a phone in my office trying to mute my squeals.

I knew that I would break down at some point and pee on a stick, if only because I had been hoping to prep myself one way or the other before the big day. But I was worried about testing too soon and ending up with a result I could not actually count on. The hormones I had been on prior to transfer were capable of contributing to a false positive if they were not completely out of my system before I tested. I did not want my hopes to be raised like that, only to be crushed in the end if I was not actually pregnant. Then there was the possibility of testing too soon and breaking my heart with a negative result that was not accurate. It was a delicate balance. I did not want to hurt myself unnecessarily with a false negative, but I also did not want to face the devastation of a false positive.

I promised myself I would make it until at least day 10 before trying, but then that twitching began on day eight. I read about women who tested positive as early as I was and who went on to have perfect little babies. I started to convince myself that if they could know so soon, then I could too. And wouldn't knowing be better than *not* knowing?

I did not mean to do it, but on the way home from work that night I pulled into Walgreens. It was like I was being lured there by some uncontrollable force. Before I knew it, I had purchased enough home pregnancy tests to last me right up to the day of my blood draw. I had officially plunged myself into infertile lunacy.

I confessed my little shopping adventure to my dad, only to have him beg me not to do this to myself. He implored me to wait until the blood draw, lest I make myself crazier than I needed to be in the process. My only reply was, "Not possible." I had officially crossed the line. I told him that when I started rocking back and forth and reciting nonsensical syllables to myself, he would need to fly to Alaska and cart me off to the loony bin. But if he knew what was good for him, he would send my pee sticks with me.

The test I took that night was negative, but it did not faze me. I was sure I was starting to have symptoms. For instance, my boobs were sore and had been for days. I was not willing to admit that could have been because I had been poking at them every 20 minutes just to *see* if they were sore. All that mattered was that they were sore. And I was exhausted, struggling every day to wake up and drag myself to work. That was not all though. I could not control my temperature. One minute I was cold and pulling on a sweater, and the next I was sweating and stepping outside for fresh air, feeling as though I was going to suffocate if I did not start tearing clothing off. There was no regulation. No comfortable. No normal.

I knew this could all be attributed to the progesterone I was now taking twice a day, but I did not believe that it was anything other than a baby. I could not shake the conviction that I was pregnant. There was a pressure/tingling/fullness that I could not quite describe in my stomach, and I knew that meant something. Something huge, amazing, and incredible.

Even after peeing on a stick on day nine and seeing another negative, I was convinced that it was simply too early. I was still pregnant. No matter what any test said. I was *so* convinced, that I started telling strangers. At dinner when servers asked if I wanted a drink, I declined and cited the bun in the oven. At the grocery store as I eyed the parenting magazines at the register, and at Target as I gravitated toward the baby section, I explained effortlessly to clerks and other shoppers why. I just liked hearing the words come out of my mouth. "I'm pregnant."

Deep down in my gut, I felt it. I believed it. No matter how early it was, or how irrational it may have been to think that my body could be reacting to a pregnancy so soon, I just knew that I was pregnant. I could not imagine it turning out any other way.

When day 10 produced another negative, I continued to hold strong. It was too early, but I was still pregnant. The next day would be a big fat positive kind of day. I felt it in my bones. I believed this even more when I pulled my pee stick out of the trash that afternoon and saw what was undoubtedly a shadow on the test. I knew you were not supposed to look at pregnancy tests after a certain point, but this *had* to mean something, didn't it? That shadow had to mean that there was at least some of the pregnancy hormone inside of me. I was sure of it. I failed to recognize the lunacy as I pulled that test apart and held the strip to a flashlight. All I could see was that faint hint of a second line; proof that my baby-to-be was settling in just fine.

Day 11 did not give me that positive I was expecting either, but still I kept the faith. I continued to believe I was pregnant, still proclaiming it to strangers every chance I got.

Until that night, when I started spotting. It was not much, and it was dark brown. I convinced myself that it was not a big deal. But by the next morning there was a little more, and it had started to turn pink in tone. It was a Sunday, which meant my doctor's office was not even open. My blood test was scheduled for Wednesday. I was not sure what I was supposed to do.

I was fighting the urge to fall apart. I had read about implantation bleeding, but I was too far along for this to be that. Seeing blood now finally had me contemplating the possibility that this cycle had not worked or, that if it had, I was losing the baby. I put in a call to the emergency line at SRM, but I did not have much hope after spending some time with Doctor Google. I held back my tears though, somehow sure that if I cried it would mean I was giving up. I was not ready to give up.

Around noon it seemed as though the spotting may have stopped. I almost had myself convinced that none of it had been that big of a deal. But then it started up again a few hours later. This time, the blood was bright red. It was still very little, but it was there every time I checked. I could not see how that could possibly be OK.

When SRM called, they moved my blood test up and told me to go to my doctor's office first thing in the morning. The woman I spoke to was very sweet, but she did not sound hopeful. She explained it was possible the progesterone capsules were causing me to spot, stating they sometimes irritated the cervix. She told me not to lose hope, but explained that there was not much to do if it really *was* over. She instructed me to drink a lot of water, stay in bed, and try to remain calm. So I did just that, fighting to hold back the tears all day long. I ignored my phone and the outside world, knowing only that I had no words for anyone in this moment.

I finally answered the phone when Stephanie called that night. She offered to bring me ice cream—vowing that ice cream could work wonders. I told her that unless ice cream could make me pregnant, I did not want any. I felt guilty almost immediately, but I did not apologize. I could not force myself to think about anyone else. I was too focused on the baby I was sure I was losing. I got off the phone with her quickly, promising to let her know as soon as I heard something the following day.

And then I went back to attempting to ignore the world. But as the bleeding got worse and the cramps began, I reached for the phone. I called Stephanie back and sobbed out the words I had been avoiding all day. "I'm losing the pregnancy." Even as I said them, I did not know if they were the right words. Was I really losing the pregnancy? Was there ever even a pregnancy to lose? I did not know what else to say though, and it *felt* like I was losing a baby. It *felt* like that embryo I already loved so deeply and had a picture of on my wall was dying.

The conversation did not last long before I began to retreat back into my shell. I promised her for a second time that I would call with news as soon as I had it, and then I crawled under my covers and attempted to sleep my grief away. I woke the next morning to blood running down my legs. It was bright red and full of clots. I did not want to give up hope, but I did not know what else I was supposed to believe now. Everything hurt. I could not even choke down water. My back was aching, but I was afraid to take anything for the pain on the off chance that there was still a baby inside of me.

It was not supposed to turn out like this.

I tried to hold myself together as I drove to my doctor's office. I wanted to maintain hope, but with so much blood, I was not sure there was any hope left. I cried almost from the moment I walked in the doors until the moment I walked out. I cried as they drew blood, and I cried as my doctor and nurse tried to comfort me. I cried as I checked out, and I cried as I walked to my car. It all felt so pointless. We all knew I was not pregnant. We all knew it had not worked.

I went into my office, attempting to distract myself from the inevitable. I did not know what else to do, so I threw myself into my daily duties. I was waiting for a call that I knew would crush me.

That afternoon the call came. I was not pregnant. I had never been pregnant. According to my levels, the embryo had never implanted.

It did not seem right.

I hurt too much for something to not have died.

Chapter 23

I left work as soon as I hung up the phone. I could not function any longer and I simply did not know how to pretend. Once home and curled up in my bed, I sent a mass text to those I knew were waiting on the news:

I'm not pregnant. And I don't want to talk about it.

I was flooded with love and support, but I failed to respond to anyone. I couldn't bring myself to assure them I was all right. I was not even capable of crying anymore. I had shed all my tears that morning. All I had left now was this emptiness inside of me.

Michael's sister showed up on my doorstep, concerned and wanting to be a friend. I stared at her blankly, unable to converse in any way that would have ever been deemed normal. I never let her get in past the entryway. I just could not deal with her. I could not deal with anyone.

I spent that night wrapped up in a ball at the edge of my bed. Not crying. Not sleeping. I was just lying there, in silence, by myself. For hours.

The next morning I attempted to get up and go to work, but by the afternoon I realized I was not accomplishing much of anything. I told my boss I was going to need to take half days for the rest of the week, and then I checked out for the remainder of the day.

Instead of heading straight home though, I drove to the grocery store as if on autopilot. Suddenly I was convinced that I needed a butter dish. I was not sure why I needed a butter dish (since I used margarine that came in a tub), but somehow I had decided this was important. There I was in my grief, combing the kitchen aisle of the grocery store until I found a butter dish. Just one. I put it in my cart, because I had an entire cart for one butter dish. Then I went and bought butter. Not because I had any need for butter, but because my butter dish could not be empty.

As I was checking out, the woman ringing me up said, "I haven't seen butter dishes in a while!" It was only then that I realized how crazy this was. I was grieving. I was mourning. And I was buying a butter dish. But I did not care.

I drove home and I put the butter in the butter dish before setting it out on my table. Like this was normal. Like it was the missing piece necessary to complete the look. Then I grabbed a large trash bag and took it to the bathroom, where I threw in all of the pee sticks I had lined meticulously across the back of my toilet. Every pregnancy test I had taken against my better judgment over the previous few days went into that bag. But now I had an entire trash bag for just a handful of tests. So I threw in the box of unused tests as well, before grabbing the progesterone capsules sitting on my counter and trashing them too. Then I chucked the panty liners that were also out—even though I would likely need panty liners again at some point in my future. They were there, so they went into the bag.

I searched for anything else related to this fiasco that I could throw away. I walked into my bedroom and saw all the pamphlets and packets I had collected from the start, information on hormones and early pregnancy symptoms that had been cluttering my bedside table. I threw those in. I glanced at the information my acupuncturist had given me about how to support a pregnancy in the first month. I tossed that. I spied the picture of my embie hanging on the wall. I marched over, tore it down, and ...

I couldn't. I just couldn't. It was ridiculous and silly and far too sentimental for an embryo that had never even attached, but I could not throw it away. Instead, I put it in the sperm donor book I had made, which contained all the information about my donor. It was tucked safely away in my closet where I did not have to look at it, hiding the heartache that I did not want to feel.

These were the irrational moves of a brokenhearted infertile woman. I was now the proud owner of a butter dish. And butter. My house was pee stick free, and I was left trying to determine what it was I was supposed to do next. I felt like a lunatic and I knew that my reactions to just about everything were stunted and wrong, but I could not figure out how to pull myself together.

At least now I had a butter dish.

In the days that followed, there were moments when I felt myself falling apart. They were the seconds in time when I became lost in the thought of, "I am *not* going to be OK". The periods where I actually succumbed to crying at my desk. For reasons I could not even explain, I felt worse with each passing day—more raw and less stable with every attempt to move forward.

I knew women who had taken for granted the gift they had been given in motherhood. Women who had used their children as pawns in ugly divorces. Women who had blamed their kids for the loss of their party days. Women who had neglected and ignored. Women who had simply walked away, because parenting was not what they had thought it would be.

I could not help but wonder why those women were allowed to have children and I was not. Why some of these women got pregnant when they were actively trying *not* to, and I could not get pregnant when a healthy embryo was placed directly in my uterus. People had babies every day. People who did not even know what to do with them and who did not even want them. It just happened, because that was how the body was made. That was how it was supposed to work. We were created to procreate. It was not *supposed* to be this difficult.

I often wondered if this meant something more, lost in the fear that there was more wrong with me than anyone realized. Maybe there was something about me that would prevent me from getting pregnant. Ever.

All I kept thinking was that I had done everything right. I had taken care of myself, I had followed the rules, and I had stayed positive. I had been Suzie Fucking Sunshine I was so positive. I had done everything I was supposed to do. This whole time I thought that I was just being challenged, but that as long as I stayed strong and kept fighting, I would get my baby. People have babies every day. So how could I *not* think that if I did everything right I would be one of them?

I was consumed by how hard I tried, how much I sacrificed, and how little it mattered. I was up to my ears in debt now. I had borrowed so much money from credit and my grandmother. It would take me years to pay it all back. And for what? I had nothing to show for it.

I experienced more moments of complete numbness than of pain. I slapped a smile on my face and had conversations, comforting those close to me and reassuring *them* that I would be OK. I was doing my best to pretend, because I always believed that you could choose how you reacted to the circumstances life handed you. Except that I was fairly sure my fake-it-to-make-it attitude was not working.

I was too broken. And all the pretending in the world could not fix that.

Chapter 24

Two weeks after officially finding out that my cycle had failed, I received a call from Michael's sister. She was throwing a surprise party for her new husband's thirtieth birthday, and she wanted me to come. She said she understood if I was not up for it, but that everyone was anxious to see me.

I had been isolating myself since learning I was not pregnant. While part of me wanted to remain locked away from the world forever, I knew that was not something I could do. I told myself it would be nice to be around the people who loved me.

I knew that Michael would be there. We had only spoken once since the wedding, about an issue involving his daughter and nothing more. I had not heard from him since finding out that my cycle had failed, and I had not reached out to him in any way either. I was not sure what to expect, but I was also not overly concerned about it. I simply did not have it in me to worry about anyone else.

Of course his was the first face I saw as I walked through the door that day. I practically ran into him upon entering. So I did the only thing I could think to do—I handed him one of the beers out of the case I was carrying and asked that he open it for me. He did, and then we each turned to talk to other people as though we were merely acquaintances and nothing more. The awkwardness was masked by my inability to care.

I hoped that the beer in my hand would serve as a clue to anyone who did not already know that I was not pregnant. The multiple beers that followed probably screamed of a girl trying to heal in all the wrong ways. But these were people who loved me. They were people who clearly hated to see me hurting and were waiting to catch me if I fell. As I continued drinking far past my limit while playing beer pong with Michael's sister, his family kept a careful watch on me while he kept his distance. In all the time we had known each other, he had never seen me drink in excess. It seemed as though even he was waiting to see how bad this was about to turn.

When the tears began to flow, it really came as no surprise to anyone. We had all wandered away from the party to a local bar, but it was time for me to go home and I knew it. I went to Michael and asked point blank if he would be joining me. I was drunk enough not to care about the implications of my words, and he was sober enough to turn me down. When I stormed out the door intent on walking myself home, he sent his sister after to give me a ride. She comforted me as I cried, and then she made sure I got safely inside before leaving.

I walked in and stripped down, crawling into bed and letting loose the tears that were so much easier to cry now that I had enough alcohol in me to diminish the need to pretend. I cried myself to sleep, waking a few hours later only because my phone was ringing. It was Michael. He had called four times and sent multiple text messages before I woke to the sound. He was obviously now at a point where we were equals in intoxication. He slurred his desire to come over to comfort me. I told him he could, because in that moment all I wanted was his comfort.

When he showed up, I answered the door naked (just as I had been sleeping) and he crawled into my bed fully clothed. He wrapped his arms around me and said how sorry he was that it had not worked. Then he told me he would always love me, explaining how much he hated to see me hurt. He said he just wanted to be able to fix this for me, but that was the extent of our interaction. We did not even kiss. We just curled into each other before both passing out. We woke up six hours later in the exact same position we had fallen asleep in.

It was awkward. I was still naked, and he was still fully clothed, right down to his jeans and socks. We did not say much of anything. We just ... fell into each other. Embracing old habits that had always been difficult to kick. It was almost like neither one of us really knew what else to do, as if we had sex solely because we thought we were *supposed* to. I knew it was a bad idea, but I was hurting and I wanted nothing more than to feel something. So when his hands began to wander and he made it clear that this was what he wanted too, I could not care about anything else. I just wanted to feel something besides what I was already feeling.

Unfortunately, sex did not solve anything. And when it was over, I knew that we were in no better place romantically than we had been just a few days before. I loved him. And he loved me, but not enough to try again. It left us with nowhere to go from there. My heart was still broken and he had not fixed it. He had only distracted me from it for a moment. It was a flash in time that did not live up to the potential we had, because we both knew it was a mistake.

Even as we were doing it, we knew it was a mistake.

Chapter 25

Time continued to pass, while I only grew more numb. I was not sure when exactly it happened, but I had simply stopped feeling anything. There was no happiness, anger, or even grief. It was all gone. I felt nothing.

I knew this was not right, that I should not be feeling so empty. I knew it was not me, but I did not know how to fix it.

I was living my life: talking to friends and family, going to work, eating, sleeping, and surviving. Yet still I was numb. I could not convince myself to move forward with my frozen embryos because I felt like I owed them better than this. They deserved more than the nothingness I had in my heart. Besides, I could not stand the thought of what would happen if I transferred them and they too failed. Could the world possibly get any dimmer than it had already become?

I began doing things in an attempt to incite feelings. I picked fights that the old me never would have engaged in, hoping to get myself worked up. I erupted into stupid laughter with friends, counting on the mood to catch. I even curled up into Michael, believing that *he* would make me feel something again.

But he didn't. Not anger or lust or even the hope and love I had once felt for him. He left, and I felt just as numb as before.

I had never been this shut down, and I had no idea how to wake myself up.

♌

Just when I was sure I would never feel anything again, I managed to convince myself I was pregnant. I realized even in the moment how much this brought my sanity into question. On top of all the obvious reasons why I could not possibly be pregnant, I had been taking the pill since finding out that my previous cycle had failed. I had not been open to another round of Lupron, but I needed to be on something to regulate my hormones while waiting to decide what would come next. So every night I dutifully popped birth control, even though it stood in direct opposition to everything I actually wanted for my life.

Ever since I had allowed Michael into my bed though, there had been a voice in my head whispering, "What if?" That voice was ignoring the fact that I was on the pill, and it was ignoring all the times I had been told how unlikely it would be for me to ever get pregnant naturally. I knew better than to allow myself this kind of hope, but I could not seem to shut that voice up.

It only grew louder one night when I started bleeding off schedule. It was random and out of nowhere and in all the years I had been on the pill, this had never happened to me. I had spotted in the past, but I had never outright started my period when it was not time. So I convinced myself that this was not my period, that I was pregnant, and that I was bleeding because taking the pill was bad for the baby. In a panic, I decided I needed to confirm this right away so that I could get to the hospital in time for them to save the pregnancy.

Even though logically I understood how crazy this was, I could not make my heart listen to reason. I had the whole scenario built up in my head: this fairy tale where I was pregnant and the doctors would be able to save the baby and all of my dreams would come true. I was not even concerned about what Michael's reaction would be. Whatever did or did not exist between us, I believed that he would never begrudge me this. Plus, I reasoned he knew me well enough to know that I would never be the girl banging down his door for child support. I would be the mommy and he would figure out whatever he wanted his role to be. It would not really matter what he decided. Either way, *I* would be the mommy.

I had thrown all my pregnancy tests away in a post-cycle rage. Having nothing left in my house to fuel this insanity, I drove to Walgreens at 9 p.m. on a Saturday night. It was the peak of my mental break. I walked straight to the aisle with the pregnancy tests and grabbed a three-pack, somehow reasoning that I may need confirmation from more than one source. Then I worked my way up to the counter to pay, where a kid in his early 20s emitting the faint stench of pot was listening to music and swaying listlessly by himself.

When I handed my pee sticks to him, he took one look at the package before meeting my eyes and asking, "Good news or bad news?" In all the times I had made similar purchases over the last year, I had never once had a clerk question me on it. I was slightly taken aback (after all, who *was* this kid?) but I beamed all the same as I replied, "Hopefully good."

"Right on!" he said. And suddenly we were having a conversation about it—me and this kid who could not possibly know or understand what I had been through. I was telling him that this had been a long time coming, as though I already knew the result was going to be worthy of celebration. He looked at me with a compassion I was not quite able to place and responded with, "It's tough, isn't it?"

Now I was seeing this kid in a different light entirely. *Did* he understand? Was that even possible? Was there someone in his life who had given him insight into infertility? Or was he just high enough that the words he was saying only magically happened to line up with those of someone who had been there? What were the chances that he actually empathized?

As I was leaving he shouted out a "Good luck!" before returning to his swaying with the music. Maybe he did get it. As improbable as that seemed, maybe he understood.

I rushed home, by this point truly allowing myself to buy into this crazy story that I had concocted. Already I was falling into the fairy tale that indicated a baby in my belly. The one that suggested after trying so hard and failing, it could actually be this easy now.

The test (of course) was negative, and I (of course) was not pregnant. In the instant that the control line on my pee stick popped up, I was somehow shaken back to reality. The fact that I had even allowed myself to take this test in the first place was baffling. I had started my period, and somehow I had convinced myself that meant I was pregnant. It made no logical sense. But now there I was, crying over one more negative pregnancy test when I never should have been peeing on another stick in the first place. It was momentary insanity of epic proportions, and while I was heartbroken all over again, I was also ashamed.

I did not know how I had ever allowed myself to become so broken.

♌

With that one jolt to my emotions, the numbness was replaced by an overwhelming fear. That voice in the back of my head was now telling me I would be alone and childless for the rest of my life. Night after night I went to bed fine, only to begin shaking beneath the tears within 20 minutes. I was so afraid that *this* was all my life would ever have to offer me.

I tried to pretend that eventually everything would go back to normal. That *I* would go back to normal. I did not want to admit I was struggling, because it felt like admitting that infertility was winning. The last thing I ever wanted was for infertility to win.

I was not sure I was strong enough to fight this though. As the tears flowed when no one was looking, I wondered if I was even capable of surviving. Because as things stood, vacillating between nothingness and agony, everything else felt dead.

So even though I knew I was not ready, I started to contemplate that frozen transfer. After calling SRM and discussing the costs involved, I decided I could make it work. Throwing another couple thousand dollars at a frozen cycle felt like a drop in the bucket compared to what I already owed. I would start the new round of hormones almost immediately.

I was willing to do anything if it could just make me feel something other than this.

Chapter 26

Right away a piece of the protocol differed from my fresh cycle. In addition to hormone injections, I was now also prescribed estrogen patches in order to increase my uterine lining for a frozen transfer. I hated them. They were sticky and irritated my skin, but worst of all, they caused the endometriosis to flare and my pain levels to grow exponentially.

I had always prided myself on my strength, but as the days passed and the protocol called for more patches, I began to question how strong I actually was. The pain was becoming worse every day, and I was scared. Scared of something happening to ruin this cycle (a cyst bursting or inflammation that would make my insides so toxic my ice babies could not possibly stick) and scared that as the protocol required more estrogen, the pain would grow to something I could no longer endure. It was an ache that was constant, like someone stabbing me in my sides with hateful ferocity. The thought of it getting worse panicked me.

I spoke to both my RE and gynecologist about the discomfort I was experiencing. They were sympathetic and each offered me a fresh prescription of pain pills, but I did not *want* to be popping pills for this. I was already concerned about the toxicity of my insides and how that might affect my lining, and I had been going out of my way to ensure that my body was as healthy as humanly possible for this cycle. Numbing myself on pills seemed to be the exact opposite of what I should be doing if I wanted to remain committed to that goal.

Refusing pain pills meant that my only option was to grin and bear it though. I kept telling myself the increased pain would be worth it if I wound up with a baby in my belly at the end of this. If I got those two lines, nothing else would matter. But in the meantime, I was stuck carrying around a heating pad and trying to do anything and everything possible to distract myself from the throbbing in my midsection.

It was in the name of distraction that I bought myself a plane ticket home for Thanksgiving. I had vacillated back and forth on making this purchase, knowing full well that I would find out whether or not I was pregnant just days before my flight. That meant a trip home could either turn into an amazing celebration or a disastrous meltdown in which I would inevitably be taking my broken heart out on everyone who loved me most.

It was a gamble, but I had to believe that all the pain, heartbreak, and stress surrounding this ordeal was going to be worth it. In just a month's time, I would be celebrating with my family over a turkey dinner.

And all the rest would simply feel like a bad dream.

Chapter 27

There were days when I was utterly confused about how this had become my life. Not too long before, I had been living a fairly carefree existence. So carefree, in fact, that I had ditched all my belongings and moved 3500 miles north on a whim.

What happened to that girl? When had she signed up for this life instead? How had she become someone who now dealt with a 9-to-5 job, mortgage, car payment, responsibilities and ... infertility? I could not help but feel as though I had taken a wrong turn somewhere.

And then one day, just as my cycle was beginning, I came home to a leak in my house. My countertops, flooring, and the storage unit below were all destroyed.

It was too much. I could not deal with this now. Not with everything else I had going on. But I had no choice. This was what being an adult was all about.

As I sat there crying in the middle of the mess, I was damn near ready to give up and turn my adult card in. Instead, I called the condo association. They were quick to send over a plumber who assessed the situation and declared the leak had originated from within the walls, making it the association's responsibility to repair. It was still stressful, because while I was in the middle of trying to make a baby a stranger would be tearing my home apart. But the silver lining was that this little leak meant I would be getting new countertops and floors for a kitchen that had not been updated in almost 30 years. I tried to remind myself of that fact as I pushed to ignore the logistics of the rest.

When the contracting company arrived a few days later, I answered the door hastily, attempting to prepare for a day spent juggling work, baby making, and home repair. I was tired from a lack of sleep, hurting from the increase in estrogen, and feeling as though I had far too much on my plate to be dealing with this now as well.

I caught my breath and stumbled over my words though, as I realized how good-looking the man standing in front of me was. I briefly panicked over the state of my house, which was in no shape for this attractive stranger to see. My heating pad was thrown on the floor alongside a pile of gossip magazines I had yet to read. A stack of unused syringes sat on the table next to the red medical waste bucket meant to place them in after each shot. Best of all, my IVF calendar was prominently displayed at eye level on the refrigerator.

This gorgeous man had kind eyes, a full beard, and a shy smile. He was exactly my type, and he was entering my house to work in the room where I had taped my protocol for the next few weeks in a location he could not possibly miss. There was nothing I could do about it now.

He introduced himself as John, and I showed him and his partner to the kitchen where I left them to work while I hid in my room. Each time John came to speak to me about another aspect of the job, I grew more flustered. I barely recognized this feeling. It had been so long since someone had piqued my interest in this way. I did not even know anymore how I was supposed to react to a man who gave me butterflies like this.

I was sure he must have seen the baby-making paraphernalia by now. He couldn't possibly return my interest after that. But then ... there was the way he was looking at me. A look I recognized from some distant point in the past, before my life had gone in this other direction. When men had watched me as this man now was. As if I was something actually worth pursuing.

I walked back into the kitchen to find both men working away on their hands and knees. Without thinking, I turned to the older contractor and said, "I'm going to owe you both a drink after this." From behind me John proclaimed, "That sounds great!"

My mind began racing. Had I just inadvertently asked him out, or was I simply in the middle of a hormone-induced delusion? I could not tell. I did not even know what had happened. So I ducked back into my room to contemplate, and it was there that I formulated a plan.

I needed to go to work. As much as I wanted to hang out staring at John all day, I knew that I could not. I realized it made perfect sense for me to write my number down before leaving though. I waited until his partner headed out to the truck for supplies, and then I brought that piece of paper to John. I said that it had been great meeting him, and that if anything came up while they were working to give me a call. I then smiled and ran away.

On my way out the door I bumped into John's partner. I relayed to him the same message I had given John about needing to head in to work, but then suddenly something took over. A voice in my head was telling me to take a leap. I looked him in the eye and said, "And if your friend is single, let him know he can call me anytime he wants."

I could not believe I had just done that. I was a girl who had never boldly picked up a man in her life, but I had just made the first move. His partner looked at me, smiled, and said, "I'll make sure to tell him that …"

I must have shrieked for a solid 15 minutes in my car before making it to work, where I then sat staring at my computer screen and fidgeting uncontrollably for the next three hours. I was completely and totally incapable of accomplishing anything. When my phone rang that afternoon and the screen showed a number I did not recognize, I knew immediately that it was John.

I *almost* did not answer, panic quickly taking over. Somehow I convinced myself to pick up though, and we talked for a few minutes about the work they had done that day. Then just before getting off the phone he said, "And I would love to take you up on that drink if you were serious?" I emphatically replied in the positive, and we made plans for the following evening.

It had worked. I had been bold, and now I had a date with John. The only problem was that calendar hanging conspicuously in my kitchen. How was it possible he had not seen it after all those hours he had spent working in that room? It clearly stated that it was from Seattle Reproductive Medicine, and it was littered with instructions about things like vaginal suppositories and periods. It was mildly humiliating to think about someone looking at it with no knowledge of what I had been through or where I was headed. Yet he had agreed to go out with me anyway?

I was not sure how to play things now. It had been over two years since I had been on a first date with a guy I was actually excited about, and I certainly had not been in the middle of trying to get pregnant at that point.

But I had a date with John.

And in the moment, that felt like something worth celebrating.

♌

By the next day, I was so nervous I was unable to eat. I finally made myself grab a sandwich around 4 p.m. solely because I did not want to be starving and incapable of interaction when we got together. When I arrived home from work, I attempted to get ready despite my shaking hands. I could not believe how anxious I was.

John and I wound up meeting at a tiny bar on my side of town with leather couches and a decent wine menu. Almost immediately our conversation flowed and my nerves began to ease. We talked about politics, education, travel, and a million other topics that we seemed to share similar views on.

He was a born and raised Alaskan boy who had only recently moved back after eight years of traveling and going to school. He had his masters in marketing, but he explained that he had hit a point where he was not sure if he was ready to pursue that life. So he had moved back home and started working for his dad's contracting company. He said it was as good a job as any while trying to figure out what else he wanted.

At some point we touched on the subject of music, and I was telling him how much I missed the live music scene from California. He briefly mentioned a concert going on that night, and suddenly we were closing out our tab and heading straight there. It was the kind of totally spontaneous move that I had always loved.

We arrived to a completely packed house and—it being November in Alaska—we were wearing layers of clothing. As quickly as we had switched gears and found ourselves at the concert venue, we were stripping off items until we were comfortable in the warm and crowded space. Before I knew it, my purse was stuffed full of our clothes and we were in the middle of the dance floor pushing closer to the stage with every beat. Then there we were, up against the rail directly in front of the band, dancing in the middle of a mob scene. We were both dripping in sweat, having the time of our lives.

For just a moment, I allowed myself to forget about everything else in my life that was weighing me down. It was then that he grabbed me and shouted, "This is the best first date I've ever been on!" And I knew I was in. I knew that this boy was just as smitten with me as I was with him.

But I also knew that the girl he was crushing on was likely a girl I would not be in just a few weeks' time. Standing in the middle of a mosh pit, being pushed at from every angle, and getting a contact high from all the pot smokers nearby. There was no way I would willingly inhabit this same scene with a baby on board.

For a split second, I grew a little sad. What if he was falling for the carefree girl I did not have it in me to be much longer? What if the side of me he liked, was the side that would soon be getting pushed even further to the background in the name of motherhood? I knew I was ready to move on to that next step, but was he? So soon after meeting me, would he be willing to witness that transition?

There were other things too. Comments he made throughout the night that made it pretty clear he was nowhere near ready to have kids in his life. Tiny shadows of doubt crept into my head as I thought, "This boy is going to adore me … Until he finds out the truth. And then he is going to run."

I pushed those doubts to the side though, willing myself to ignore them. I attempted desperately to remind myself to live in the here and now, and here and now I was on a ridiculously fun first date with a guy who totally made my heart skip a beat. A guy who was dripping sweat and holding my hair up off my neck because he could tell it was driving me crazy. A guy who still looked at me like I was adorable, even when I tucked all that hair up under a Fedora borrowed from a stranger and stripped down to just a tank top because I had begun to soak through my shirt. A guy who jumped and danced and lost all his inhibitions, only to come back to my side and kiss my sweaty neck every chance he got.

We were both disgusting but laughing hysterically at the twist this night had taken. And when the show ended, we slowly put our layers back on and headed outside only to discover that after an entire day of wet snow and rain, everything had frozen over. As we slipped all over the road on the way back to my house, I assessed the situation. The roads were icy and we could already see a few slide outs. My house was only a few minutes away, while he had a much longer journey. He was likely sober enough to pass a breathalyzer, but he had consumed a few drinks while we were at the show. The idea of his driving all that way less than completely sober on roads that were far from ideal made me nervous.

So I took another leap. I told him that he could stay at my house. I laid down the rules (letting him know that we would not be getting naked), but I said that if he wanted, he could sleep over. Being a boy, he did not think about that offer for long before saying, "Yes."

We both took showers upon arrival at my house. Then we crawled into bed with the intention of falling asleep, only we could not stop talking. We talked about everything. Faith, family, interests, middle names. We talked about it all except for the veritable (baby) elephant in the room.

We touched on my illness a bit. I told him about my passion for writing, and when he asked what I usually wrote about I could not tell the truth without mentioning endometriosis. It was a short conversation though. He did not ask many questions, and I did not push the subject. It had become clear throughout the evening that he was clueless to my plans. Somehow he had never taken notice of that calendar I had been so worried about, and now certainly did not seem like the time to open up about something so big. Our night had been too incredible. I was afraid that when he knew the truth, he would no longer look at me the same way. So even though a part of me felt like I should tell all, I enjoyed basking instead in the light of the girl he seemed to think me to be.

We talked about the events of the previous day, and he confessed that he had been as immediately attracted to me as I had been to him. He said my eyes had drawn him in, and that he had not believed his co-worker when he told him what I had said on my way out the door. He had not believed that *I* was interested in *him*.

I laughed as I explained that it had been his eyes that pulled me in almost immediately as well. They were warm eyes, the kind that you could not help but fall into. I had always been a sucker for eyes. Well, eyes and beards just like the one John happened to be sporting in true mountain man fashion. I made this confession as I cuddled up in his arms with his beard tickling the back of my neck. He responded by saying that he had always had a thing for girls with curly hair, before running his fingers through mine. Again, I was melting.

As we laid there with my back to his chest, I took another leap. "Do you think it's a little weird?" I said. "That you're here, in my bed, cuddled up next to me, and we've never even kissed?"

This was followed by silence. Crickets. No words were spoken for what must have been hours before finally he said, "Well, you sure know how to put a lot of pressure on a moment, don't you?"

I let out an anxious laugh. This was of course a specialty of mine, creating awkward moments. Convinced that I had ruined the mood, I snuggled in, content simply to have his arms around me. But it was in that instant that he flipped me over and planted the sweetest, most gentle kiss upon my lips. I giggled through the entire thing.

We got very little sleep that night. It turned into bouts of talking peppered with more of those sweet kisses until alarms were going off and it was time to return to the real world. We kissed our goodbyes as he explained that he was leaving town for a few days. I was only a week away from leaving for Seattle myself, something I had already told him about without disclosing the details of my trip. With both of us traveling, we made no future plans.

But throughout the day, my phone continued to ding as we texted each other incessantly. There was no question in my mind that we would be seeing each other again. I had all the faith in the world that there would be a second date.

It was just possible that I would be pregnant when that time arrived.

Chapter 28

While John was out of town, I began the progesterone shots that were a requirement of this frozen cycle. Unlike the suppositories I had used previously, these were big needles that needed to go straight into my backside each night before pushing the thick progesterone oil in.

I had not believed it could be possible, but this was actually worse than that trigger shot I had rushed through prior to egg retrieval. Getting the needle in turned out to be the easy part, even though it required twisting in a way I had not thought I was capable of. From there though, the thickness of the oil meant that it took almost a minute to push the plunger down entirely—a practice made all the more difficult by the awkward angle achieved with the syringe behind me. I was bruised and sore right from that very first shot. Nothing about this was simple, but if this cycle worked I would have 10 more weeks of these injections to look forward to. As much as I recognized that to be the best-case scenario, the idea of repeating this shot every night for the next 70-plus days made me feel ill.

It was on night two when I began rifling through the box looking for information that I hoped would include tips or tricks. I wanted to believe that there was some way to simplify this process, and possibly even reduce the pain involved. Unfortunately, that was not what I found. Instead, the only thing to fall out of that box was a stern caution:

WARNING FOR WOMEN:

Progesterone or progesterone-like drugs have been used to prevent miscarriage in the first few months of pregnancy. No adequate evidence is available to show that they are effective for this purpose. Furthermore, most cases of early miscarriage are due to causes which could not be helped by these drugs.

There is an increased risk for minor birth defects in children whose mothers take this drug during the first four months of pregnancy. Several reports suggest an association between mothers who take these drugs in the first trimester of pregnancy and genital abnormalities in male and female babies.

The risk to the male baby is the possibility of being born with a condition in which the opening of the penis is on the underside rather than the tip of the penis (hypospadias). Hypospadias occurs in about 5 to 8 per 1,000 male births and is about doubled with exposure to these drugs. There is not enough information to quantify the risk to exposed female fetuses, but enlargement of the clitoris and fusion of the labia may occur, although rarely.

Therefore, since drugs of this type may induce mild masculinization of the external genitalia of the female fetus, as well as hypospadias in the male fetus, it is wise to avoid using the drug during the first trimester of pregnancy.

As I sat there reading the words that had fallen directly out of the box, my panic mounted. How was this OK? How was this drug, which the Food and Drug Administration was telling me should absolutely *not* be taken during pregnancy, the same drug that was involved in and required for every single cycle of IVF?

I could not wrap my head around any of this. I understood the risks that some of the drugs involved in this process carried for *me* and *my* body. I had accepted those risks. But risks to my unborn children? I did not know how I could possibly feel OK about taking that on. There were some things that just could not be forgiven, and I was pretty sure if I had a son who was born with a malformed penis as a result of my choices in this, there would be no forgiveness.

I was hormonal and scared and unsure. I was still harboring so much sadness over my first failed cycle. That had been my baby. Even though it had never attached, it had still been *my* baby. I had loved it, just as much as I loved those ice babies of mine now waiting in Seattle for me to come get them. Something about this did not feel right.

For the first time, I was truly questioning myself and these decisions I had made. I wanted to be a mother more than anything in the world.

But what cost was I willing to pay to get there?

Chapter 29

Over the course of that weekend, I made the decision to tell John everything. I knew that most people would have argued for allowing more time before revealing this piece of my life, but we lived in a small town and my story was too well known. I had begun to fear his finding out from someone other than me and, besides that; I did not like feeling as though I was hiding this from him. It had become too large a part of who I now was to keep secret.

When he arrived home, he called to ask if he could see me before I left for Seattle. I lobbied for a mellow night in the following evening, suggesting he come over to my place for dinner so that we could talk. I had already scripted out in my head exactly how this conversation was going to go, practicing every word until it no longer seemed so crazy for me to say. Then about an hour before he was supposed to arrive, he sent a text asking how I felt about changing our plans and instead going out to drink with an actress he knew I idolized. It would have been a hilarious joke, had it not been for the fact that I knew he was serious. One of the many things we had talked about the night of our first date was a movie with a slew of big names attached to it that was filming in town. One of the actresses in the film had long been a favorite of mine, and John just so happened to have a buddy who was working on the set.

So when he offered up the opportunity to meet her, saying his buddy knew exactly where she would be, I immediately shifted gears. I managed to inject my nightly progesterone in record time before quickly getting dressed and ready to go. I had been growing more nervous about this conversation with each passing hour anyway. This was the only bait I needed to scrap my plans entirely. As far as I was concerned, coming clean would just have to wait for another day.

I met him and his friends at a bar, and we wasted the evening away talking about anything and everything. We laughed and drank, but we never did see anyone famous. Flanked by members of the crew, the promises of who might show popped up throughout the night, but none of them ever came to fruition. I found myself not even caring though. I knew there was something to be said for a guy introducing a girl to his friends on a second date, and knowing I had made that cut was enough to keep a smile on my face.

As the night wound down, John whispered in my ear that he was ready to go and asked if I wanted to see his house. After an evening spent attempting to impress his friends, I hopped at the chance for some time alone. Before long, we were in the same position we had been in just the week before, once more lying in bed, talking the night away, and distracting each other from sleep.

We kissed and cuddled, but nothing more. It was sweet, almost like being 14 years old again. As we drifted off to sleep still wrapped in each other's arms, it dawned on me that I hadn't spilled the beans. There had never been a right moment though; no necessary segue where it had seemed appropriate. I fell asleep composing in my head the e-mail I would send to him later in the week. I knew he needed to know the truth before I came back from Seattle. Something about writing it rather than speaking it felt far less intimidating anyway.

At 6:00 a.m. my phone rang, Stephanie calling to check in on how my night had gone. I did not answer, but it woke us enough to prompt another make-out session. As we kissed, his hand slowly drifted down toward my stomach and under my shirt. Immediately I remembered the four estrogen patches currently plastered squarely around my belly button. I froze, sucked in my breath, pulled my shirt back down, and blurted out, "Ummmmm … Yeah. My stomach is covered in estrogen patches. That's really *not* hot."

He started laughing though, as he replied, "Sure it's hot! I want an estrogen patch!" He just kept kissing me, as if finding four patches on a girl's stomach was not bizarre in the least. It was clear he had no idea what he had just happened upon.

I was thrown, even if he was not. Slowly our kissing stopped, and I curled up into him with my back to his chest. I knew there likely would be no better opportunity than now to come clean, and I knew that doing this face-to-face was better than taking the coward's way out with an e-mail. So I inhaled again and started, "I have something to tell you." I said. "I think it might be a deal breaker, but I have to tell you anyway. And for the record, if it *is* a deal breaker, I get it. So you don't have to worry about hurting my feelings."

He wrapped me up tighter in his arms before replying, "You've got to love a conversation that starts like that."

I laughed, and then continued on with the plan I had crafted the previous day. I took one final pause before saying, "I was born a man."

It was a statement I then followed with complete silence.

I thought it was funny. I had decided that if I gave him completely inaccurate but bad news first, hearing the actual story would not be nearly as traumatic when I finally got around to it. I was pretty sure this plan was scientifically foolproof, but when I turned around to see his face, I knew he did not believe me for a second. He was holding back the laughter and let it loose only when I cracked a smile first.

Then I launched into the truth. And he let me tell it. Without interjecting, he allowed me to relay the whole story while he listened in silence. When I finished, he took a deep breath of his own before replying with his arms still wrapped tightly around me. "I've just got to tell you that I honestly don't know if I see myself being a dad … ever."

I stopped him there, assuring him that I was *not* looking for a baby daddy in whatever it was we had started. I reminded him that we had only known each other for a week and that for all I knew he bred goats or liked to pee on people in his spare time (to which he responded "I do—on both counts"). I made sure he knew that at this stage in the game, I was not looking for a lifelong commitment. I was simply enjoying getting to know him.

I told him that I understood this was a lot, and I would not take it personally if I never heard from him again. And then I got up and prepared to leave, throwing on clothes that I had left neatly folded on the floor when I had put on his shorts and a tank top the night before. He stopped me and said I did not need to go, but I could feel myself beginning to panic. I had been prepared for his rejection, not his kindness. The buildup of this conversation stressed me more than I realized, and now that it was over, my only instinct was to run. Every part of me was anxious, and it was obvious I was coming undone after spilling the truth. It was not him who was reacting poorly to this confession. It was me.

And so he grabbed me, pulled me back into bed fully clothed, and wrapped me up in his arms. His tone was soothing as he held tight and whispered for me to calm down, repeating that everything was going to be OK. Once my breathing evened out, he said that while he had never known anyone who would do something like this, he understood *why* I was doing it. He repeated that he was not sure how he would feel about dating a pregnant woman, but then he said, "If you do get pregnant though, I would totally come over to your house and fix stuff for you. You probably won't be able to do much yourself once you've got a big belly to drag around."

Even though I knew all he was promising at that point was a friendship, I felt myself relax into him. It was sweet that he was trying to understand, and it was even sweeter that in this moment when I had been so sure he would freak out, he was actually the one attempting to put me at ease.

I left shortly after that. He walked me to the door, kissed me goodbye, and told me good luck. Everything was left hanging in the air, but not in a bad way. I felt as though there was a weight lifted off my shoulders, knowing that I was not hiding this from him anymore. He was now in a position to decide how he wanted to proceed with me based on the facts, rather than some fairy tale version of perfection I could not possibly live up to. If this did turn out to be a deal breaker, I knew that the end result would have been exactly the same even if I *had* waited another month or two before telling him. The only difference would have been in the amount of time I would have continued to be dishonest.

I drove away with no regrets, heading home to get my bag and then leaving for the airport in one more attempt to fulfill my dream of motherhood. Just as I was walking through security, I received a text message:

> **Thank you for the conversation this morning. I just wanted you to know I appreciate the honesty; thanks for trusting me with all that. It was cool of you. Nice to wake up next to you. :) Safe travels!**

It was not the reaction I had expected. He had not freaked out or run away. Perhaps he would take the next few days to contemplate the whole thing and decide that it was all too much for him. It was possible. And if I did manage to make this cycle work, I was pretty sure it was even plausible.

But the truth was, it did not matter. I had told him everything, and he had not flipped out. Now I could turn my focus toward what was really important this week, without worrying any more about him. I knew that those ice babies of mine meant far more than the reaction of a man I had known for only a week. If I had been asked to choose right then and there between him and a baby, I knew that I would have chosen to be pregnant.

Suddenly though, I was starting to wonder if maybe I would not have to choose after all.

Chapter 30

Just like that, I was back at Seattle Reproductive Medicine trying for a second time to make my dreams come true.

Many of the unknowns that had existed the first time around were not there now. My eggs had already been retrieved and were waiting for me to arrive. My transfer was scheduled for the day after I landed in Seattle. This part was very similar to the first round. I sat with my legs up in the same stirrups after filling myself with the same overabundance of water. There was an entirely different doctor from any others I had met before, but even that was the same. At this point I would have been surprised to see a familiar face.

The doctor came in and talked to me about my two ice babies, both of whom had come out of the deep freeze beautifully. We discussed only transferring one and refreezing the other, but I knew that was not an option for me. I wanted both of my babies to have the best chance for survival, and if that meant the possibility of twins—so be it. I had come to believe I could handle twins if that was what I was blessed with. I certainly preferred that option to none at all.

Once he finished transferring two perfect embryos safely into my womb, he set that familiar egg timer for 10 minutes and then left me alone with my thoughts and prayers.

This time around I had decided to do things differently, moving right into acupuncture after the timer dinged. It was an hour of relaxation and focus that I wanted to believe would make all the difference. I stayed in Seattle for an additional three days as well, opting for bed rest over getting straight on a plane. I followed every naturopathic tip for pregnancy I could find, eating pineapple and putting my feet in warm baths during the rare occasions I allowed myself out of bed. I rested, meditated, and did not allow a single morsel of food to pass my lips that was not considered baby friendly. I promised myself that this time around, I would leave no questions to ask in the end.

I spent those days simply cooking my ice babies and praying for them to stick around. When it was time for me to get on a plane and head home for the rest of the wait, I did so knowing that I had given this my very best shot.

The only thing I had left to rely on now was fate.

In the days that followed, I managed to hurt the feelings of those I loved. My dad in particular. I didn't mean to, but it happened.

The problem was that he was hovering. In truth, *everyone* was hovering. My phone rang off the hook with people checking on me, and while it was incredible to know I had so much love and support, it was also overwhelming. I had enough on my plate worrying about myself without worrying about all those around me as well.

I tried to remind them of the time that remained before I would know anything. Somehow, I found myself consoling everyone else, my dad included. I was continuously assuring people that I was fine, when in truth, they were the ones who sounded anxious.

I could hear the worry in all of their voices, but also the hope and concern. It was about the future they wanted for me, but also for themselves as grandpas, aunties, uncles, and friends. These were the wishes that I knew could go unfilled, and it left me with more than just myself to agonize over. So many people were invested in this process now, and I was starting to wish they did not know.

I was staying calm and level headed, but every time someone asked how I was doing, it made me wonder if perhaps I should not have been doing so well. And *that* was putting me on edge.

So I ordered my dad to back off. I told him to stop hovering, and then accused him of smothering me. I felt awful almost immediately afterwards. I knew he loved me, and I knew his concern stemmed from that love. But I was at a stage in this process where I could not worry about anyone else. I could not worry about how they might be affected by the turns this cycle could take, because it was those worries that threatened to break me. There were too many people who stood to be hurt if this did not turn out exactly as I hoped it would.

If I broke all of their hearts in this process as well, how would I ever heal my own?

Chapter 31

My two-week wait passed with agonizing slowness. I grew desperate to distract myself from the absolute lack of pregnancy symptoms I was experiencing. I wanted so badly for those babies to be growing inside of me, but I sensed nothing. It became harder to believe this had worked with each passing day, until I remembered how sure I had been that I was pregnant during the previous cycle. Obviously those gut feelings of mine had turned out to be wrong, and I wanted that to be case now as well, when I truly did not feel a thing. Still, all I could think about was the fact that my boobs did not hurt and my stomach was devoid of flutters. I did not *feel* pregnant, and I was not entirely sure what that meant.

So I turned my focus instead toward John.

Since having the conversation no two people with such a brief history should share, we had only exchanged a few text messages. None of it was overly heavy or gave me any indication of where his head was at. I was beginning to think he was keeping me at arm's length until he knew whether or not I was pregnant, and I couldn't blame him if that *was* the case. But I needed a distraction, so I took matters into my own hands one night toward the end of my cycle, texting:

> **So, are we getting together soon, or are you avoiding the possibly pregnant (definitely neurotic) girl until you know whether or not she's about to reproduce?**

Direct, while still attempting to maintain some semblance of humor. It was the first time I had mentioned the possibility of my being pregnant since our initial conversation. I had no idea how it would go over, but I figured one way or another, his response would help me to gauge his thought process. It took more than an hour for my phone to ding back at me with that clue:

> **Well the fact that I know I'm not the father takes a lot of the pressure off. I actually have plans with my family tonight, but sometime this week we'll have to get together. I am curious about this baby making process now that I've had a moment to wrap my brain around it.**

His use of the word "curious" forced a laugh out of me. Curious was so much better than freaked out as far as I was concerned.

I was ecstatic the next day when he invited me to a wrap party for the movie that had been filming in town. His buddy had somehow managed to get both of our names on the list at the last minute. I fretted over what to wear and how to do my hair. I spent over an hour on my makeup, preparing in a way I had not prepared for anything in ages. Everything leading up to our arrival felt frenzied, and then there we were: in the middle of this packed room filled with celebrities, taking it all in. Like anything about this, or us, was normal.

For a brief moment before spotting anyone famous, we slipped back into reality and touched on my situation. With a playful smile, I boldly asked how much alcohol it was going to take for him to want to kiss the possibly pregnant girl at the end of the evening. He looked down at his glass (only his second) and said, "I think I'm already there."

I could not figure out how this man was being so sweet. It was clear there were parts of this that freaked him out, but not enough to want to wash his hands of me entirely. He was still looking at me like I might be something special, despite everything about me that should have had him running. It was a look that left me melting inside.

When he finished his drink, I made my way to the bar with one of the drink tickets I had been given upon entrance. I obviously was not in any position to be drinking myself and was more than happy to let John take advantage of my inability to consume. While I was waiting for the bartender, I glanced back over in his direction to find him trying to get my attention. He was motioning toward the girl standing beside him. I allowed my eyes to fall on the person he was pointing at, and there she was: the actress I had been so hopeful about meeting just a few weeks before.

I frantically mouthed at him not to lose her, and then set about getting that drink as quickly as possible. Never in my life had something so simple taken so long. I was back by John's side in a matter of minutes, after shoving my way through the crowd with his drink in hand. She had her back to us, but was close enough to reach out and touch. So, that was what I did. As soon as the guy she was talking to walked away, I reached out and touched her shoulder. It seemed like the right move at the time, and only after I had done it did I realize I had *no idea* what my next move should be.

When she turned around and met my eyes, I said the only thing I could think to say. "I love you. I really love you." I could have died. Even as I said it, I knew it was ridiculous. What kind of a person would come to a party like this and turn into a stalker fan so quickly? Yes, this girl was easily one of my favorite actresses, and I had long ago convinced myself that we would be friends if we ever met in real life, but this was insane.

She could not have been any sweeter though. She looked right at me and said, "Oh, I love you too!" It was all the encouragement I needed to just keep going, the fan girl inside of me gushing about everything she had ever done. John was looking at me as though I had grown two heads, but I could not seem to stop. She stood and talked to us for a few minutes before politely excusing herself. I had completely spazzed out on this girl, but she never once acted as scared as she probably should have been.

After she left, John spent a good 15 minutes making fun of me. It was well deserved. Everywhere we looked it seemed there were celebrities wandering about. They were all so mellow, as if this were just any other night. I continued to be star struck while John continued to enjoy both his and my drink tickets. He quickly became intoxicated, but we were both in such good moods that it did not seem to matter.

As the night grew late and the party thinned out, we huddled in a corner to talk. His alcohol showed in how freely he began speaking to me. He explained I had thrown him for a loop with my baby-making revelation, but that the more he thought about it the more he at least understood where I was coming from. He again made it clear he was not ready to be anyone's daddy (and I again reminded him that I had not asked him to be) but then he said, "I think I would be the cool friend though. And that kid is going to need some testosterone! So I'll totally be the guy who comes over and does guy stuff with him."

I fought the grin overtaking my face as I replied, "And what if it's a girl?" His mouth dropped. It was clear he had not thought of that possibility. He really did seem to have come around to the idea though. At one point in the night he even proclaimed, "I really hope you *are* pregnant." I was not sure how much of that was honesty and how much of it was red wine, but it was nice to hear. Almost as nice as his gushing to a stranger at the bar about how beautiful I was just as it was time for us to go.

I grabbed his hand as the bar closed down and we rushed out into the cold to my car together. When we were almost to his house, I realized that we would not be spending this night together. He was being incredibly sweet, but with him drunk and me stone-cold sober, it was not a fair pairing. As we sat in his driveway and he planted sloppy kisses on me, I marveled at the fact that drunk make-out sessions were only ever fun when both parties were drunk. I was happy he was showing me this attention, but I knew in this moment that I wanted to get home to my own bed until we both were on a level playing field again. He pouted a bit when I said I would not be spending the night, but he kissed me goodbye and promised to call in the morning.

And he did. We spent the whole next day texting and recounting the events of the previous evening. We bragged to each other about the stars we each had seen and laughed over how unbelievable the entire night had been. He complained about his hangover and I complained about the impending dread I had building over a blood test now only a day away. I allowed him to continue to be as much of a distraction as possible, while I attempted to ignore the unknown status of my insides.

I was only 24 hours away from knowing whether or not I was pregnant.

Everything that really mattered was now riding on the next day.

Chapter 32

I woke up the morning of my blood test and, for the first time during my frozen cycle, I allowed myself to pee on a stick. When the result was negative, my heart sunk. Most women would have seen two lines by this point if they were pregnant. It was still marginally possible that I could get a positive blood draw, but it was difficult to hold out much hope for that now. So I cried, because I could not believe that I was about to go through this again. I was not sure I would ever forgive myself for allowing this kind of heartbreak into my life once more.

I went in for my blood test feeling defeated, but at least by that point the tears had dissipated and been replaced by a numb resolve. I told the nurse about my negative home test and she encouraged me not to give up yet. She reminded me that at least with this cycle I had not started bleeding as I had the last time around, which had to count for something. The results would be in that afternoon. I just needed to find a way to remain calm and hold out hope until then.

I went straight from the blood draw to an appointment with Tina, my acupuncturist. I had timed this intentionally, knowing that one way or another I would need her help in remaining calm. But almost as soon as my session began, she ceased talking and got a strange look on her face as she focused all of her attention on my pulse.

"Don't get your hopes up," she said. "But your pulse feels *different*. Good different. Like your body is working extra hard." She paused. "Like a pregnancy pulse."

I had seen her around this same time during my fresh cycle, but she had never said anything along these lines. I wanted to heed her warning and not get my hopes up, but I could not help it. Suddenly I wanted to believe that maybe there was something to be hopeful for.

I went to work and did my best to remain patient as the hours passed by. My ability to focus was blown, but I was grateful for even the smallest distractions that came my way as time passed more slowly than it ever had before.

When the phone rang and the caller ID revealed it was SRM, I made the last-minute decision not to answer. Whatever it was they were calling to tell me, I hoped they would leave a message I could to listen to on my own—without someone on the other end of the line playing witness to my emotions. The caller left no such message though, and a few minutes later the phone began ringing again. This time I picked up.

I knew almost immediately from the sound of the voice on the other end of the line what the results had been. The echo of pity made what she was trying to tell me unmistakable, even as I could not comprehend how the words could be true.

It had not worked.

I was not pregnant.

There would be no happy ending.

Chapter 33

The next few days passed by in a blur. I shut down completely, going through the motions of life but not allowing myself to think or feel anything beyond the mundane. And then it was time to travel home for Thanksgiving.

My flight was scheduled to leave at 12:55 a.m., but a delay notice appeared as I sat in the airport waiting to board. The delays continued for the next 5 hours, by which point I had long since missed my connecting flight. I got on the plane anyway, because I did not know what else to do. I did not have the strength to deviate from what had already been planned, and I assumed the airline would accommodate me once I arrived at my layover location.

When we landed I learned that the next connecting flight with available seats was another six hours away. So there I sat in another airport, not sleeping, barely eating, and hoping to make it through this hellish trip home. I was tired, frustrated, and hormonal. Most importantly, I was not pregnant.

I was fairly sure that nothing could make this any worse, until my period started. Right there in the airport, with all of my pain medications tucked away in the baggage I had stupidly checked over 12 hours before. When I had stopped my progesterone shots and torn off the estrogen patches, I had done so knowing that the pain would be inevitable. The IVF drugs had worked too well at causing the endometriosis to flare, even if they had failed at everything else. I assumed this period would not appear until I was in Arizona though, and if my first flight had been on time, that would have been the case. But it hadn't been. I was by myself, without my drugs or heating pad, in a level of pain that was threatening to break me. I was not pregnant, my insides were literally tearing apart, and I did not have anything available to help make it through. This all felt like some sort of cosmic joke, only I did not understand the punch line. I was simply trapped by my own misery.

It was past 7 p.m. when I finally landed in Arizona after more than 20 hours spent in airports and on airplanes. For over eight of those, I had been in excruciating pain with nothing at my disposal to help ease the hurt. By the time the plane landed, I was far past the point of agony. I walked toward baggage claim, gingerly counting my steps, thinking my dad was waiting for me just outside and wondering if it was possible to bleed out before ever even getting there.

But then, there he was. My daddy standing tall amidst the sea of people. I stopped in my tracks when I saw him and began sobbing right there in the middle of a crowded airport. I finally let loose the tears I had been holding back since this debacle began. They were tears that flowed until he was by my side with arms around me, and finally I was able to breathe again. Because my dad was there, ready to take care of me.

We got my bag and I immediately inhaled the Percocet I desperately needed. As soon as we arrived at the house, I crawled into his giant tub, scalding myself with water so hot it left my skin blotched in hues of purple and red. I was grateful just to be there. My strength had been squandered, and more than anything I needed someone taking care of me now. My dad was the only person in the world I trusted enough to be able to do that, and for a brief moment it felt safe to relax into my grief. Relax into my grief and cry.

♌

Those first days home were consumed by pain and tears and hiding from the world. It was not until the weekend that I finally felt ready to see people outside my own family again. Close friends of mine from a past I could not even seem to remember anymore were throwing a party that Friday night, a reunion of sorts for everyone now back in town. I had my dad drop me off, reminding myself that only a week before I had been excited to catch up with everyone. I was determined to spend this night pretending everything was fine, putting on a happy face for my friends if only to make *them* believe I was OK.

Unfortunately, that did not turn out to be as simple as I had hoped it would be. While listening to my friends discuss all the ways in which their lives were moving forward, I felt stunted, stuck in this place of heartbreak and despair where I was not accomplishing any of the milestones they were all reaching together. It was as though I was being left behind, and in that feeling I was unable to converse with these people I had known my entire life. I tried to drink in an attempt to blend in, but that only increased the physical hurt I was experiencing. Cramps sent shooting pains through my chest and up to my shoulder, making each breath more difficult to take. I knew this was related to endometriosis because it started precisely with my period, but I could not figure out how it had spread so high. It destroyed any hope I had of using this night to forget my problems.

After only an hour there, I gave up trying. I texted my dad, begging him to come back, and I blamed my early exit on him when I said my goodbyes. I did not want to own up to how much pain I was in. It was embarrassing enough to fall apart mentally, but now I was crumbling physically as well. I did not want my friends to see that. I wanted them to believe I was stronger than this. I wanted to *be* stronger than this.

On the ride home, the subject of my aging grandparents came up. Looking for a distraction from the pain, I began explaining to my dad that I would not want to continue living a life where I could not take care of myself. I did not say it outright, but in the back of my mind I knew I also feared living a life in this constant state of hurt. As I spoke though, I realized my dad had 25 years on me and would likely be dying long before I was ready for him to. "I take that back," I said. "*You* are not allowed to die. Ever."

He did not respond the way I thought he would. Instead he said, "Well, it has to happen eventually …"

My head immediately began screaming.

Wait. Stop. Don't even go there!

I was too emotional already to contemplate what he was saying.

"I've lived a good life," he continued. "I've raised two good kids and done what I've needed to do. If I die tomorrow, it will still have been a good life."

I can't think about this right now. Stop talking like this!

"Not before you're a grandpa," I interjected, bringing up the topic we had both been avoiding for days. "You still have to be a grandpa."

I think he thought he was comforting me with what he said next. I think he thought he was saying the right thing. "No. I don't need to be a grandpa," he replied. "It will be OK if I'm not."

My head was bellowing at me above any reasonable thought.

*No it **will not** be OK. You not being a grandpa **will not** be OK. Why aren't you angry about this? Why aren't you pissed? **This isn't fair**! Be angry! Be angry for me! Be angry for you! Just be angry!*

But don't say that it will be OK if you aren't ever a grandpa.

Because it won't be. It just won't be.

I had to fight back tears the rest of the ride home, not wanting to break down in that moment, not wanting to break down at all. But as soon as we got back to the house and I found my way up to my room, the flood gates opened.

As I washed my face and brushed my teeth, the tears fell. Soon after I crawled into bed, the pillow was soaked through. I stifled my sobs, keeping them quiet as I could. But I cried. I cried over my empty womb. I cried over the idea of my dad dying before he ever became a grandfather, over the idea of him dying at all. I cried over old friends who had all moved on to the next stage of their lives. Who had all gotten married and at least *started* talking about babies while I was still stagnant. I was doing the same things and maintaining the same less-than-substantial relationships, and already I was facing the fact that I would probably never carry a child. I cried over that, and the money which had been lost on this endeavor. I cried over the choices I had been forced to make, the ones it seemed no one else in my life ever came up against. I cried because of the pain I had been in for the last several days, and because I felt like a weak person every time I complained about that pain. I cried because I did not want to feel like this, with my heart ripping out of my chest.

And I cried because in just one more day I would have to go home to my real life. My job, my house, and my responsibilities. I would have to go home and face how clueless I was about what was supposed to come next. I could not even begin to imagine how I would recover from this.

So, I cried.

Because I had no idea what else to do.

Chapter 34

I returned to Alaska still shattered, raw, and incapable of taking ownership of my life. I knew I had lost my chance of ever becoming pregnant. With $30,000 now down the drain, and no embryos left to go back for – I would never be able to justify trying again. Not when the drugs were so hard on my body, and there were no guarantees of a better outcome.

I needed to find a way to accept the fact that I would never carry a child beneath my heart. But every time I attempted to do that, I was faced with a future I wanted nothing to do with. Some days I was so overcome by emotion that I could not seem to stop the tears. Other days I would go entire 24-hour periods feeling nothing but numb. Then there were the days when I was almost able to forget that empty space beneath my heart, only to be jolted back to reality as soon as I allowed myself to believe I might be alright. I never knew what to expect from one day to the next. They all blended together in a mess of hurt and confusion.

I was falling apart, and on the descent I was frantically searching for anything (or anyone) to stabilize myself with. I had only been home for a few days when I reached out to John and we made plans to see each other. I wanted to believe that maybe he could fix me, a level of pressure that really wasn't fair to put on any man.

I woke the day of our date an emotional mess. I could not control my tears, no matter how hard I tried. It started as I prepared for work surrounded by the remnants of my last cycle: the calendar, the leftover syringes, and that picture of those two ice babies of mine attached to the refrigerator. They were all the things that for whatever reason, I had not yet been able to throw away.

I wiped at my cheeks as I drove to work, wondering if I would be able to get through the day without a full breakdown. I did not even make it to lunch. I had an acupuncture appointment with Tina that morning, which served as the catalyst to my self-destruction. While attempting to update her on how I was feeling, I heard myself say, "I'm just … I'm having a really hard time accepting the fact that I will never carry a child." My lips quivered with each word, and the tears fell without control. When I looked up and realized that she was crying now as well, it only made things worse.

I spent most of my time on her table alternating between fighting back the tears and giving into them fully. I left that session feeling defeated and worn down. Everything inside of me hurt. I did not know how to fix this ache I was experiencing. I just wanted it to go away.

When I arrived back at work, I received a text from John asking what I wanted to do about meeting up that evening. We lived on opposite sides of town and were planning on heading to a location between our homes. I knew he was wondering whether it might just be easier for us to meet there, but I said he should come over to my house first, telling him to pack whatever it was he needed for work the next morning. I figured there was no use pussyfooting around it. My heart was broken, and I was determined to salve the wound with him. He would be sleeping over.

That night we headed off together to the same concert venue we had gone to on our first date a month ago. The opening band was nothing impressive, so we sat away from the stage drinking and catching up. It was awkward at first, as we both felt each other out and attempted to determine where we now stood. I tried desperately to put on a happy face and act as though my life had not just fallen apart. He knew I was not pregnant, but I could tell that he did not really know what to say on the subject. So there we each sat, anxiously avoiding the thing that was on both of our minds.

When the main band came on stage, we wandered back toward the crowd but were quickly disappointed to find that they were not anything to get excited about either. We tried to get into the music for a few songs, but neither of us was feeling it. We left shortly thereafter. The night thus far was not working, and I was tired of pretending I was fine. I just wanted to let him distract me from this hurt.

As soon as we arrived back at my house, the pretense disappeared and we seemed to regain whatever it was we had experienced that first night together.

We found ourselves fluctuating between varying stages of fooling around and talking until eventually we took it all to the next level. Less than two weeks after finding out I was not pregnant and likely never would be, I was sleeping with this man I had been so excited about only a month before. But as much as I had been counting on this to ease my broken heart, the distraction only lasted for moments at a time before I remembered how much I had lost.

He did not seem to notice though. We drifted in and out of sleep, never staying down for long before waking back up to kisses and conversation. Eventually he mentioned the elephant in the room, laughing as he explained that upon my exit the morning I told him of my IVF plans, he had spent the next 20 minutes in bed experiencing an escalating state of panic. This new information caught me off guard. He had been so calm when I gave him the news, so stoic and put together. I had originally been expecting the panic, but there had been no signs of it. So to hear about it now surprised me, but it was what came out of his mouth next that truly stung me.

Still laughing over his own stress regarding my situation, he informed me that he had told his sister and a few friends the story in the midst of that panic. "My sister thinks you're crazy," he teased, with arms still wrapped around me.

My mind began spinning. The story he had gotten from me that morning had lasted no more than 10 minutes. I had shown very little emotion as I gave him the most basic of details. He could not possibly have understood the intensity that existed beneath those details, the complexities of the situation, or the circumstances surrounding each of the decisions I had made. Apparently, when he had regaled his sister and friends with my news later that night, it was after one of the guys had asked him how things were going with the new girl he was dating. It was in a moment when he had decided that this whole thing was a deal breaker and had already convinced himself he would never see me again. So he had spilled all. As though it was some humorous dating story, rather than my life.

Even as he told me this—and informed me of his protective sister's understandable reaction to the small "she's in Seattle trying to get knocked up" piece of the story he had shared—he was laughing.

Meanwhile, I was shrinking away from him in bed, appalled by the whole thing. Perhaps it was the freshness of this wound, but the idea of anyone laughing about the decisions I had made stung deep. Had I gotten pregnant, I probably would not have cared nearly as much about hearing the details of this conversation after the fact. But I had not gotten pregnant. There were so many raw emotions lingering behind that failure, it felt like a slap in the face to picture anyone laughing at the effort.

I knew he did not see that though, because I had not allowed myself to show it to him. He had even made a point earlier in the evening of noting how great I seemed to be doing. I could sense his hesitation when he said it, no doubt wondering if there was a breakdown lingering beneath the surface. But I had maintained the smile plastered on my face, putting forth the picture-perfect image of a girl meant to be the life of the party, rather than one crumbling beneath the weight of her own losses. I had fought to show him that I was fine.

While I was hiding behind my very fake smile, he was only taking his cues from me. The confusion that washed across his face as he registered my hurt now made perfect sense. Still, I could not manage much beyond looking at him and spouting off, "Yeah. Well, my dad probably wouldn't like you all that much either." Because in this moment, reacting like a 12-year-old felt like all I was capable of. I rolled over and turned my back to him as he continued laughing, still under the impression that this was a joke.

As much as I hated to admit it, I could see how a conversation like this could have evolved. I had dropped an insane amount of crap into his lap and then gotten on a plane and left. It made sense that he would tell the people in his life about it, especially when in his mind he had already decided we were over. If he never planned on seeing me again, why *wouldn't* he share those details? Even as I fought back the tears of betrayal, I knew that it was hypocritical of me to be upset when all along I had been blogging about our courtship. From day one, I had been writing about the boy who had shown up to date me just as I entered my second round of IVF. That was an infraction I realized in retrospect was actually far worse.

So when he said, "You're worrying about an awful lot of other people right now. People who aren't in this bed and who really don't matter in regard to the two of us," I knew he was right. It was much easier to pretend everything was OK if we weren't actually discussing all the reasons why it wasn't. I had no idea what had changed his mind from the point when he had been so sure we were through, and I wasn't sure I wanted to know. I didn't want to focus on any of it anymore. Within twenty minutes, the subject was dropped and we were right back to kissing as though nothing else mattered. He became my excuse to pretend.

And in that, I was choosing to ignore all the rest.

Chapter 35

I relied more on John in the days and weeks that followed, but not in the expected ways. I hardly ever spoke to him about how I was feeling, and it was rare when I allowed him to catch a glimpse of me in an emotional state. It was not that I did not trust him; rather, I needed him to be a distraction from my grief. He could not fulfill that role if I plunged him into the middle of it.

So our nights spent together became nights focused on pretending. I smiled, laughed, and cuddled up into him as though nothing was wrong. We were now together a few times a week and talking every day, but we had retreated into our own little bubble of quiet nights in, rarely ever venturing out. It was easier this way. I was able to pretend better when I only had to worry about fooling him. And when it was just the two of us watching a movie or curled up in bed, there were actually moments when I was able to forget how much my heart was hurting.

Over time, it became a joke between us. Fully aware of what I had been through, he clearly expected to see me to break down by now. I never showed him that side though, leaving him instead to continue making comments about how well I was handling everything. They were comments that I took to be well-meaning attempts at getting me to open up. As such, I made a point of brushing them aside. Eventually he began to tease me for clinging so tightly to my "strong, independent woman" status. I knew I should try to let him in, but it was just so much easier to pretend.

Eventually he started asking more questions about my health. Physically, I had been experiencing a lot of pain since my failed cycle. He knew that, but he did not fully understand the extent of what it meant or what could be done to fix it. One night in particular I was deflecting his questions as I had so many times in the past, when he finally let out a sigh and said simply, "I've just been thinking about it all, and it seems like a lot for you to have to deal with on your own."

I was not sure what he was getting at with this—if he was imploring me to open up, or if he was simply expressing frustration over the fact that I did not seem to want to. So I did the only thing I knew how to do. I made a quip about being a strong, independent woman before positioning myself in a way that made it clear I was intent on distracting him with my feminine wiles.

I could feel him looking at me sometimes though. He was watching to see if this all meant as much to me as it must. As much as it should have, given how hard I had tried. But I was not ready to show him that. For so many reasons, I could not bring myself to let him know how broken I truly was. Part of it was probably because I knew he could never be as invested in this as I had been, and I did not want to have to describe my pain (both the physical and the mental) to someone who would never truly understand it. But then there was also the part of me that was simply far too committed to being the strong, independent woman now—in both his eyes and my own. That part could not let down the wall, no matter how much he was ready for me to.

♌

The time we spent together was typically fun, sexually driven, and exactly what I needed to ignore the ache in my heart. Over the next month, we fell into a groove and were swiftly approaching relationship territory, even as I fought to keep the broken pieces of myself away from him. If anything, it felt as though he was the one most invested in what we were building.

So when he dumped me, I did not see it coming.

It was a Friday night and he knew I had plans with a group of girlfriends. We had discussed the details the night before amidst fevered kisses in his bed. So when he began texting me a little after seven, I could not help but smile. We had not planned on seeing each other, but now he was asking if I would come over after my girl's night. I told him I would head his way as soon as we wrapped up, before turning my attention back to my friends, where I made a fatal mistake. I referred to him as my boyfriend. For the first time ever, I called him mine.

When I showed up at his house a few hours later, we sat downstairs talking and listening to music until the early morning hours. It was one of those comfortable evenings where everything felt just right and we were perfectly at ease in each other's presence.

Only when it was far too late did we crawl into bed and begin playing our usual game of alternating between unending conversations and passion-driven moments. Somehow the subject of New Year's Eve came up. It was only a few weeks away, and I had suggested we go out with my group of my friends. I was anxious for him to get to know them, never expecting the reaction I would receive.

"I'm not sure I really want to meet your friends." He said it while still wrapped tightly around me, so that I was not even sure I had heard him correctly.

My voice was momentarily paralyzed, stunned for only an instant before we tumbled into a conversation neither one of us seemed to have been planning on. It was a conversation about what we were. Or I guess what we were not. That was when he told me for the first time that he was not looking for a relationship. It was funny because I had not believed I was either. Not until this very moment. But then I realized that was exactly what we had been building up to, and I could not help but ask him what it was he thought we had been doing.

He said he knew we were heading in that direction and that it was not anything I had misread. He explained that he really did like me, but that all these little steps toward a relationship were not something he was ready for. And that was when he launched into the excuses.

He described a relationship which had ended only a few months prior to meeting me, explaining he was not yet ready for another. I had always assumed we never spoke about past relationships because of my desire to keep the still-lingering feelings I harbored for Michael out of whatever this new endeavor was. It turned out he had been avoiding the subject all along as well. He told me he liked his space, his independence. He liked being single and enjoyed the nights spent by himself without obligations or commitments to anyone else.

I stopped and reminded him that *he* had invited *me* over on this night, not the other way around. If he wanted his space and the night to himself, he could easily have had that.

He paused before saying I was right, but that he really had wanted to see me. He said he enjoyed talking to me and the time we spent together. He just was not ready for another commitment.

For the second time in a row, it seemed like a guy was telling me he wanted me in his life but that we had no future together. I got up and started to get dressed, knowing only one thing for sure: I was *not* going to spend the next however many months or years trying to convince him to want more from me than he did.

As I prepared to leave, he panicked. He said he did not want me to go and that this was not how he wanted things to end. He began to tell me how much he cared, but I stopped him. I looked him in the eye and said, "You just told me that you have no interest in meeting my friends, because doing so would feel like too much of a commitment. What kind of girl would stay after that?"

He started to backtrack. I could tell this was not a conversation he planned on having. I didn't believe it was a conversation he *wanted* to have. But it was happening. It was out there. And at three in the morning, there was no escaping the words that had already been spoken.

We talked for maybe 20 minutes longer. At one point I looked at him and said, "It's not like we're going at lightning speed here. I wanted you to meet my friends. That was it. I just thought that was the direction we were heading in, moving forward like people do. I'm a little embarrassed right now, because I really did think we had something."

He admitted that we did and that I had not been making it all up, but it just was not what he wanted. I kept thinking about how calm this conversation was. I was reserved in everything I said, and there were no heavy emotions or strong outbursts by either of us. I was confused, and it was obvious I was trying to clear up that confusion, but that was it. Nothing else in my words hinted at a girl fighting to keep this thing together. I knew that, and it seemed he did as well.

So when we got downstairs and he sat on the steps and said, "I feel like you're a little relieved right now," I almost felt bad. There were other comments about mistakes he had made in his past; things he was trying to do now to put his life back together. He kept saying that I seemed to have it all figured out, and that I handled myself so well no matter what I was dealing with. They were comments which seemed to imply I was somehow steps ahead of him, and now he was bringing up how I was handling this too, making it clear I had inadvertently tricked him into believing I was more put together than I really was. My desire to hide all the dark from him had apparently backfired.

But I could not change it now. Not as I was being dumped. I was not sure I even wanted to at this point. So instead, I sat down next to him and explained that I did not have it in me to get emotionally worked up over one more thing in my life. I did not have it in me to break down and beg him to reconsider. I told him I was not going to fight him on this, but that he did need to know it was not what I wanted.

Then I put on my boots and left his house at 3:30 in the morning. He was still sitting on those steps, just as blown away by what had gone down as I was.

The next morning I woke to a text message from him:

> I'm sorry for being a dick head. I woke up this morning feeling pretty low about the way I conducted myself last night, but it was just clear we were at different points. Hope you don't hold it against me too much. Maybe we can hang out some time away from the confines and pressure of a relationship, because at the end of the day I really just like talking to you.

I responded by telling him I was fine and that I was glad he had at least been honest with me, but that was pretty much it. The end. There were no tears shed, even in the light of day. I had meant it when I said I did not have it in me to get emotionally worked up about anything else. Still, I was sad. This was not how I had wanted things to go.

And suddenly, I was not feeling so strong and independent anymore.

Chapter 36

There was no time to dwell on my breakup with John. While he had served as a distraction, the physical pain I was experiencing since IVF had become almost impossible to ignore. Only days later I had an appointment with my doctor to discuss options. Unfortunately, the only solutions she was able to offer were far cries from anything I was willing to accept: a hysterectomy, another round of Lupron, or a referral to a pain clinic.

We had discussed the first two possibilities in the past, and through my own research and personal history I had already concluded that neither was an option for me. There were too many known cases of endometriosis continuing to cause issues long after the uterus and ovaries were removed. It was no guarantee, and I could not bring myself to make such an extreme medical decision without assurances that it would work. If I was going to lose my ability to have children once and for all, I needed to know it would not be a wasted sacrifice.

As far as the suggestion of Lupron, I simply was not willing to go through that again. Not when it hadn't even worked the first time around.

I had been expecting her to offer me these two options and had gone into this appointment knowing I would turn them down. What I had not been expecting was the third and only other choice she presented me with.

A referral to a pain clinic. It just felt so hopeless. I had managed to avoid becoming reliant upon pain medications in the two years I had been dealing with this disease, solely through sheer determination and an aversion to being drugged. But now, this was the only thing left in her magic bag of tricks to offer. Once more she reiterated that I had one of the most aggressive cases of endometriosis she had ever seen, growing somber as she explained that she no longer knew how else to help me.

I knew a pain clinic could do nothing to prevent further damage from endometriosis. It would simply numb me to it all until I was willing to do something more permanent. I pictured myself living the rest of my life in a drugged-out haze, and it hurt to breathe. I knew she was not trying to blow me off, but I could not shake the feeling that my doctor was washing her hands of me. In that, I felt incredibly helpless. None of these options were acceptable. And yet, it seemed as though they were all I was left with.

It was not until a day or two later that I remembered an e-mail I had received months before from a woman who read my blog. She had written following one of my failed cycles to recommend The Center for Endometriosis Care in Georgia as a last line of defense. Describing her personal experience, she explained that after years of pain it had been that center where she finally found relief. I wrote back thanking her for the information, but at the time I had been too overwhelmed by grief and heartache to think about my next step. Now that I was suddenly remembering her words, there was renewed hope in another choice.

I began diving into the CEC's website and devouring every morsel of information I could find. They practiced excision surgery, which according to the center was the only true way to treat endometriosis. Unfortunately, very few doctors seemed to be trained in the method. As I continued to research, I learned that most doctors were taught to treat endometriosis with drugs such as Lupron and birth control pills. They resorted to surgery only to diagnose or when the pain became unbearable—and when they did cut, it was not really cutting at all. It was rather a burning and melting of bad tissue, time-saving measures to remove the disease without being overly invasive. According to what I was reading now, this burning and melting was not permanent. It was known to leave remnants of the endometrial tissue everywhere, allowing it to grow right back in severe cases.

But with excision surgery, everything would be cut away. These specialized surgeons worked to excise every last ounce of endometrial tissue to prevent the chance of recurrence, almost always buying the women who went this route at least a few years of relief. Only a handful of specialists in the United States were treating endometriosis this way, and I quickly tracked down the names of those touted as the best—the doctors at the CEC and a Dr. Cook in California. He had his own practice, The Vital Health Institute, where he worked primarily to treat women with endometriosis.

Before I knew it, I had submitted inquiry forms to both places. Each of their websites promised free phone consults, so I was quick to get them my medical records as well. I heard back from Dr. Cook's office almost immediately and arranged an appointment for a few days later.

I had no idea what was involved in going out of state for surgery or whether my insurance would even pay for a dime of it. But I refused to accept that my only options were giving up, embracing a drug I hated, or submitting myself to a life of pain management rather than treatment. There had to be something better out there. And I was determined to find it.

♌

I went into that first phone consultation with Dr. Cook expecting a sales pitch. After all, there had to be a reason he did these consults for free. I was almost immediately taken aback by his gentle demeanor though. He was incredibly receptive to my questions and seemed concerned about my general wellbeing.

The way he explained excision surgery to me was as a treatment option, not a cure. He said that with cancer, you may see 70 percent of patients go into remission and never have problems again. In cancer treatment, that was considered a success. He explained that we needed to look at endometriosis the same way. Women who went on to live pain free after these surgeries needed to be looked at as the successes, while recognizing that every woman may not have the same results.

According to Dr. Cook, the problem with most surgery to remove endometriosis was that the doctors were burning off the layers of bad tissue but still leaving the roots behind. Much like pulling out a weed, *everything* needed to be methodically removed in order to avoid recurrence. I knew as soon as he said it that I had never had *everything* removed. There had always been tissue left behind, and my doctor had always been honest about that. I realized now those roots had never been detached.

Dr. Cook assured me that his priority in surgery was to get every last bit of endometriosis, explaining he was meticulous in accomplishing that goal. If I had this surgery, it would last four to five hours. Each of my previous procedures had been completed in fewer than two. His track record boasted only a handful of patients who had gone on to have a recurrence within a year. That fact alone filled me with hope.

When we got off the phone that day, I was sold. This was the surgery I believed could give me my pain-free life back, and Dr. Cook was the doctor I wanted to perform it. I liked him and the way he spoke to me. Or rather, the way he *did not* speak down to me. He had shown concern beyond the realm of just physical health and seemed to want to treat me as a whole person, not just one more uterus gone awry.

I scheduled a time the following day to speak to his financial office in order to get an idea of what this all would cost me. I had assumed my insurance would at least cover the same percentage they had for my previous two surgeries, but I quickly learned that would not be the case. Because this was a surgery with a specialist located out of state, my insurance was putting a cap on how much they were willing to pay. The nurse on the other end of the line explained that my share of the surgical costs would come out to a little over $12,000. I had paid just a few thousand more than that for my first IVF cycle, and I would still be paying that debt off for the next several years. So when she began mentioning financing options, it was all I could do not to throw up.

How much more debt could I really go into? If I lost my job, how long would it be before I also lost my house? My car? My dignity? Even with great health insurance, I had been consumed by medical debt. I did not know how I could responsibly take on more.

This surgery was not about having a baby. I was past that, working every day on coming to terms with the fact that it would probably never happen for me. Even with this surgery, the damage that had already been done would never be repaired. But this was about finding relief. It was about fighting in a way I had not yet tried, without feeling like I was losing even more of myself to the battle.

I could not afford it though. There was simply no way I could come up with that money out of pocket, especially not in addition to airfare and hotel expenses.

I felt defeated and tired of fighting. I had been trapped on a hamster wheel for two years now, running my hardest but never getting anywhere at all. Learning about this surgery had renewed my hope, but in realizing I could not pay for it, I was not sure I saw a way to win anymore.

It was almost Christmas, yet nothing about my life left me wanting to partake in jovial celebrations. I canceled all my holiday plans at the last minute in favor of cocooning up in my house and succumbing to the sadness. For the first time, I truly allowed myself to grieve. There was sobbing so hard I could barely breathe and moments where I simply curled up in a ball, immobilized by the heartache of the last year. I bargained, pleaded, and begged for answers and relief. In my darkest moments (when I pictured a lifetime of pain and no one ever to call me "mommy"), I collapsed under the weight of it all. This was not the life I wanted, but I was not sure there was any way for me to change it.

I could not shake the voice in my head now telling me this disease had won and would continue to win, always.

Chapter 37

A few days before New Year's Eve, I went to see Tina for an acupuncture appointment. My nights had been overtaken by tossing, turning, and pain, so I was explaining to her how difficult sleep had become. I could not remember having ever felt so exhausted. She began attacking me with needles, allowing me to continue my complaining as my eyelids grew heavy. I woke over an hour later as she was removing those needles from my body, feeling more rested than I had in a long time.

Our session had already run long and should have been over, but I was her last appointment of the day. She said she wanted to work on a few more points on my back if I had time. I flipped over as we began discussing the year to come, my dark mental state over the holidays, and even my breakup with John.

She asked if I had been fighting the urge to call him, but the answer to that question was easy enough to give. The man simply had not been on my list of things to concern myself over. In admitting that, I began to wonder if perhaps he may have been on to something when he accused me of being relieved in the end. At the time I had believed he was completely misreading the situation, but maybe somewhere deep down inside I had known all along that it was never going to work; that we simply were not right for one another.

As I expressed this possibility to Tina, she posed a question to me. "So what do you want?" she asked. "*Who* do you want?" We talked about it for a minute, the qualities I was looking for from Mr. Wonderful, and then she ordered me to write it down. "Make a list, and send it out into the universe," she said. "Make it real."

She then told me the story of meeting her fiancé. A year before, she had written a list herself on New Year's Eve while trying to recover from a bad breakup. She said it was meant to serve as a guideline of qualifications she would refuse to deviate from with the next man she gave her heart to. That list remained in her purse all night, and at 1:30 in the morning she lit it on fire in a symbolic gesture, sending it out into the universe before then meeting the man whose ring she now wore. They were planning a wedding the following summer.

I had heard this story before, but I could not hide my smile as she retold it now. Make a list and put it out into the universe. It sounded simple enough. A list for everything I wanted, romantically or otherwise. A list that would make it clear I was not willing to settle for less.

Michael taught me I was ready. I had wanted him to be my happily ever after, but just because he had not been did not mean I shouldn't go out and find the man who was. After experiencing the heartbreak of failure on my own, I knew now more than ever that I wanted a partner. I was tired of making these decisions by myself and tired of facing the world without someone who loved me by my side.

And so I began working on *my* list, reminding myself with every addition that this was what I deserved: a man who fit the mold instead of simply keeping the bed warm. I worked on it for days before finally committing the words to quality stationary in my own 4th-grade scrawl:

- All the makings of an incredible father-to-be.
- Comes from a genuine and warm family. One with a mother willing to wrap me up in her arms and adopt me as one of her own.
- Passionate. In a thousand different ways and about a thousand different subjects. But most of all, passionate about me.
- Honest. To a fault even. A man capable of being an open book.
- Intelligent.
- Motivated. Not necessarily rich or driven to the point of forsaking all else, but simply motivated. Towards something. Towards anything.
- Someone who holds my hand, touches me when I don't expect it, and runs his fingertips along my body in bed. A man who gives me massages just because.
- Witty. Capable of sparring with me for hours on end.
- Undeterred. By me, my life, my health issues, my random bouts of insanity, my incessant neurosis, and my unending verbosity. In fact, not simply undeterred, but actually all the more smitten as a result.
- Open minded. About anything. About everything. Capable of seeing the world through the eyes of others, and of exhibiting compassion in even the most uncomfortable of circumstances.
- A zest for travel and seeing the world. Together and with our children.
- Loyal. Dedicated. True.
- Mine. For keeps.

I folded it up like a secret love letter and tucked it away in my purse before heading out on New Year's Eve with my friend Lindsay. I made her write a list too, just for good measure. I then went to great lengths making myself presentable. It had been a long time since I put any effort into my appearance after spending months angry at my body for failing me. But that night, I shaved, perfected my makeup, and straightened my hair just so.

At the first bar we went to, I began taking shots and downing champagne. I was determined to have a good time, but after so much sadness I was not entirely sure how to do that without drinking myself into oblivion. I sauntered up to the bar and requested an entire bottle of champagne for our group. I was thinking I was pretty hot stuff at that point, but when I received the bill for $77, I faltered in my confidence. I had been far too stressed about money in the previous weeks and months to be spending that kind of cash on alcohol. Somehow in my already drunken stupor though, I found in this moment an opportunity to actually take something away from money thrown down the drain this year. As my friends and I drank straight from that bottle, I declared it my trophy. I had gotten nothing at all out of those two IVF cycles, but I was determined to keep this bottle. It would be my symbol for a broken year—the one thing I threw money away on while still managing to walk away with *something*. As soon as it was empty, I tucked it away into my purse.

When the countdown began, I exchanged innocent kisses with each of my friends. There was not a single man in sight who caught my eye, but I did not care. I shouted a big "Fuck you!" to the year now gone by. Liquid courage had given me an ability to acknowledge my bitterness for the night, but I was still doing so with a smile on my face.

Now past midnight, we found our way to a courtyard filled with ice sculptures that seemed built specifically for the ritual burning of our lists. We laughed hysterically throughout the process, but still there was something symbolic to it. I felt a purpose behind every last flicker of paper, a commandment sent out to the universe before we began walking to the next bar.

It was there, while sipping water and attempting to sober up, that I locked gazes with a man sitting just a table over. He had gorgeous blue eyes and I immediately wanted to know him. So when he and the group of people he was with got up to leave, I caught those eyes again and questioned where they were headed. He smiled before mentioning a bar a few blocks over. As soon as he was gone, I turned to my friends and announced I had found the man I wished for with my list. I was sure of it. And so we closed out our tab and followed his path.

As soon as we entered the bar, I spotted him. With alcohol coursing through my veins, I walked right up to introduce myself. His smile was wide as I told him my name, and he in turn told me his before grabbing hold of the woman standing next to him and introducing her as his wife. I was immediately embarrassed, realizing I had somehow been so fixated on him that I had never even noticed her standing by his side. They could not have been nicer about it though. He was clearly flattered, and she quickly struck up a conversation with me. We sat there talking for over 20 minutes about a variety of things before she asked for my number and mentioned a friend they had who she wanted to set me up with. It was one of those conversations you have with strangers while drunk in a bar, knowing you will probably never see or hear from them again. We exchanged numbers, but they each escaped my memory as soon as we parted ways.

Lindsay and I went on to have a little more fun that night before heading home. Neither of us did anything overly stupid or embarrassing. It had been a good night, although we each nursed hangovers the following day. As soon as I was able to pull myself out of bed the next morning, I dug that empty bottle of champagne from my purse and placed it on display in my living room.

The year of heartbreak was over. I had officially lost Michael, endured an awful drug that did nothing to combat the disease I still fought, and gone through two failed IVF cycles in the span of 12 months. My world had been ripped apart at the seams.

But a new year was here.

And there had to be hope in that.

Chapter 38

Only a week into the New Year, I received a phone call from Dr. Cook's office asking if I would be available to speak to him that afternoon. I explained I had already had my consultation with the doctor, but the voice on the other end of the line said simply that he was hoping for a chance to speak again. Curiosity got the best of me and I agreed.

When the time arrived, I called his office back and waited for him to join me on the line. Within minutes of our conversation beginning, I determined he was quite possibly the most amazing man I had ever come in contact with. Dr. Cook explained he had been thinking about my case and had spoken to his financial consultant about the fact that I was not able to afford the costs associated with this surgery. He went on to tell me that he had entered this field because he wanted to make a difference, because he knew this was a horrible disease and he was passionate about helping to combat it. Cases like mine were his reason for that passion. He knew he could help me and, more importantly, he *wanted* to.

I sat on the other end of the line dumbstruck. This was a busy man with a very popular practice. When I began searching for the top endometriosis specialists, his name came up over and over again. Yet here he was, taking the time to call me after our initial consultation simply to express a desire to help. I was at a loss for words, and I knew then and there that Dr. Cook was *the* doctor who I needed to perform my surgery. He was the one I wanted taking on this aggressive case of mine, if for no other reason than because he obviously cared so much.

I had spoken to my doctor in Alaska a few weeks before about some of the research I had been doing. Initially she had expressed skepticism about the benefits of excision surgery, concerned it was too invasive and that the doctors performing these surgeries went too far in their quest to rid the body of virtually all endometriosis. But she started asking around and doing some research of her own, and the day before this unexpected call from Dr. Cook she had gotten in touch with me herself. While she was still wary about the aggressive nature of this surgery, she now believed it was my very best chance at finding relief and preserving whatever fertility I still had. Hearing that from her solidified for me the fact that I *needed* this surgery, but all the same hurdles still existed and I did not know how I could possibly make it work.

Now I was talking to Dr. Cook though, and I was suddenly sure we were going to find a way. He took the time to discuss with me the financial aspects of the surgery and what could be done to convince my insurance company to cover more. He went over some of my options and the ways in which he could help. He went above and beyond what I ever would have expected any medical professional to do in order to find a way to make this surgery a reality. By the end of our conversation, we had come up with a plan.

Everything happened incredibly fast. Within a month, I was scheduled for surgery. Arranging the time off work and booking hotels and flights occurred in the blink of an eye. My dad and sister-in-law, Anna, arranged to drive to Northern California from Arizona in order to take care of me in the days post-surgery. Two of my closest friends from San Diego made the trip north to offer moral support as well. Before I knew it, I was in San Jose waiting for my friends and family to arrive and anxiously anticipating my first face-to-face appointment with Dr. Cook.

I did not have to wait long, as I was scheduled to meet with him bright and early the morning after my arrival. I was even more impressed with him in person than I had been over the phone. He was so laid-back and easy to talk to that I quickly forgot how important he really was. It was comforting to converse with a doctor who had such a vast understanding of this disease. I felt validated in having someone tell me that everything I had been dealing with in the past two years had been real. And even more importantly, that it was treatable.

Obviously I had always known this was real, but there was something about this pain that no one else could see that often left me feeling as though others did not buy it. From that very first doctor who said my issues were just the result of moving stress, I had been guarded when it came to discussing this disease and what it had done to me. I never anticipated it would be such a relief to deal with someone who knew so much about it. Someone who believed they could actually help me without a hysterectomy or pumping my body full of poison.

Dr. Cook was completely on board with my hopes to treat as naturally as possible after this surgery, explaining that if he did his job correctly and got rid of everything, there would be no need for drugs or hormones or body-altering substances after the fact. I could focus on acupuncture, herbs, supplements, and a workout routine and diet meant to provide me with balance. It felt like such a relief—an MD with all the respect in the world for natural therapies. I wanted to hug him right there.

After about 45 minutes of talking, we finally went in for the first exam. Once that was complete, Dr. Cook stated that everything looked just as he would have expected it to. The ultrasound revealed the same large endometriomas that had been found on each ovary fairly recently, and he also found what he believed to be some endometriosis and adhesions in the area behind my uterus. He explained that he would not really know how bad everything was until he got in there, but all signs were pointing to a fairly extensive case of endometriosis.

The following morning my dad and Anna arrived and I began the pre-surgery cleanse meant to empty out my insides. There was a possibility of endometriosis throughout my bowel, and if that was the case, a bowel resection would be necessary during surgery. I was officially on clear liquids and no solids for the 24 hours leading up to the first cut. About two hours in, all I could think about was how much I wanted a burrito. The time went quickly though, and before I knew it we were waking up bright and early the following morning to drive to the hospital.

I had that familiar pit in my stomach I experienced during previous surgeries. I was a bundle of nerves as I dressed down into nothing but a gown and was hooked up to an IV in my room. Dr. Cook and the surgeon that would be assisting came in and introduced themselves to my dad. I smiled and laughed and made jokes out of everything in my own attempt to deviate from the parts of this that terrified me. I knew this surgery was going to be different from my previous two, and it was in that difference that I found both hope and fear. I had no idea what to expect upon waking, and my anxiety had me on edge—both for myself and for my dad who was looking on as though he was about to send his only daughter off someplace he could not possibly protect her.

But then it was time. The nurses came to wheel me away and the anesthesiologist came into the surgical room to shake my hand before asking me to begin counting backwards from 99. I immediately noted that something in my arm was stinging, but he told me that was normal and requested again that I just begin counting. So that was what I did.

99…98…97…

Out.

Chapter 39

I had been under anesthesia before, not only for my previous two surgeries, but also for the egg retrievals involved in my donations and IVF. Then there was the time I had my wisdom teeth out and the time I needed plastic surgery after being attacked by a dog as a child. I had been under anesthesia before, but I had never woken up so incapable of functioning as I did upon waking from this surgery. It was like one of those nightmares where you are conscious but cannot speak or move. Surgery was over and there was a nurse standing above me explaining that everything was fine and I was just waking up, but still ... I could not speak. I wanted to ask for my dad. I wanted to ask for juice. I wanted to ask how everything had gone. But instead, I just remained there immobilized.

By the time I was finally wheeled back into the room where my dad and Anna were waiting, I had come to believe it was the morphine drip making me so fuzzy. So as soon as the regulation of that was given to me to manage through a button placed in my hand, I made a conscious decision not to push it unless I absolutely could not stand the pain any longer. I hated being out of it, and I wanted to feel like I had some control over my brain and body once more.

I requested the catheter be removed immediately and promised I would be capable of getting up and going to the bathroom on my own if it was. So as soon as the fluids streaming in through my IV made that necessary, I declared my intentions of keeping good on that promise and allowed a nurse to help me from my bed to the bathroom. I was annoyed at how long it took me to go once there, but I was determined to prove I could do this on my own. When I finally finished, I grudgingly allowed her to walk me back to bed.

The plan had always been that I would stay the night in the hospital after what turned out to be over five hours of surgery, but I knew all along that I would attempt to bypass that plan if given the chance. I hated the idea of staying there. So around 7:30 that evening, I began putting in the hard sell for an early release. The hospital was beautiful and the staff was incredible, but I just did not want to be there. I did not want an IV in my arm for one second longer, I did not want to deal with hospital noises while trying to sleep, and I did not want any more morphine clouding the thoughts in my head.

I started in on the nurse first, explaining to her that I was feeling fine and wanted desperately to be unhooked from the IV. My dad sat next to my bed with panic washing over his face. The thought of my leaving early clearly terrified him. He began to protest, citing how painful the drive would be for me, how far away from the hospital we would be if something went wrong, and how much I would miss the morphine once it wore off. Unfortunately, he had raised a strong willed daughter, and once I set my mind on leaving, I was going to stop at nothing short of a jailbreak.

The nurse began by turning off the morphine, stating we should first gauge my ability to take the pain. I think her thought process had been that perhaps I would realize how much easier the drip of drugs was and change my mind, but that did not happen. She then called Dr. Cook, who asked to speak to me directly. I pled my case, letting him know I wanted nothing more than to check out of the hospital and crawl into my quiet and comfy hotel bed. At first he was a hesitant, but eventually he saw things my way. At 9:00 p.m., I was discharged.

Sore, drugged, and relying upon a lot of help simply to walk, I made my way back to the bed I had woken up in that morning. And then, I began the road to recovery.

♌

I was slowly updated on the details in the days following surgery. My dad explained that Dr. Cook appeared exhausted when he came to speak to them while I was still in recovery. The doctor described the massive amounts of endometriosis he found. But he had managed to remove it all while still saving both of my ovaries and my one remaining tube. It was an incredible feat when you considered the fact that a hysterectomy had been offered to me as the last viable option only a few months before.

When I got the chance to speak to him myself, he informed me that my bowel had been completely fused to my uterus. Separating the two had been one of the biggest pieces of this surgery. There was also scar tissue and endometriosis up near my spleen, which he believed had been contributing to the shooting chest and shoulder pain I had recently been experiencing.

I began reducing my pain pills on day two, making my distaste for being doped up clear from the start. Yet I was quick to acknowledge this surgery had knocked me down hard. It was a struggle simply to get out of bed, and there were moments when I literally felt as though I had been hit by a truck. In the past I had been back to normal within just a few days of surgery, but I knew that would not be the case this time around.

As the days passed, I was increasingly grateful to Anna for making the trip with my dad. Having her there to help me with dressing and showering proved invaluable. I knew beyond a shadow of a doubt that I never would have been comfortable with my dad being the one to assist me in those endeavors. Eating was a chore now as well. I had gone under wanting nothing more than a burrito, and woken up incapable of consuming even just a few bites of anything. I quickly began dropping weight in the post-surgery days.

I had my follow up with Dr. Cook the morning before I left for home. I explained that healing was happening slower than I would have liked, but according to him I was right on schedule. We went over the pictures from surgery, and he showed me all the places that had been "covered in disease." He truly believed he had gotten it all though, and he was hopeful that over the next few weeks I would begin feeling better than I had in years.

When it was time to travel, I still did not feel well enough to navigate an airport. Rather than further postpone our stay, I had my dad call ahead and request wheelchair services. I wanted to get home and into my own bed, and I was anxious for my dad and Anna to be able to do the same. I was grateful to them for being there, but I felt awful that they had been cooped up with me for the entire trip.

Saying goodbye was harder than I anticipated. I was quickly transformed into a sloppy, snotty, sobbing mess while being wheeled away from the people I loved the most in this world. A customer service rep navigated the chair as I cried my way through the San Jose airport. I could not figure out where these tears had come from or why they had come on with such a vengeance, but I knew I could not control them either. Within seconds of being separated, all I could think about was how much I already missed my daddy. I wanted to believe this was the drugs still talking, because otherwise I was reacting like a 12-year-old.

A 12-year-old being wheeled through the airport like an invalid in a chair. A 12-year-old who simply could not stop crying, no matter how hard she tried.

Chapter 40

During one of my pre-op appointments, Dr. Cook spoke to me about something that had very little to do with my *physical* health. He explained that for many women, their lives revolved around this disease and the pain they could not escape. As hard as most tried not to allow that to define them, sometimes it was a difficult fate to avoid. He told me that once the pain was removed, along with the disease, there were often times when a momentary feeling of panic and disillusionment would set in for patients as they attempted to figure out what their lives were meant to revolve around now. He wanted me to prepare for the dip in mood that might accompany that phenomenon.

Initially, I thought he had to have been joking. I anxiously yearned for the day I would be free to go back to living my life just as I had before endometriosis. I could not imagine feeling anything other than elation over relief from this disease. But within a few days of returning home, I realized that Dr. Cook might have been on to something. I was not sure what I was feeling exactly. Shell shocked? Suffering from post-traumatic stress disorder? Dazed? Confused? Just plain exhausted? I did not know what it was, I simply knew that something was off.

The last two years had been a marathon, a test of endurance with no end in sight. And now, it was possible I had reached the end, with at least a few good and pain-free years laid out ahead of me. I should have been ecstatic, but instead I was weepy. I did not know why or how to explain it, I just knew that there was a bit of heartache on my part in the days and weeks that followed.

It was daunting, imagining life again without this fight. I could not picture how I would spend my days now if not in pain. I did not want to waste it. I was already afraid of waking in agony two years down the line and feeling as though I had not lived life to the fullest when given the chance. But I was also exhausted and unsure of how to truly start over. I could not figure out how to push endometriosis and infertility to the back of my mind and return to a life that had not been defined by hormones, sadness, and pain. So in the moments when I should have been healing and rejoicing in the gifts I received, I was instead unexplainably dejected—both over the fight I had already endured and the future that felt so permanently scarred.

I still worried I would never have the family I longed for, and the finality of that was suffocating. That grief became the loneliest thing I ever experienced. During those weeks, I felt tormented by the things I could not control, all the dreams that seemed to have been lost and all the hurt that had been piled on top of me. I did not know how to pull myself out of this ache. Even though I felt as though I should have been over this and focused on the future, I instead became painfully entrenched in the past.

I was at the height of my sadness now. In the previous year, there had been distractions after every fall; next steps and moves that still needed to be taken. The devastation of that second surgery (and the news that came as a result) had led to the drive towards IVF. The heartbreak of that first failed cycle had only given way to preparation for the second. And the shock of that second failed cycle had been abruptly ignored in favor of finding relief from the pain.

But now, here I was. Out of pain, endometriosis free, and finally having to face the events of the last year and a half. I was forced to acknowledge that there was no baby in my womb and that there likely never would be. There were no distractions left. No next steps or options to pursue. There was nothing more to do besides throw in the towel and deal. Something about that reality had me drowning beneath the misery.

When it came time for me to return to work, I was not ready. I needed another day off, and then another, always telling myself that *tomorrow* I would go in. When I finally managed to make it there, it was another week of only half days before I was able to work a regular schedule. Part of that was pain and fatigue, but I also knew it was a side effect of the depression I seemed to have fallen into.

I had always known that life had a way of changing when you least expected it to. You could be walking along at a pace you were comfortable with and on a path you recognized, but there was always the possibility that suddenly and without warning something could shift and everything would be different.

Sometimes it was for the good, for the amazing even. You could meet the love of your life, get offered your dream job, or even win the lottery. And sometimes it was for the bad. You could get diagnosed with cancer, lose your spouse, or find out that someone you held dear had betrayed you.

Occurrences that you had not been anticipating only a few weeks before suddenly had the power to change *everything* and morph your life completely. The only thing I had ever learned for sure was that nothing remained stagnant for long. And I began to realize as the days passed that I was counting on that. Because as

I healed from surgery, I was forced to face how stagnant my life had become.

The drugs from trying to conceive, the mess of hormones, and the heartbreak had all worn me down. They left me feeling completely disconnected from everything and everyone. I was not even sure how to recover from that now, still so consumed by my grief.

It was during an appointment with Tina that I explained how I was feeling and begged for her to fix it. As I lay there naked on her table attempting to describe my current mood, the tears flowed down my face. I was in varying stages of breakdown throughout our appointment.

She talked me through the trauma my body was still recovering from and explained the biological components in all of that. She even encouraged me in my grief and my need to let it all out. At the end of our session, she sat me up to face her before saying, "The light is not out of your eyes. Your soul has not been crushed. You are still there, fighting to come back to the surface. You just have to get through this."

For some reason, I felt comfort in that. One of the things that had been setting me off lately had been people asking what I would do now, what my plans for future motherhood would entail from here. It was a perfectly reasonable question given how singularly focused I had been on that goal during the previous year. The people in my life simply wanted to know what the plan was and how I was going to fulfill my dreams.

The problem was that as soon as I tried to answer that question, my lip would begin to quiver and the tears would form. Every single time. I had tried. I had put everything into trying. I had attempted to carve out the life I wanted and force parenthood as a single mother, because I believed so strongly that being a single mother was better than never being a mother at all. But it had not worked. And now, I could not help but feel that maybe these were decisions I had never been meant to make on my own.

I lost faith in myself, but Tina had not.

I realized I needed to wait for a shift, the moment in time when everything would yet again change. I had to see what would *come* next, before attempting to determine what to *do* next. Because the only thing I knew for sure was that it was coming—a flash in time which would once again change everything. Even at the depths of this depression that had overtaken me, I knew this to be true. Change was imminent.

And it was going to hit in the least expected way.

Chapter 41

I wanted to start working out. It had been over a year and a half since I had engaged in any truly physical activities—a huge shift from my days of running on the beach, biking, hiking, and always being active and outdoors. Once upon a time, I had been a girl who was fit. Now, I simply seemed to be "soft."

I waited anxiously to receive clearance for a return to normal activities. Once I had it, I decided almost immediately to sign up for boot camp at a local Pilate's studio. I became fixated on the goal of getting back into shape. It was easier to fixate on that than to continue dwelling in sadness. I knew only that I wanted to be strong again. I wanted to trust in my body once more.

My introductory class was only three days later. I was nervous but excited, and I seemed to be doing fine until about midway through the class when I was suddenly overtaken by the need to cry. I managed to keep that urge at bay until I was safely in my car with the keys in the ignition, but then the tears flowed freely. I had no idea why. I had been having a good day and it had been almost a week since I had last succumbed to the waterworks. Being in the middle of some beginning Pilates pose when my heart began to ache barely made sense at all.

I reasoned that it was partially because I was tired and cramping. My first post-surgery period had exhibited the awful timing of appearing that very day. My back hurt, my stomach was tight, and only after it was too late had I realized that I was bleeding through my pants. A pad had simply proven to be no match for the heavy first days of my period combined with the butt-in-the-air poses I was twisting into at the instructor's guidance.

But maybe it also had something to do with the release of finally doing something physical after far too long spent sedentary. I partially believed that release had simply opened the dam, allowing the rest to come tumbling through.

I was not sure. All I knew was that I should not have been crying. I was moving (just as I had been yearning to do), I was breathing (slowly, calmly, methodically), and according to the instructor I was even picking up some of the nuances of Pilates like a pro. I had no idea what had set me off, but it was a surge of emotions that was over as quickly as it began. By the time I got home, my tears subsided. Whatever caused the mini breakdown had not lasted long enough to worry about.

I quickly fell in love with Pilates, even while struggling through poses I was not entirely sure I was designed for. I liked leaving classes with the shakes and feeling like I was retraining my body to work for me now. When the boot camp was over, I emphatically signed up for a regular membership. For the first time in a long time, I felt as though I was gaining control of my body again. I was proud of myself, and in that pride, I was coming out of the haze of depression I felt so trapped beneath following surgery.

Weeks passed and my 28th birthday came and went, still with no husband or baby to call my own. It had been two months since surgery, and I was finally starting to feel like myself again. My girlfriends banded together and took me out that night. We laughed and drank and ate an elaborate meal where we shared everything on the table. I felt lucky just to have them.

Every single day, my pain was growing less. All signs pointed to this surgery having been a success. While I was still working with a therapist on reconciling the pieces of my heart that had been broken by infertility and endometriosis, I could feel myself surfacing again, finding things in life to be happy about once more. Typically this involved pushing the emptiness in my womb to the back of my mind, as I did not yet have it in me to think about what would likely never be. But I was surviving. Thriving even.

It was the end of April when I found myself walking out of a Saturday afternoon Pilate's class with a smile on my face. I was feeling refreshed, strong, and confident in the workout I had just completed. The sun was shining and the last of the snow was melting on the ground. I was excited about the summer to come and open to any new adventures that might present themselves.

I sat in my car and put the keys in the ignition. Before taking off for home, I took a long sip out of my water bottle and then glanced down at my phone. There was a missed call from a number I did not recognize. I turned the radio down and then hit the speaker button as I replayed the message:

> **Hey Leah, this is Nick. You met me on New Year's Eve. You may remember, you may not. Either way ... give me a call back.**

That was it, the entire message. I had no idea who the caller was, but somehow I knew that this was the shift I had been anticipating all along.

Life was about to get shaken up, and I would be stagnant no more.

Part 3: Rebounding

(Or: About a Boy)

"Nothing is perfect. Life is messy. Relationships are complex. Outcomes are uncertain. People are irrational." – Hugh Mackay

Chapter 42

I sat in my car, bewildered as I listened to the message once more. I couldn't even guess who this man was, and it was almost May. It made no sense that someone I had apparently met on New Year's Eve was just now picking up the phone to call.

I went over the details of that night in my head once more, but I was sure my memories were clear. The only man I had shown any interest in on New Year's had been the married guy, although I could not even remember his name now. As soon as he introduced me to his wife, I had immediately placed him in the off-limits zone.

She and I had chatted for a bit though, and were getting along well when she mentioned that friend of theirs she thought I would like. We had exchanged numbers under the pretext of a set-up, but that had been the extent of it. I never heard from her again, and I never went out of my way to initiate contact either. Only the week before I had noticed her number in my phone and thought to myself that I should delete it, but for whatever reason … I had not.

I was positive she was the only person I had given my number to that night, and I knew for sure that she was not the one calling me now. The only person I could think it might be was her husband. But I could not wrap my head around some married man I had met for a brief interval months before now calling, out of the blue, as though it was the most normal thing in the world to do. It could not *possibly* be him.

Still, as much as I wanted to simply delete that voicemail and move on, I couldn't do it. The more I thought about this the more driven I became to know who the voice on that message belonged to. Almost four hours passed before I finally gave in to that curiosity and sent him a text:

> Got your message ... Sorry, but I really don't remember giving my number to any guys on New Year's? Curiosity is killing me though ... Where did we meet? And just because it's cracking me up ... What kind of guy waits almost 5 months to call?!?

Within the hour he responded:

> I like to take things slow. Would you like to meet for coffee and see if you remember me? I will send you a picture so you can find me at the coffee shop.

Something about his response had me sure he was a creep. He wanted to send me a picture and lure me to a coffee shop? This did *not* sound like a good idea, and I quickly replied:

> Um, yeah ... Meeting a guy that I maybe met in a bar months ago who I don't remember giving my number to at all kind of sounds like a good way to get murdered. Think I'm going to have to pass on that one ... Thanks though!

He responded again, this time mentioning the bar we had locked eyes at and the black cap he had been wearing at the time. I suddenly knew, based on these details, that this was in fact the married guy. But I could not comprehend why he would be calling me now, so I continued to pretend as though I had no idea who he was:

> **Yeah ... Sorry ... Nothing ... Clearly I didn't make much of an impression myself though. Otherwise, I'm pretty sure I would have gotten a call at least by February.**

I was laughing to myself as I sent it, thinking that if this guy was looking to cheat on his wife, I wanted no part of it, but I was going to give him hell for being such a creeper. I thought I was going to be pretty clever about it too, until he replied:

> **You met my ex-wife the same night. I was married then. If my wife would have left me that night, I could have called in February.**

And there it was, in black and white. This was *definitely* the married guy. The one who I remembered nothing about, beyond the instant attraction I had felt for him. I knew that nothing good could come out of this, but suddenly I had to know what was going on here. So after a few minutes of fighting with myself over whether or not to blow him off, I finally sent a text agreeing to meet for coffee. He responded almost immediately:

> **Wednesday or Thursday in September works for me, or we could jump right into it and meet this Wednesday.**

I laughed out loud. I had been giving him a hard time, but he was giving it right back and remaining persistent in the process. I liked that, and even though I knew it was ridiculous to feel the least bit giddy about a man I knew nothing about beyond his recent separation status, I had been waiting for something to shake things up, and this felt like it could be that. A chance to have fun, flirt, and allow a good-looking man to take my mind off all the rest.

Even if it was just for an hour over coffee.

♌

The day we were supposed to meet, I thought about standing him up a thousand times. My gut told me this was crazy, especially because I still could not figure out how he had gotten my number. I distinctly remembered giving it to her, and I did not like the idea of his digging through his wife's phone to get it. But in the end, I could not quell the curiosity that led to my agreeing to this in the first place. Once the workday was over, I drove straight to the coffee shop he had suggested.

Walking in, I realized that the place was packed, and for a brief moment I worried I would not recognize him. I had been so drunk when we met, and it had been months before. I could not even remember what he looked like now. I was almost convinced this was a lost cause, but then I spotted a man sitting at a table by himself in the middle of the room. When he looked up and our eyes met, there was no doubt in my mind it was him. They were the same clear blue eyes that had sucked me in that night.

I plastered a tentative smile on my face before walking his way. He stood as I approached, and it occurred to me that he was leaner than my typical "type." I could not remember if he had been this thin when we met, but it did not matter. My attention was focused on those eyes.

He asked if I wanted anything and I explained that I did not drink coffee, offering a laugh over the irony of a coffee date. But I noticed that he was not drinking anything either, nor did he make a move to place an order. We eased into a conversation about our day and what we each did for a living. He was intelligent and thoughtful with his words. Even in those first few minutes of conversation, I knew I was in trouble.

I had gone into this skeptical, wary of any signs that he might have been lying about the state of his relationship. Within two minutes of talking to him though, I knew that this was not a man out to cheat on his wife. He was too nervous and unsure of himself, only holding eye contact for a few seconds at a time before anxiously looking away. He smiled and our conversation flowed, but I knew this was not something he was at ease with. I had walked in so incredibly nervous myself, but somehow my confidence grew by the minute—not necessarily in any connection we may have had, but just in the fact that I was sure he was not looking to screw anyone over.

When I finally gained the courage to ask him what had happened to his marriage, he opened up more than I expected. He told me about a couple who met in their early 20s and dated for three years before marrying. They built a home together, supported each other through graduate school, adopted two dogs they each adored, and lived three more years in wedded bliss. In his version of events, she had blindsided him with her decision to end it all a little over a month before. Throughout their relationship she had wistfully discussed her dream of becoming an actress, but never actively pursued the goal. Then she randomly spotted an open casting call online for a low-budget film, decided to audition, and landed a part. She convinced herself that it was a sign of greater things to come and over the next few weeks determined that her marriage was a hindrance to the other life she wanted to be living. No amount of pleading on his part seemed to make a difference once she came to that conclusion.

He had believed they were happy and had never seen this coming. I knew just by listening to him that he was telling the truth. I also knew that he was still devastated by the implications of that truth.

I could not help it. My guard was pummeled. It was painfully clear how difficult the entire situation had been for him. The hurt was plastered across his face. Because of that though, I could not figure out what it was he was doing here in this coffee shop with me now. It was too soon. It made no sense for him to be dating. Besides, I still was not sure how he had ever gotten my number.

I decided that was a question I should ask, but when I did he simply looked at me confused (as though I should have remembered this part of the story myself) and said that her phone had been dead that night. When we exchanged numbers, she had entered mine into his phone.

He explained that the previous week he had been scrolling through his contacts and remembered me when he saw that number staring back at him. Then he admitted that he called initially because he had not known what else to do. According to him, attempting a first date made more sense than sitting at home wallowing in self-pity.

We talked for a while longer and it became clear to me that if I had met this guy under different circumstances, I would have been all in. But these *were not* different circumstances, and knowing what I now knew, I was positive the only thing he needed was a friend. So I made the decision to be that. As far as I could tell, his entire world had just been ripped out from underneath him. He had called for no other reason than because he was hurting and he felt like he *should* be dating. He had simply lucked upon my number. I could have been anyone. There was nothing about him that screamed scumbag to me though. He was a good guy who had been dealt a crappy hand and had no idea what he was supposed to do next. I wanted to help him. I wanted to be his friend.

When we parted ways, Nick thanked me for meeting him and then threw out an invite to a BBQ at his house that weekend. He announced it as his bachelor party, with a sly smile spreading across his face. It was one of the few times he hinted at having a sense of humor during that first meeting. I said "yes" and mentioned bringing a friend, knowing that Lindsay would be dying for an opportunity to meet this guy again herself. We made plans to see each other just a few days later.

Once I arrived home that night, I did an extra bit of sleuthing that I knew deep down I did not need to do. I started by looking up the project he mentioned his wife had gotten involved with, knowing only the genre and town it had been filmed in. When I found a news article referencing it, I took the producer's name and sought him out on Facebook. From there, I searched his friends list for the girl whose first name I only knew. Once I found her, I had her last name as well as his. I was able to use that to look up court records on the state database. Within 15 minutes, I had my proof that he had been telling the truth about when they filed for divorce. The official finalization date was still almost two months away, but I knew that it was real and felt better for having taken the time to dig.

I believed every word he told me during our coffee date without the coffee, but I also believed that he was not in the least bit over her and what had happened between the two of them. Nor did I expect him to be at this point, leaving me convinced that the only role it made sense for me to play was that of his friend. I was not sure what was going to happen between us beyond that, or even if anything would ever happen at all. I just knew already that I cared about this man. If he needed a friend, I was going to be that to him.

Chapter 43

I wrote about our first meeting on the blog, careful to keep any identifying information out of the story I told. I was feeling strangely protective of him, so the post I wrote was rather vague. I had been writing daily for almost two years, committing every thought, feeling, and interaction I experienced to what I considered to be my online journal. I never questioned what I was sharing or who it I was sharing it with. Now though, I had something that I wanted to keep just for me.

So it shook me when only a few hours after I posted such minimal details, I received an e-mail from someone I had formed a friendship with through blogging. Leigh was another Alaskan girl with endometriosis who had reached out to me months before, shortly after my second failed cycle. She had initially written to express her condolences, but over time our e-mails became more an exchange of information as she and her husband prepared to pursue IVF for the first time themselves.

She was writing now to say that she was fairly sure she knew the guy I had been alluding to in my recent post. I had not shared much beyond the fact that he was clearly hurting over the abrupt demise of his relationship, and I left out all details pertaining to why that demise had come about. Because she knew him though, she immediately picked up on the story line of a man dealing with a broken heart after being left by his wife. As I read her e-mail, tentatively naming him and asking if he was the guy I had met, I panicked over who else may have recognized him from the limited picture I had painted.

I immediately felt guilty for having shared any details at all about our meeting. She assured me it had simply been luck that she knew him, and that her big clue had actually been the BBQ I mentioned I would be going to that weekend. Her brother-in-law was going as well, as he and Nick had grown up together and been close friends since childhood. Leigh then confirmed what I had believed all along: that Nick really was a good man who had been screwed over.

It was strange, having this connection I made only a few months before turn out be someone who could reassure me now. But in a way, it also felt like a sign I should not ignore.

♌

The night of the BBQ, Lindsay and I made the 40-minute trek out of town to Nick's house together. We talked the whole way about the bizarre set of events that were now leading us to this party. I maintained my stance that Nick and I were going to be nothing more than friends. In the back of my head though, I think I knew even then that I was lying. There was something about this guy. He had me hooked already.

We had shared a few text messages in the days since meeting for coffee. I could tell he was not quite sure what to make of me and what we were embarking upon either, but there was an ease to our interactions that left me smiling every time I heard from him. I could not remember the last time I had felt butterflies like this. In only a few days, he had proven to be the best distraction I could have asked for from the parts of my life I still had not dealt with.

When we showed up, Lindsay and I made our way slowly up his drive. He spotted us as we came around the corner and immediately walked over to introduce himself to Lindsay once more. He then went about making introductions, and I quickly realized that every person at this party knew who I was. They knew the story of how we had met and every detail of our conversations up to this point. Everyone was friendly, but I could feel the eyes on me from all directions.

I smiled nervously, attempting to comfortably converse with these strangers who seemed to have such high expectations of me. Within five minutes of our arrival, an older gentleman walked over and introduced himself. It was Nick's dad. I had not realized his parents were going to be here, but they too seemed to know exactly who I was. My smile was starting to hurt as I worked to hide the anxiety over this situation. I had never been great in large groups of people I did not know, but I wanted so badly to make a good impression now. Even though I kept telling myself that Nick and I would be nothing more than friends, it suddenly seemed important that these people like me.

It did not take long before I had a drink in hand as I fought to calm my nerves. One of Nick's work buddies sidled up beside me and introduced himself as James. I somehow knew immediately that he was an ally. He was funny and sarcastic and right off the bat we were bantering back and forth. It was because of him that I started to feel at ease, and in his presence I began to genuinely laugh and let go of the tension I had been holding on to up to this point.

I could tell Lindsay was dying for an opportunity to talk to me away from prying eyes. She pulled me aside as soon as the chance arose, explaining that she had been watching Nick as he had been watching me. She practically squealed as she described the way his eyes followed me around this party. Lindsay had seen me struggle through the previous two years. She had seen my heart broken again and again by life, and she had known some of the men I dated along the way. Now though, she was adamant that she had never seen a man look at me quite like this.

When we returned to the group, I caught his mom watching us. It was obvious she was trying to determine what she thought of me. She had to have been worried about her son in the way only a good mother would be. So when she approached me to talk, I was quick to follow her inside, where we sat on a couch in the beautiful home he had only just a few months before shared with his wife. Despite how awkward it should have been, our conversation flowed.

She opened up about the concerns she had for her son, describing the fear she felt for him as he had ceased eating and sleeping immediately following his wife's exodus. She told me he had lost 20 pounds in those weeks, and asked if I had noticed how much more gaunt he appeared from when we originally met. The love she had for her son was clear, and the trepidation she must have been carrying toward me seemed to be overshadowed by a desire to simply see him happy.

His mom revealed that when he found my number in his phone, he had looked at it for three days before getting the nerve to call. She then explained that after meeting me for coffee, he had gone to her house and told her how beautiful I was. But as she told me more about his marriage and the woman who had left, I could see how much she too had been hurt by the abrupt ending. She described his ex as a daughter. Nick was an only child, and it was obvious she had relished the bond she had been able to form with his wife. She was hurt and confused by his wife's exit from their lives and the fact that there had been no recent contact between them.

All of this was a precursor to her asking me to be careful with his heart. I explained that I had no idea where this was going, and that my intentions at this point were only to be his friend. I told her I did not think he was ready for anything more, and that while I was absolutely attracted and interested, I could not foresee us jumping too quickly into something he would not be able to maintain.

She looked at me, explaining that as sad as she was about the events of the previous few months, something about him lit back up from the first time he spoke to me. She said she was a strong believer in everything happening for a reason, and that there was just too much fate in this situation for her to think it was not meant to be something more.

I had to admit I was starting to feel that way as well. The same night I had written and burned a list meant to tell the universe exactly what I wanted out of my next love, I had picked him out of a crowd driven only by instant attraction. He had immediately introduced me to his wife, who simply laughed off the fact that I had hit on her husband. Her phone happened to have been dead, so she put my number in his. And months later, after she left, he thought to call it. Then there was Leigh, who after connecting with me months before online, had been able to reassure me that he was not a creep. Even sitting here now talking to his mom when I still had no idea what was happening between us felt too coincidental to ignore.

It was ridiculous really. If someone had told me a week before that I would be having such an intimate conversation with the mother of a man I had just met, I never would have believed it. But here I was, already caring about her as well. She was warm, genuine, and invested in making me feel comfortable, even though part of her had to have been simultaneously grappling with a loyalty to her daughter-in-law. It was clear she wanted only for her son to be alright, and she seemed to think that maybe I would be a piece of helping that to happen.

When we wandered back outside, another partygoer grabbed me before I could make my way out to the group huddled around the fire. It was his friend Chad, who I had met earlier in the night. He was a few drinks in now and revealed things he likely should not have said. He explained that Nick had been staying with him and his wife Kara a lot in the weeks following the separation, and that the night he remembered my number, he had not simply been scrolling through his phone and seen it. Apparently he had thought of me all on his own and had then needed to search for the old phone he had been using on New Year's Eve in order to retrieve my number. The day he finally gained the nerve to call me, he repeated to both Chad and Kara every text I sent in response—laughing for the first time in weeks. After we met face-to-face, he went to dinner with the two of them and explained that I was the kind of girl he was sure he would want a relationship with, even though he was not sure he was ready for that. In fact, he was pretty sure he wasn't. He had pursued it anyway though, taking the plunge and moving forward despite the hurt he was still in the middle of experiencing. Chad stood there and thanked me for putting a smile on his friend's face again, before predicting that I was about to become a permanent fixture in their circle of friends. He seemed so sure and so prepared to embrace me as one of their own.

Everyone I spoke to seemed eager to offer a similar vote of confidence. As I was passed around among Nick's friends (each enthusiastic to get to know me themselves), I snuck glimpses of him sneaking his own glances back at me. It felt like hours before we finally found ourselves together again, and only then when James decided to grab pictures of Nick from high school to show me. We were laughing over the body-building poses made by a cocky 16-year-old version of Nick when Lindsay mentioned that she was ready to go. It was almost midnight now and she had to be at work early the next morning. I was not ready to leave, but I knew my friend had already been a good sport about staying so late. I began saying my goodbyes, only to have Nick step in front of me with a look on his face that said he did not want me to go. That was when James suggested I stay the night. He and his wife and a few others were sleeping over as well after having too much to drink, and he assured me that someone would get me home in the morning.

All my better instincts were telling me I should probably go, but then there was Nick looking at me with those big beautiful eyes asking me to stay as well. In that moment, all I wanted to do was say "yes."

So I stayed. I walked Lindsay to her car, and she gave me a hug goodbye while whispering that she had a feeling he was the one. I brushed her off and called her a sap, but her words stuck with me as I wandered back into the party. She had met plenty of the men I had been interested in before, but never once had she given this same endorsement.

As people started to leave, the rest of us congregated by the fire. Finally Nick and I found our way to each other, sitting side-by-side and holding hands as though it was the most natural thing in the world. When the hour finally came for everyone to head inside, I did not hesitate as he led me to his room. We had not discussed what we were doing or who we were to each other, but there we were crawling into his bed together. It was not lost on me that this was the same bed he had shared with his wife, and for a moment I was uncomfortable, wondering if he was as well.

That moment quickly vanished when he leaned over and kissed me.

Chapter 44

I allowed that first kiss to sink in before pulling back and asking what we were doing. He looked at me with a sly smile and said, "I thought that was obvious?" I smiled back, but could not hide my apprehension. I outlined for him my master plan to be his friend and nothing more. The master plan I had obviously veered away from now, curled up in his bed with our lips meeting.

Still slightly intoxicated, I joked that he had a choice: I could be his friend and wingman (helping to meet the girls he should be rebounding with) or I could be his rebound chick. But I could not be both. He told me I was crazy, and that I was neither a wingman nor a rebound chick. Then ... he went right back to kissing me. They were kisses so sweet, I was distracted from all reason. We spent the rest of the night laughing and talking and making out as though he was not a man who had been happily married only a few months before.

When I opened my eyes the next morning and his arms were still draped around me, I worried that he was going to wake clear from the alcohol he had consumed the night before and regret my being there. As he began to stir though, he only wrapped me up tighter. When he opened his eyes, he kissed me again before asking if I would go on a date with him that night. I melted into him, comforted by the fact that he was not itching to get away.

We went out to breakfast that morning with James and his wife Amanda. The four of us ate eggs and bacon while laughing over the events of the previous evening. I was surprised at how comfortable I felt with them, as though we had always been friends and this was a typical Sunday morning.

Lindsay called to check in once she got off work, offering to meet us nearby and give me a ride home. As I got out of the car and said my goodbyes, Nick promised to call to finalize our plans for that night. I smiled back at him as they drove away. Lindsay was waiting anxiously for a full report. When I described to her everything that had taken place after she left, she swooned and declared herself even more convinced that he was the one. I had never been a girl to believe in "the one" and knew how crazy it was to claim Nick as such after only one night spent together. Still, I was having a harder time shooting down her proclamations now.

That afternoon he came through on the promise of a date, suggesting we go to a movie I had mentioned wanting to see that morning. Once we arrived at the theater and were looking for seats, he unexpectedly grabbed me from behind before anxiously whispering, "Shit! There's my ex-wife!" I immediately stopped in my tracks, heat rushing to my cheeks as I feared the confrontation that would inevitably ruin our night. When I turned around and looked at his face though, he was laughing and smiling back at me. Already he had discovered how gullible I could be. I shoved him for making me panic, and then we both laughed as we found our way to seats near the back. We did not touch at all upon sitting, maintaining the barriers of a respectable first date. Halfway through the movie though, he placed his hand on my leg and did not take it away until the credits began to roll. I relaxed into that, into him.

Everything inside of me was shouting for attention, telling me to be wary of this man and the broken heart he carried. Logically I knew that he could not possibly be in a place to live up to the feelings I was already experiencing, and that voice in my head was imploring me to take a step back to the friendship I had already decided would be for the best. But from that very first kiss, I knew I could do nothing to stop this from catapulting forward.

When we got back to my house that night, I poured us each a glass of wine and we sat in the living room talking. Eventually I broached the subject that had been weighing heavily on my heart the entire day. I asked him again what it was we were doing—this time without the distraction of a bed to keep us from fully focusing on the topic at hand. He paused for a moment before looking me in the eyes and saying that he had never expected to meet someone he felt as strongly about as he did me, certainly not now with his divorce filed but not yet final. We discussed our actions and the possible ramifications of our choices if we decided to move forward with anything more than a friendship. I said I felt strongly that now was a time for him to be rebounding and that he should be dating women without any intention of getting serious. I implored him to look at me simply as a friend, explaining that I was not the girl who could be his rebound chick, no matter how much we joked about it. I would need more, and in truth, we had *already* crossed the boundary into more. I knew myself, and I knew I had started to fall. It terrified me. So it was then that I told him I was willing to step back. To be his friend (even his wingman) because I truly believed that was what was best for him, and us, in the long run. I was sure he needed to cycle through a few meaningless relationships until he got back on his feet.

I had been rambling out of a nervous need to keep myself from getting hurt, but finally he stopped me. He reached for my hand as he explained that dating other girls and jumping into countless meaningless relationships was not what he wanted. As lost and hurt and broken as he was, he seemed so convinced that *I* was who he wanted to be spending his time with. He was not sure where this was going or what it would become, but he was adamant that *I* was who he wanted—and he was willing to take the risk if I was.

Thus began the epic battle between my heart and head. Even then, I wanted with everything inside of me to believe what he was saying. But I knew better. *Of course* I knew better. Even as I told him I wanted to see what we could become as well, that voice in my head was calling me a fucking idiot. Perhaps it was possible that I was also still too broken (from infertility, from endometriosis, from loss) to listen to logic at that point. Because as I looked into his eyes and allowed him to profess these strong feelings he already harbored for me, logic did not stand a chance.

It was that night when I also made the decision to tell him my story. I felt like he needed to know about my previous year—the pregnancy attempts, the blog, all of it. He had been through enough betrayal. He did not need to find out months down the line that I had been keeping such a big part of my life from him, especially when he was being such an open book with me.

So as we crawled into bed, I began to share my own truth with him as organically as I knew how. I pulled my standard move of trying to make jokes about the whole situation, even though there was nothing funny about any of it. Before I got very far though he stopped me, saying that he already knew what I was about to tell him.

He then explained that when we met on New Year's Eve I had unloaded my entire story upon his wife, giving her every detail right there in that bar. I remembered talking to her, but I had no recollection of baring my soul. Still, given the amount of alcohol I had consumed that night and my typical lack of a filter, I knew as he said it that it was true.

He grimaced as he explained that was why she had never called to set me up with their friend as planned. She had walked away from our conversation saying, "Leah is really nice, but that whole story is a bit much. And it's really weird that she would tell it all to a stranger."

It *was* weird. I was horrified and embarrassed and turning 18 different shades of red as he told me this. I knew I had been drunk that night, but I could not believe I had been *that* drunk.

Still, she had taken my number. Perhaps because she had already brought up the idea of a setup and had not wanted to appear rude, or perhaps because it had felt like the only thing left to do that would allow her to escape me and my over-sharing. Except her phone had been dead, leaving her with his phone to put it in instead.

When I recovered from my shock and embarrassment, I looked at him as seriously as I could and said, "Why? Why would you ever have called the crazy chick from New Year's Eve who unburdened her sad story upon your wife in a bar?"

He did not hesitate before saying, "Why not?" He explained that he had remembered only being excited in my presence that night. That he had wanted to feel that again, and had thought maybe if he called me he would. Once he remembered having my number, he said dialing it had been a no-brainer. It was something he had needed to build up the courage to do, but not something he ever questioned actually following through on.

So that was it. He knew, and he did not care. It did not change anything. He did not even think it was all that weird. He just knew he liked me, he liked being around me, and he wanted to get to know me more.

This man knew everything, and he wanted me anyway.

Chapter 45

Something shifted that night as we settled once more into sweet and frenzied kisses. The entire evening I felt as though I was the one on edge about what we were doing, while he had remained confident in the path we were taking. But with lights out and the absence of the alcohol that had fueled us the night before, it finally hit him that he was now in an intimate setting with someone other than his wife.

He stopped abruptly mid-kiss and laid his head upon my chest. Each of us was still fully clothed, and we had done nothing more than this. When I asked him what was wrong, he said he was not sure he could continue. "You're too nice," he fretted. "You're too nice and you're too perfect and I don't know if I can sleep with you. I don't want to hurt you. I just really don't want to hurt you." I was stunned. I had not been planning on us sleeping together, and I could not figure out where this anxiety had come from. I began running my fingers through his hair as he remained rested on top of me. I whispered that everything was going to be OK and reassured him that we did not need to do anything further. I held him tight as it seemed the reality of what we were doing finally hit him. From the moment of that first kiss, he had been so intent on reassuring me that this was what he wanted. Now though, he was as lost and confused as he had been the first time we met for coffee. I wanted to be the one to calm him in this moment. I wanted to be the one making him feel safe.

We laid there in silence for what felt like forever, his head still rested upon my chest and his arms still wrapped around me. I continued running my fingers through his hair and over his temples as I attempted to comfort him. But then he was shifting, lifting my shirt up and kissing my stomach as he pulled off the yoga pants I had been planning on sleeping in. I did not say anything. I did not know what to say. This was not what I had intended for the night, but now that it was happening, I did not want to stop it either. I was suddenly so caught up in making him feel better—and also in solidifying myself in his life—that I was not thinking clearly. As he moved ahead, I simply followed his lead. Neither of us spoke another word as our bodies came together, but in that moment of physical connection, we could not have been more distant. He was not looking at me, and he was not kissing me. This was not how it was supposed to be, but I somehow understood exactly why it was. When it was over, we both laid there in silence, equally dazed by what had just occurred and unsure of what to say next.

Finally I sat up, looked him in the eye, forced a smile, and said, "Well … at least you got that out of the way." He looked at me for a split second before laughing out loud and pulling me back down beside him. He apologized that it had been so weird, explaining only that he had never believed he would have sex with another woman besides her. He said he could not shake the feeling that he had cheated on his wife, even in knowing that was not what had just occurred. I quipped that I was pretty sure we had just done the entire thing wrong, but he joked back that we would simply have to practice until we got it right.

Slowly, he was coming back to me and returning to the mood he had been in leading up to this awkward encounter. It was not exactly the most romantic moment of my life, but I knew better than anyone the desire to distract from a broken heart with the body of another. I had done it myself after each of my failed cycles.

I was choosing now to ignore how each of those dalliances had turned out.

♌

Nick had believed with all his heart that he was in a happy marriage. He never cheated or thought about straying. He never contemplated his life without her. He was committed—for keeps.

Then she had changed all the rules. As he opened up more in the days and weeks that followed, I learned that their parting had been fast and furious. She had provided very few warning signs to clue him in to the impending end. One day they were happy, and the next she wanted out. I realized even then that there were obviously two sides to every story, and I was sure it was something she had been battling with for longer than it had seemed to him. But regardless of what factored into the decision for her, it was clear he had never seen it coming.

Because of that alone, I knew better. So I decided early on to stop writing about us and whatever we may become. I had never felt this need to keep a piece of my life so private before, but I felt it now. The only thing I knew for sure was that this was going to get messy. I believed in my heart that it would all work out in the end. After all, the entire story was too seeped in fate for it not to. But I knew that nothing about it was going to be easy. I also knew that if I started writing about the roller coaster as it was happening on my blog, it would paint him in a horrific light. He deserved better than that from me. He had been hurt and broken down, but he was a still good man. I wanted to protect him. I wanted to protect us.

For as many times in my past as I had formulated lists in my head of the undesirable qualities the man in my life possessed, with Nick I could come up with none. Those lists had always come easily to me before. Typically within hours of knowing a guy, I had been able to pinpoint why it would not work. Nothing about Nick stuck out to me as something I would not want in a future partner though. He was loyal, funny, and intelligent. He was a good man, and I saw our future when I looked at him.

I knew that if Nick felt for me even half of what I felt for him (even half of what he *said* he felt for me), we would make it work. It would just take patience, commitment, and sacrifice on my part. I would have to be the cool and collected one for once in my life. This was not my forte, but I was prepared for it. I was ready. I truly believed it would be worth it in the end.

We fell into each other's routines, touching base regularly and spending most nights together. On good days and bad, we never ran out of things to say to one another. Everything about our beginning was far more comfortable than it should have been. I felt like I had been with this man my entire life, rather than just a few short weeks. I hurt when he hurt, and I soared when he smiled. There were no secrets. I had never before felt so connected to anyone.

At the same time, my friendship with Leigh was growing stronger. Having never known another person who shared my same hurts, she quickly became my sounding board for all things infertility. Her connection to Nick was what initially catapulted our friendship forward, but it was this much deeper shared connection that bonded us. Even though I was still recovering from my own post-IVF scars, I enjoyed being in a position to guide her through the process. There was something healing about helping someone else on this path. As we grew closer, I found myself more invested in her cycle than I had previously believed I would become. I wanted her to succeed where I had failed. We shared information on doctors and medications, side effects and IVF protocols. We touched on all the topics that typically remained out of our day-to-day discussions, a result of us each attempting to assimilate into a world that did not revolve around endometriosis and infertility.

Our conversations often turned to Nick as well though. It was nice to talk to someone who knew him, but who somehow felt more like my friend than his. She was quick to encourage me in this relationship, always reminding me what a good guy he was and how devoted he had been to his wife. Everything seemed to be pushing me toward him, even as all logic argued I should be running away. I wanted to believe in the fate of it all. I wanted this man to be the one to rescue me from myself, my heartbreak, and my own sad story.

And I wanted to be the same for him.

Chapter 46

Things between us progressed quickly in the beginning. Any rational person would have argued that they progressed *too* quickly. We spent the majority of our time together and were always talking, mostly about his marriage. We discussed at length how they had met, the details of their wedding, and the events leading up to the end. I did not mind that she was so often the topic of our conversations—in fact, I encouraged it. I got the impression that he had not been able to open up quite so freely when discussing the details with his friends, but that like me, he needed to examine the situations life threw at him from every angle. We both had a knack for over-sharing in the pursuit of that mission.

We talked about my past as well. There were plenty of conversations that revolved around my wounds. It was just that what was going on with him seemed so much more prominent. There were many nights when he and I analyzed the facts together in his infinite quest to "get" what she had done to him. I was OK with that. I wanted to be there for him as he processed it all, and there was a piece of me that was happy to allow my own issues to take a back seat. I had simply run out of ways to sift through my infertility baggage. In some ways, I was grateful for the distraction.

There were times I would catch him looking at me though, in a way that made it clear he was wondering how he could be having so much fun with me when just weeks before he had been so miserable. I knew he sometimes felt guilty because of it, or like it in some way diminished what she had done to him if he was able to move on so easily. I knew he struggled with those conflicted feelings. With knowing he *had* loved her and she *had* broken his heart—but that what he felt for me was real too.

I did not think any of it needed to be as complicated as he was making it. His feelings for me had nothing to do with her. They were two separate entities as far as I was concerned. Because of that, I never got particularly jealous when she came up. She was something he had to work through, and I understood that. I just figured that in the end, when he was past what she had done to him, I would still be there. What we had would still be real.

♌

A few weeks in, Leigh found out that her first IVF cycle was being canceled. She was not responding to the hormones the way she should have been, which made scrapping the current cycle and trying again in a few months the only option. Talking to her that afternoon, my heart broke. Both for her and for myself, for the sorrow I knew I still had not fully recovered from. It brought me swiftly back to my own failures.

Nothing about this was fair. This girl had her life together. She had an amazing husband by her side who loved her, a great job, a beautiful home, and an overwhelming desire to be a mother. On that day, I felt held hostage by infertility once more. I could not understand why it should have to be so hard for someone who would make such an incredible parent. It plunged me into a bout of infertile PTSD as I attempted to wrap my head around why this sadness seemed to follow me. I wanted to take her hurt away and to diminish my own in the process. I felt helpless in knowing that I could do neither.

I needed Nick more that day than I had at any other point in our very brief courtship. But something was off. He had not called after work as he usually did, and I had gotten preoccupied with Leigh myself. Up to that point, we had been fairly inseparable. If we were both in town, there were very few instances when we were not together. This night had been one of those exceptions. We had exchanged a few text messages throughout the day, and everything had seemed normal. As I hung up the phone with Leigh that night though, it finally occurred to me that I had no idea where he was. And that I desperately wanted his arms around me.

As I was thinking this, the phone finally rang. But I heard the sadness in his voice immediately and knew that something was wrong. In an instant, my attention turned away from what I was feeling and focused on what was going on with him. At first he started telling me about his day, a lot of small talk that did not add up to much of anything. Then (out of nowhere, almost like he had been building up to it all along), he said that he wanted us to take things a little slower than we had been. He took a deep breath before admitting, "I'm just really screwed up right now." He was incredibly sweet about it, listing all the things he liked about me and saying how much happier he had been since I had come into his life. But he kept coming back to what a mess he was and how unsure he was suddenly feeling about being ready for a relationship. He said he was terrified of hurting me, and that I had quickly become one of his closest friends. He did not ever want to be the reason that I cried.

We had never clarified *what* we were, and at least on my end, there had never been any pressure. He had initiated our time together and our conversations up to this point. We had never been anything more than what he had pushed for us to be. None of that really mattered now though. I could tell he was freaking out, and all I cared about was putting him at ease.

I remained calm as we spoke, explaining that I liked him, but that more than anything else, I *cared* about him. If he could not do this, I could handle that. We could step back and just be friends if that was what he needed. I told him that in my gut, I knew we were going to come out the other end of this as friends no matter what. Then I said that I trusted him to be careful with me and my feelings. I trusted him to move forward with honesty.

He seemed to relax as I spoke. He assured me that he did not want us to be only friends, and that he did hope for a future for us together. He was just scared. Scared of hurting me and getting hurt again himself. Talking it out seemed to help him find the balance in us again though, and by the time we got off the phone we were making plans for a bonfire with his friends that weekend.

I never did tell him about Leigh. About her heartbreaking day or about the sadness it had unearthed for me. I never took the time to fill him in on how I was feeling that night. It just seemed as though he was hurting too badly himself to be capable of taking anything else on. I wanted him to take care of me, but I recognized that he was the one who needed taking care of at this point. So I kept it buried, determined to deal with it myself.

While also determined to keep holding him together in the process.

♌

I knew that Nick and I had slept together too soon, and he knew it too. It was something we discussed on more than one occasion, as he adjusted to what it meant to be intimate with someone other than his wife. Once we had started though, it was not something we could easily stop. The line had been crossed, and our relationship was there.

About a month into dating, his buddy invited us to go camping with him and his new girlfriend. It was still chilly in Alaska, and the four of us spent the night huddled around a fire laughing and drinking to stay warm. He and I parted ways the next day—each planning to get a few of our own errands done—but less than an hour later my phone rang and his face flashed across the screen. I picked up, assuming he just wanted to tell me I had earned yet another vote of approval from his friends, but as soon as I said "hello" I could tell that he was laughing. He was barely able to contain himself as he explained that he had something he needed to tell me. If it had not been for how clearly funny he thought the whole thing was, I probably would have been worried.

He started by saying he had called his mother shortly after getting home from our trip. Nothing about that was surprising, as I knew he had a very close relationship with his mom. It was one of the things I liked about him. The way he opened up to her about everything reminded me of how I was with my dad. But what he said next was not something I was prepared for.

Apparently his mom had inquired about the seriousness of our relationship, as any concerned mother likely would at this point. His response had been to tell her that yes, we were sleeping together. Even though she had not explicitly asked that question and even though I had only met his poor mother once.

"Oh no!" I panicked. "Your mom totally thinks I'm a whore!" This reaction only incited further laughter from him. The kind of laughter he had a hard time speaking through.

"What," I implored, my irritation now palpable, "is so funny?"

Finally he calmed enough to say, "It's just that right after I told her, I immediately said that when I told you your first reaction would be 'Oh no! Your mom totally thinks I'm a whore!' Word for word! I called what you would say exactly!" He was so proud of himself that he did not even think to apologize for this embarassing little revelation to his mother. He just proceeded to invite himself over that night and to tell me he was on his way, clearly over the idea of us spending a few hours apart.

From then on, his mom began affectionately referring to me as "the whore" whenever my name came up. I could only ever laugh when he told me this, because while I was sure she wished we had proceeded with a bit more caution, I knew she was glad to see him engaged in someone else, finding his way back to happy again, whatever route would eventually lead him there.

I, of course, wished we had proceeded with a bit more caution as well. After that first night of awkwardness, I chastised myself for allowing sex into our relationship so soon. There were even occasions where we discussed taking sex out of the equation. He still struggled with feeling like he was betraying her by sleeping with me. It was not a feeling he had anticipated, and I did not blame him for it, but it did manage to create an additional pressure that neither of us wanted. Every time we talked about slowing down the sexual aspects of our relationship though, it was only a matter of hours before we found ourselves naked again.

Neither one of us was very good at putting the brakes on something we had already started. But with time, it did not seem to matter as much anymore. As we grew closer, this piece of our relationship began to fall in line with everything else we shared. It became more "normal" and less forced.

Until one night, I realized it finally felt more like *he and I* in bed.

Instead of he and I and ... her.

Chapter 47

Nick invited me to a BBQ that weekend with several of his friends. I made a point of being social while there, but the entire night I could feel his eyes on me. I would be across the yard talking to one of the many people I had gotten to know over the previous weeks, only to look up and find him staring and smiling. When we were anywhere near each other, he was touching me. Holding my hand and making sure that even if we were not engaged in a conversation with each other, we were somehow connected. He seemed to have no qualms letting these people see he cared for me, and in that I felt safe.

I got to know Chad and Kara much better that night. He had been one of the first to embrace me at Nick's faux bachelor party, but while I had met his wife briefly then, we had not gotten much of an opportunity to talk. Now that we were standing by the fire exchanging life stories, it came out that she too had advanced endometriosis and they had been trying for quite some time to conceive. I was shocked to discover this connection between us. With the exception of Leigh (who I had met through the blogging world, nowhere near as organically as this), I knew no one in my real life who had dealt with infertility. Nick had mentioned what they were going through when we discussed my own situation, but I had not realized how similar some of the details actually were. In a few months they would be embarking upon their first IVF cycle, so we immediately bonded in discussing the preparations for that. I could not shake the feeling that night that she and I were meant to meet, as much as anything else in this relationship had been meant to occur. I had so few people in my life who truly understood what I had experienced in my battle with endometriosis and infertility. Talking to her at this party and being able to serve as the voice of someone who had been there was freeing in a way I had not realized it would be until I was right there in the middle of it, forming this friendship that I was sure would be a lasting one.

As the night wore on, a group of us headed out to a local bar. I had started my period and was not feeling much like drinking anyway, so I volunteered to play the role of designated driver. For a moment Nick seemed concerned and asked if we should just go home, but I insisted that I wanted him to have fun with his friends.

His outpouring of affection only grew as he began downing drinks with his buddies. We were in the middle of a conversation when he stopped me mid-sentence by leaning abruptly forward and touching his lips to mine. It was the first time he had kissed me in public. It would not have been such a big dating milestone if it were not for the fact that he typically seemed fearful of running into her when we were outside the privacy of one of our homes. The moment was clearly not lost on him either, because when he was done he pulled away with a grin on his face and said, "There! Now that's out of the way too!" He quickly caught himself for almost ruining a sweetly simple moment, touching his hand to the back of my neck and whispering in my ear, "You look really pretty tonight."

I knew he had been drinking and that I should not take any of it to mean much, but seeing him let go of these fears made me melt. It was one thing for him to be this way when it was just the two of us curled up together in bed. It was another thing entirely for him to behave like this in public and in front of his friends.

That night we were in bed, his arms wrapped around me, when he said it. "I don't know what I would have done without you this last month. You are the best thing that has happened to me in this divorce." It was the first time he spoke those words to me, but it would not be the last.

We spent the next several days in a nearly perfect place in our relationship. We were bonded and in tune, seamlessly fitting into each other's lives. It was on one of those nights that we found ourselves entangled in bed after what had arguably been the best sexual encounter of our courtship. He had *been there* with me, engaged and connected rather than distant and distracted. And when it was over, we had laughed and cuddled and talked. My knees were still weak and it was past midnight when I decided I was ravenous. I peeled myself away from his embrace to get up and make a sandwich, a fact which he found hilarious. As I sat in bed facing him and eating, he relentlessly poked fun at me for needing to refuel after our rendezvous. He was quite proud of himself for being the one responsible for the famished state I was in.

There we were, laughing and talking and getting so much enjoyment out of each other's company. Her name had been coming up less and less, as his affection toward me continued to grow. James and Amanda had invited us to spend Memorial weekend with them at their cabin, and we were excitedly preparing for that trip. Nick had not even asked me if I wanted to come. He had simply assumed I would and started planning for the two of us from the start. We were in a good place. We were happy.

And then, about 15 minutes after midnight on a Tuesday night, as I was eating my sandwich and he was teasing me with every bite, his phone beeped. We both stopped. Stopped laughing, stopped talking, just … stopped. It made no sense that we each knew it was her. There had been limited communication between the two of them since her departure, and they had not seen each other since we had begun. The divorce would be final in less than a month, and she had not once reached out to express remorse over her decisions.

There was no way we could both have known that it was her texting. But we did. And in that moment, we each also seemed to know that everything was about to change. He reached slowly for his phone, looking at it only for a moment before wordlessly handing it to me.

I love you so much. ;) XOXO

My heart stopped.

And for a split second, I forgot how to breathe.

♌

Before that night, I never realized how many thoughts the human brain was capable of processing in a matter of seconds. I sat there, staring at the phone and then back at him. I was trying desperately to figure out what to say, not wanting to make a wrong move or do anything that could make this moment even more uncomfortable than it already was. I felt trapped. And more than anything, I felt like I needed to know what *he* was thinking before I breathed a word myself.

But looking at that text ... it just did not make sense. I would have understood *"I miss you"* or *"I'm sorry"* or even *"I **still** love you."* But *"I love you so much! ;) XOXO"*? It did not make any sense. Not given the circumstances. Not considering how she had ended things. And not when you took into account the fact that in two months, she had not once expressed any kind of regret over her decisions.

And what was *with* that smiley face? It was not the kind of text you would send to a guy— certainly not under these circumstances.

"It doesn't make any sense ..." He said. They were the first words he had spoken since the text had come through. I breathed a sigh of relief, realizing that we were on the same page and that I could proceed with caution.

"I don't think she meant to send it to you," I said. "I think she must have meant to send it to someone else." That was the only thing I could wrap my head around. I had done that before, on accident of course. Texting one person, when I had absolutely meant to text another. Unfortunately, this theory sent him into a mini panic. "Was it meant for another guy?" he questioned out loud. I could see the fear washing over his face.

We had discussed this possibility before. He had asked her early on if there was someone else, and she had denied it. But my opinion, based only on what I knew, was that there had to be. Given the way he described the situation to me, it was the one thing that made all the pieces fit together. Initially he had been resistant to this idea, but as time wore on he had begun to acknowledge the likelihood of it as well. Now though, with the use of the 'L' word and the chance that it could have been meant for another man, I could see it tearing him up inside.

Still, I was convinced that was not the case. There was no way this text had been meant for a man. Not *any* man. It seemed more like the kind of text you would send to a friend after they had just said something inspiring, motivational, or uplifting. It was the kind of text you would send in response to hearing exactly what you had needed in a moment of sadness. Not the kind of text you would send to a potential *or* past love interest.

He then began to question whether or not she knew about me. In his panic, he even asked if it was possible that she knew he was with me now. He wondered aloud if she had sent this text because she was jealous and was intentionally trying to make things between us uncomfortable. I did not buy that either though. When she had walked away from him, she had pretty effectively walked away from all of their mutual friends as well. Those friends had now embraced me with open arms and were steadily becoming *my* friends. I could not picture any of them running to her to give the details on the new woman in his life. Even if they had bumped into her somewhere and it had come up, I was sure we would have heard about it.

Anchorage was a big small town though, and I did acknowledge that it was at least marginally possible she knew about me. Even still, it did not make sense. There was certainly no way she could have known he was with me in this moment. Whether or not she did know about me, I did not believe it had anything to do with this text.

After discussing it for almost 20 minutes, we decided that he should respond. He *deserved* at least some kind of explanation. So he typed in a question mark and sent it. Thirty minutes later, when she still had not replied back, I could see him starting to break. And I was angry.

There were many times I had felt sorry for this girl. I obviously did not know her, and what I did know had come only secondhand from Nick and those close to him. I was not in any position to make a judgment, but it seemed to me as though she was simply lost. Like she had gotten married too early, before she had taken the time to figure out who she was and what she wanted out of life. Based on everything I had been told up to this point, it seemed to me that all the decisions she had made since choosing to leave had been made quickly and without a lot of rational thought behind them. From the moment he and I started, I had always believed the day would come when she would regret her choices. To some extent, my heart went out to her for that. After having lost Michael years before, I could relate to throwing away something good with someone you loved for no other reason than because you were broken, lost, and confused.

But in this moment, I was angry with her for playing with his heart and mind. For being so careless, and for popping up now to screw with his head when we had been falling into such a good place.

I convinced him he should push the subject. I knew he was likely to let it go, but all along I felt he had made things far too easy for her. He had never really held her accountable for the promises she had made to him, and it was difficult for me to see because I knew how much he was hurting. He kept that from her though, both out of pride and out of not wanting to force her into staying if it was not what she wanted. He had given her whatever it was she needed in the end of their marriage, without putting any more burden or responsibility on her than was absolutely necessary. In some ways it was admirable, but in others … the side of me that wanted to see people brought to justice for their actions wished that he had made her face the damage she had caused a little more.

I knew it was my influence that finally encouraged him to text again:

> I don't think you meant to send this to me, but would you mind explaining? You really should be more careful...

Initially, I did not expect she would respond. I certainly did not expect her to respond in the way that she did:

> I don't know what you're talking about? I haven't sent anything. I'm sleeping. You woke me up, and I have to work early in the morning. I'm going back to bed.

Now I was *really* pissed. We all knew she sent it, so why couldn't she have the balls to own it? Why lie like that? Why try to make him feel stupid?

I showed him how to take a screen shot of the text message and send it to her. I figured there was no denying it if he confronted her with proof of exactly what she had sent. I was right, and she immediately started backtracking, apologizing, and swearing it had not been her. She claimed that her phone had accidentally sent her sister a similar text earlier in the week as well, and that she could not figure out what was going on but that she really had been asleep.

At this point, my eyes were about to fall out of my head from rolling so hard. But I was keeping my mouth shut, allowing him to handle this however it was he needed to. So when he penned his next text, I could not help but laugh:

> **Whatever. Must have been the text Houdini.**

It was the first time (to my knowledge) he had confronted her with any kind of venom, despite the fact that I knew he was fully capable of being sarcastic. I was proud to see him put her in her place a bit now, and we both laughed as he put his phone back on the nightstand before suggesting we try to get some sleep.

It did not work of course. We were up most of the night talking, dissecting the entire situation. He did not hear from her again that night, but that did nothing to ease the adrenaline we both had pumping. Neither of us got much sleep before our alarms began to sound the next morning.

We were talking, but we were not touching. It was as if suddenly there was a wall between us, an invisible barrier that we both seemed wary of now. We stayed on our own sides of the bed. Talking, but never once physically connecting. I *wanted* to reach out to him. I *wanted* to comfort him. I *wanted* to hold him and let him know I was there.

But for some reason, I couldn't.

Meanwhile, he made no attempt to alleviate the space between us either.

Chapter 48

Nick and James had to travel out of town for work the next day. While he was gone we texted back and forth, but did not speak again. Even in our texts, something was off. There was a giant elephant in the room we were both trying desperately to dance around.

When Friday finally arrived, I got off work early and drove to meet him at his house for our Memorial weekend camping trip. The sun was shining and the temps had risen to almost 80 degrees, the kind of weather we dreamed about in Alaska. When I arrived to find him basking in the sun with his shirt off, I told myself the shift in weather would warm the chill between us.

From his house the drive should have taken 30 minutes, but traffic was so backed up that it was a good hour and a half before we got to where we were headed. He barely looked at me most of that time. I began to regret agreeing to this trip. James and Amanda's cabin was fairly remote—something I had initially been excited about. Spending time with him out in the middle of nowhere for three days was going to be beyond difficult though, if I kept feeling like he did not really want me there.

I knew why he was being like this. I understood that it was because of her text, and the fact that neither of us was talking about it just felt wrong to me. We talked about everything. We were *always* talking. To have this thing standing between us now was suffocating. So finally, I brought it up by asking if there had been any further developments in the "I love you" drama. He hesitated, and I knew there had been. I also knew he was sitting right in front of me contemplating whether or not to tell me about it.

Eventually though, he pulled out his phone and said she had sent him an e-mail. He was trying to pull it up for me to read, but we were too far out in the middle of nowhere by then for him to get a reliable signal. So he began to describe it to me instead, saying that she had written the next day to apologize. She admitted in this e-mail that she *had* sent the text and, that contrary to my initial assumption, she had actually meant it for him. Apparently she had been drinking and had typed it out on her phone before realizing how inappropriate was. But when she went to delete it, she hit "send" on accident instead. In a moment of panic after realizing what she had done, she chose to simply deny she sent it when he questioned her.

From there she went on to tell him that while she did not regret her choice to end their marriage, she wanted him to know that it had not been easy for her and that there were times when she still missed him. She explained that she still thought about him often, before ending the e-mail by saying she hoped he was doing well.

Most of what she said left more questions for him than anything. He had decided not to respond, and said now that he had not planned on telling me about it because of his own decision to ignore it. It was the first time he had not immediately volunteered information and the first time I felt he intentionally kept something from me. I understood, and I knew I was owed this information, especially since he had not responded. But I could tell that e-mail (and the whole incident) had shaken him. It had created a rift between us. Her popping back up now made him want to keep certain things from me, rather than discussing it all openly and honestly as we had up to this point. I was not sure if this damage would heal itself. For the first time, I was nervous.

Nervous about whether or not we would ever get back to that good place we had just been in.

And nervous about the next three days we were meant to spend in very tight quarters, in the middle of nowhere, with just one other couple.

Most of my fears were still lingering as we parked next to his friends. Before I took two steps out of Nick's truck, James was by my side sweeping me up in a bear hug. Amanda was there to do the same quickly after, and I remembered immediately how much I liked these two. I felt at ease with them, somehow instinctually knowing that even though they were *his* friends, they still wanted the best for me too. They were rooting for me and for the two of us as a couple. There was comfort in that.

Nick perked up once we were in their proximity as well, and we all excitedly moved supplies from the trucks to the ATVs for the off-road portion of our journey. It was a 30-minute trek out to the lake. While Nick drove, I snapped pictures and took every opportunity I could find to get him laughing. We were going to be fine, I told myself. *This* was going to be fine.

Once we arrived at the water's edge, a boat was waiting to take us across to the cabin. It was a one-room space with a wood floor and an outhouse about 15 feet behind it. I suddenly realized that packing all my hair essentials had been unnecessary. The loofa had probably been overkill as well. This was basically camping in a tent, but with a roof. Nick had definitely not fully prepared me for what to expect from this weekend.

Everyone had a good laugh over my clear ineptitude at roughing it, but I was excited. Just because I had not known what to expect going into this did not mean that I was not ready to embrace the adventure. Of course, when Amanda suggested we take a dip in the lake to clean off after our dusty drive in, I was sure she was teasing me. After all, the ice on the lake could not have melted more than a few weeks before. But as I was jolted awake by that first jump in the water, I realized it had been no joke. And I knew that my summers spent frolicking the beaches in San Diego had not prepared me for this.

We all began aggressively drinking shortly thereafter, if only in an attempt to warm up. Before long we were sitting around a fire eating dinner and sharing life stories. That was when James began to tell me about how he and Amanda had first come together.

He had been on the heels of a rough divorce himself when they met. He explained the similarities between his story and Nick's, while describing how his own heart had been ripped out by the woman he had believed he was going to spend the rest of his life with. The way the story was told that night, Amanda was supposed to be his rebound. Over the course of a year though, they experienced a roller coaster of ups and downs before she finally had enough. They parted ways on less than amicable terms. Months passed. *Months*. They did not speak and they both dated other people.

For some reason while in the midst of dating someone James described as a "pretty cool chick" though, he realized she was not Amanda. And even though he had not been ready before, he was now. He wanted *her*. He said he had to fight for another chance, but that when she finally came around, the back and forth between the two of them was no more. They were solid. A few years later, he proposed. Almost in the exact same spot we were sitting now.

James looked at me, looked at Nick, and said, "I know exactly where you two are. We were there too. It's not easy, and he's not ready. But still, I have a good feeling about where you're going to end up." Nick met my eyes with a smile. It was a drunken and disorderly smile to be sure, but one that still spoke volumes about his feelings for me.

I had always assumed our relationship would take a similar detour at some point. In the back of my head, I knew that right now I was only his rebound. I believed that the move our relationship had taken in another (far more serious) direction would eventually come back to haunt us. That eventually, we would have to fall apart before we could come back together. It was not what I wanted of course. I wanted everything to be smooth and easy and perfect. But deep down inside, I knew it would not be. Now though, there was a happily married couple sitting in front of us describing almost the exact same trajectory I had already begun preparing myself for. And they were looking at us, thinking we had the same potential. It was just one more of those random pieces that seemed to be pushing us together.

It became a long night of laughing and storytelling as we all drank past our limit. When it was time for us to make our way to one of the two side-by-side air mattresses for bed, Nick and I first snuck away for some alone time on the porch. James and Amanda had already headed in themselves, while the midnight sun was still hanging in the air. Rain began drizzling down on us, there at this remote cabin with no one around to catch us in our moment. There was a passion between us that we had not quite been able to reach before now. A desperation. We were far from sober, and maybe it was because of that we were able to give in to each other so completely. But it was incredible. One of those flashes in time capable of making your knees weak even years after the fact.

When we stumbled back inside, we draped ourselves in a sleeping bag and wrapped around each other.

He slept the entire night, never once loosening his hold on me.

♌

The next morning was rough for all of us. Nursing hangovers and moving slowly, we did what we could to make breakfast and acclimate to the daylight. Eventually Nick and I escaped to go fishing on the lake.

We never had a single bite, nor did we say much of anything to each other as we cast and recast into the water. I could tell he was contemplating, but he was not pulling away. He was simply deep in thought, and I understood why.

After giving up on fishing, we returned to the cabin and curled up in the back of the boat for a nap in the afternoon sun. With our arms intertwined, we drifted between sleep and occasional bouts of light conversation. There was a comfort there between us. Even though she was lingering in each of our thoughts, we both fought to keep her at bay.

The boys began drinking again that night, but I refrained and chose instead to stick to water. The two of them cracked jokes back and forth as I hung back and took pictures, glowing in the moments when he turned his attention to me.

Rain began to fall as the night wore on, and we retreated inside and away from the fire. Nick held my hand and told me how beautiful I was over and over again in varying intervals as his level of intoxication grew. But still, I melted at the sweetness. When his eyes began to droop under the weight of too much to drink, he pushed for us to go to bed. We cuddled up talking for only a moment before each quickly drifting off to sleep. He remained spooned against me the entire night, once more refusing to let go.

In the morning though, something had shifted. Even with his arms still around me, I could feel the distance between us. As James and Amanda began to stir, he whispered in my ear that he was ready to go home. We had originally been planning on staying one more night, but it was obvious she had found her way back into his head. There had been a time they had come to this cabin together. They had likely even woken up here on many mornings wrapped in each other's arms, just as we were now. He needed space to process that, to push her out of his thoughts once more. As much fun as we had been having, it was time for our isolation from the rest of the world to come to an end.

James loaded us up on the boat and took us back to the location of the abandoned ATVs. While Nick transferred our things and prepared to leave, James wrapped me in a hug before quietly saying, "Don't take his moods too personally." He looked me in the eye and reminded me that it would just take time, but that he still saw good things for us.

Nick and I did not talk the entire trek back to the road. Once there, we loaded the truck in silence as well. On the drive to his house though, he suddenly began opening up about her.

I was not sure what prompted it or how long she had been on his mind. I knew it was at least possible (maybe even probable) that her e-mail had never really left his thoughts. As he spoke though, he explained his fear that he would never love anyone again as much as he had loved her. That statement hung in the air, neither of us acknowledging what it meant about us, about me. We spent the remainder of the drive in silence as I tried to fight the feeling that a single text had changed everything.

But I was not willing to give up. The girl I had been once upon a time would have cut and run. The fear of being hurt would have been too much for her to stay. I refused to listen to that girl this time though. We had been in such a solid place before that text had come through. I wanted to believe that if I allowed him the space he needed to work through this, we would get there again. So when we arrived at his house, I hugged him goodbye and I did not push. I left him there standing in his garage knowing that I was just a phone call away if he needed me, and that I would be there as soon as he was ready to let me in once more.

I had loved and lost. I had been broken down by life and infertility. I had been the girl to walk away, simply because it had seemed too hard to hold on.

I was not going to give up this time. I was not going to walk away from him.

Chapter 49:

Only a few days passed without us talking, but it felt like much longer as I tried my best to patiently wait. Eventually I broke down and sent him a text message, saying simply that I missed him and was around, even if all he needed was a friend. He responded that he was still trying to work through some things, but then he added:

> **You are still one of the best things that has happened to me through all of this. I really mean that.**

I trusted in the fact that he cared about me, and I was willing to give him all the space he needed. But even as I was resigning myself to more time apart, he showed up on my doorstep that night.

He was drunk. I could tell that almost right away. He said a friend dropped him off as he asked sheepishly if he could come in. He began to tell me about his night while crawling into my bed, cutting a rambling story short before saying, "Thank you for being so great." It caught me off guard, and a shrug was all I could manage in response. But he pushed the subject again, stating, "No really, you are amazing." Then he busted out a maniacal laugh before saying, "You have got to be wondering where the heck you picked this guy up, huh? I mean, how did you get stuck with all this baggage?"

I looked at him, trying to figure out where this was coming from and how I was supposed to react. Did he really think for even one second that I did not *want* to be with him? I responded by saying that everyone had baggage, and then reminded him of some of my own as I crawled into bed beside him. He told me I was one of the strongest people he had ever met though, as if my baggage did not count because of that strength. He said he was not sure he would ever be as strong as me. Again, I did not know how to respond. So instead, I rolled over and allowed him to curl around me like a body pillow. We fell asleep like a couple, even as I could not shake the feeling that she was still right there in bed with us.

The next night he showed up again, this time with a bottle of booze in hand. I realized he had been drinking every single night since hearing from her, but I bit my tongue and did not say a word. The final divorce date was quickly approaching, and I made up my mind to be there for him, without judgment or rules. We spent the night talking while he drank, again falling asleep in each other's arms but not crossing the boundaries of intimacy any further.

The following night was a Friday and he had a bachelor party to attend. I had known he was going and had not expected to hear from him that evening. At 3 a.m. though, he texted simply to say he was thinking of me. As soon as I responded, he called claiming that he missed my voice. All the guys from the party were staying together at a cabin a fair distance away. He was drunk, but this was not a booty call. Apparently, it was nothing more than him thinking of me.

He stayed out of town the next day to attend a wedding with his friends. He called me several times to see what I was up to and apprise me of his status, but at no point did he ask me to join him. It was not until just before midnight that he called asking if I could pick him up. I was crawling into bed and he was more than an hour away, but I could hear in his voice how drunk he was. When he said he was there at a bar by himself and that the friend he had been hanging out with had left with his girlfriend over an hour ago, I was worried. He was out in the middle of nowhere. Getting a cab would run him at least a few hundred dollars. I knew he was drunk—by himself and drunk. So I got in the car and went to pick him up in the pouring rain, past midnight, over an hour away from my own warm bed.

He called again when I was about halfway there. I started talking to him in an effort to ensure he stayed in one place and did not get himself into any trouble. But just as I tried to convince him to find a booth to sit down at until I was able to get there, he said it.

"I love you."

My immediate response was, "Oh my hell." I did not know what else to say. His drunk ass had caught me completely off guard with that one.

He laughed hysterically and replied, "I know. I just dropped the first legit L-bomb. And I meant it." He kept going, "That wasn't an 'I want to sleep with you' L-bomb. That was an 'I seriously love you' L-bomb."

I laughed too, before reminding him that he was drunk and that I would be there soon. I begged him to stay out of trouble, and then we hung up so I could focus on driving safely in the rain.

When I got to the bar, he came barreling out to meet me. He swept me up in a giant hug right outside the doors as if I was his favorite person in the entire world. And then, he said it again. Once more I made mention of his less than sober condition, but he just looked at me and said, "No, I mean it. And you know what? You love me too."

In my head, I wanted to deny it. But in my heart, I knew I could not. So I just did not say anything. We walked to my car with him draped around me, and once I had him settled in the passenger seat I began driving to his house. He reached out and held my hand as he told me about the girls in the bar who had taken care of him until I arrived. He beamed with pride as he said he told them *all* about me. He claimed they had even given him advice, telling him that if I was as special as he said I was, he should never let me go.

Then he said, "I was thinking about you all night." I laughed again before saying that lately it seemed as though he was only thinking of me when he was drunk. But he protested. "That's not true!" he argued. "I think about you all the time. I think about you more than I should. You are always on my mind. I've never gotten so close to anyone as fast as I have to you. You are my best friend, and I am always thinking about you."

Again I stayed silent. As he moved the chair back to fall asleep (never once letting go of my hand) I kept my mouth shut, if only because I had no idea how to respond while still protecting myself.

When we finally made it to his house, we both brushed our teeth and got ready for bed. And then he stripped down naked and crawled in beside me.

Completely naked.

He ran his hands over me while attempting to get my own clothes off as well, but I turned him down pretty quickly. After a week of his keeping the physicality between us limited, I did not want him sleeping with me now simply because he was drunk. Not when it seemed that what he really needed was a friend.

He grew serious and forced me to meet his gaze before saying, "I like you, as *more* than a friend. You know I like you. No matter what else I say or do, you know I like you. And now I guess you know I love you too. But right now, I just don't know how to trust in much of anything."

Then he started talking about sex, explaining how weird it was for him, still, to be sleeping with someone who was not her. To be sleeping with *anyone* who was not her. He promised it was something he was working on, just before telling me that the only thing he knew for sure was how much he cared about me. He did not want to see me hurt, and he did not want to lose me.

He wrapped his arms around me, holding on tight once more, almost as if he was afraid I was going to disappear in the middle of the night. Just when I was sure he had finally fallen asleep, he stirred before saying, "I know you think it's because I'm drunk, but it's not. I love you. And you love me too."

I pretended to be asleep.

His final divorce date was a little over a week away. At that point, we would be just shy of having spent two months together. Only days before it had seemed as though he was pulling away from me. Yet here he was now, saying he loved me.

And there I was, believing him.

There is only so long you can bask in the glow of sweet nothings whispered by a drunken man. But the next morning, I basked until I could get away with basking no more. Enveloped in his arms, I refused to move, fearful that setting our feet on the floor would lead to the inevitable destruction of all the love he had declared the night before.

He woke to the unavoidable hangover, complaining even as he seemed intent on staying wrapped around me. It was not until we finally made the move out of bed that I remembered plans I had with a friend. I quickly threw my things in a bag and told him I had to go. He made a crack about me being the perfect girl—one who knew when it was time to get up and get out.

I caught his eye for a second and said, "What? You mean you don't want me moving in?" A look of pure panic washed across his face as he tried to assess whether or not I was serious. It was all I could do to keep my expression blank. When he still had not replied a few moments later, I took the lead. "But…" I pouted, putting on my very best *you're-breaking-my-heart* face. "You told me you *loved* me!"

I erupted into laughter before he ever had a chance to respond. Almost immediately he was calling me an asshole, but he was laughing too. He was breathing again and looking more than a little bit grateful that I was willing to make light of the situation. I could tell he was still trying to get a handle on it all. On what he felt for me, what he felt for her, and how the two could possibly ever co-exist. I knew he was struggling with the impending date and wondering how he was supposed to feel anything other than heartbroken. I expected him to increase the distance between us as he wrapped his head around what it meant to mourn the loss of his marriage. So I was surprised when he called that night asking if he could come over. Of course I told him he was welcome.

He turned up fairly morose, sitting quietly on my couch before finally looking at me sadly and saying, "I really don't want to be divorced." My heart broke for him. I knew this was hard. If I had been in his shoes, I would not have wanted to be divorced either. He really and truly had wanted his marriage to last forever. He had planned for the quiet and settled contentment that comes with committing yourself completely to someone you love. And he was losing it through no real fault of his own. I understood his sadness over that. Over the disruption of a life he had already planned on living from now until forever. And I understood why he was having a difficult time coping.

Up to this point, Nick had led a fairly idyllic life. He was the only child of parents who were still together and loved him dearly. His core group of friends were the same guys he had been hanging out with since early childhood, and they were *good* friends who would have done just about anything for him. He was by all measures successful, with a master's degree and a great job. He had been with a woman he loved for six years, and they owned a beautiful home with floor-to-ceiling windows and two dogs they both doted on like children.

Dogs she had taken with her when everything fell apart.

Nothing had ever really shaken him before this. And I knew that as the weeks passed, the instability of it all was becoming more difficult for him to take. So much of what he was feeling was normal, but so much of how he was dealing with it was not. He had never really learned how to survive the hard stuff. The hard stuff had never hit before now.

In contrast, the life I had led up to this point was very different from the one he had known, and I recognized that. In some ways, I was almost grateful for it. Because here he was, learning these lessons for the first time. I could see how unbearable it was for him, having to come to terms with the fact that people leave. They lie and betray and let you down. Not always, but more often than you expect. It was a lesson I had learned far too young, and one that in some ways he was learning far too late.

We talked a lot that night, and when he took out a bottle of whiskey and poured himself more than a few drinks, I kept my mouth shut. Her popping up again when he had just been getting to the point of letting go had thrown him. He was trying so hard to get back to a good place now, but he just wanted to be there already. I could relate to that. I had felt it so many times myself. So even though it was not how I would have coped, I understood why he had been drinking so much since that text. And I knew from talking to his friends that he had never had a drinking problem before. We were all trying to treat this as exactly what we hoped it would turn out to be: a phase.

He left for an out-of-town work trip early the next morning, kissing me goodbye as I remained snuggled up in bed. He called every night while he was gone, always at the end of the day and always drunk. But talking—just hearing my voice and knowing I was there—seemed to help.

So that was what I tried to be to him in the week before his divorce was final.

A voice on the other end of the phone, fighting to help him keep his head above water.

Reminding him, night after night, that there was somebody who cared.

Chapter 50

Nick got back into town that Friday and called as soon as he landed. We talked about meeting up with friends, but by the time I got to his house he was already a few drinks deep and seemed intent on staying in. With his divorce only three days away, I was bracing for him to fall apart. But his mood was good and he was outwardly affectionate toward me the entire night. If he was on the verge of cracking, I could not tell.

We made plans Saturday to go out with a few of his friends. I was excited to see Kara, as she and I had grown increasingly close over the previous weeks. She and Chad were currently on what would be their last IUI cycle before moving on to IVF. I had spoken to her that day and knew she was confident it had not worked (as only someone who had been through failure after failure could be), but she was planning on remaining sober anyway. Because that was the insanity of infertility—continuing to hope and pray and believe, even when knowing better. I was just glad she was coming out at all.

I showed up to the bar after everyone was already there and Nick was well on his way to drunk. We had only parted ways a few hours before, but he still seemed happy to see me. He attached himself to my hip and kept smiling down at me like he could not believe I was his. I knew it was wrong, but I liked him like this. With a few drinks in him, it was as if he forgot all the things that otherwise held him back from me, and I was able to forget all the things that had broken my heart before him as well. Infertility became a distant memory in these moments when we were able to be happy together.

Logically, I knew this was the definition of co-dependent. But I just kept telling myself that at his heart, this was a man I could see myself spending forever with. We shared the same sense of humor and penchant for bold and open honesty. We wanted the same things out of life. We could talk for hours on end about nothing and everything all at once. And more than anything, I *trusted* him. He was loyal and solid and true. I knew he would never be the guy to lie to me, sneak around behind my back, or walk away for no reason when I least expected him to leave. I knew he would be good to me, if only we could get past this place of hurting he was now in.

I still had concerns though. I was still wary of what it would mean for us if he could never get over her. As hard as I tried, I was rarely able to distance myself from that worry for long.

James was with us that night and must have sensed those concerns. We had not been out more than an hour when he pulled me aside for a pep talk. He said they discussed me all the time, and that his personal opinion was that Nick was terrified of me. He explained that I was everything Nick wanted, but that he had not been prepared to meet me when he did. James held nothing back as he told me Nick often described me as the nicest person he had ever met, and had tormented himself over the possibility of hurting me. He said he was always talking about me—always recounting something funny I said or something kind I had done for him. He seemed to be positive that Nick and I were perfect for each other.

But he also conceded that more than anything, I needed to protect myself. He did not question my ability to do that—to put me first and walk away if necessary—for a second. I had to admit that by this point, *I* was not so sure. I knew how I felt about Nick and how much I was willing to sacrifice to be there for him. It scared me. But James was confident. Not just in my ability to protect myself, but also in Nick's feelings for me. He was adamant that in the end *that* would be what would win out.

When we wandered back to the group, I found Nick sitting down talking to Amanda and looking distraught. The second he spotted us, relief washed over his face. He stood and smiled hesitantly while walking toward me. He had been talking to a girl, an old friend from high school, when James and I disappeared. He explained that he had panicked for a moment, thinking I had gotten the wrong idea and left. I looked down at my phone and realized he had texted several times. The depth of his feelings for me was written all over his face now, and all of James's words began to ring true. It was obvious he did not want to do anything to hurt me and that he did not want to lose me.

He refused to leave my side for the rest of the night. When we walked into my house a few hours later, after a cab ride in which we barely kept our hands off each other, it took only moments before we were coming together with the same desperation that had been there just two weeks before at the lake. For a moment, everything was right.

He told me that night he was happier when he was with me, and I knew it to be true. I knew I was happier when we were together too. Whether he was drunk, sober, affectionate, or pulled away, I preferred to have him by my side. To know that he was OK, and to be in a position to help when he was not.

In two days, he would be divorced. I hoped that meant we would be able to put *her* behind us, moving forward as an "us". Without quite so much whiskey. I was ready for him to be the man I knew he was capable of being.

The man I knew I wanted to be mine.

For keeps.

♌

We woke the next morning and went to breakfast with James and Amanda before parting ways. The following day would be the first time in months he would actually see her face-to-face, for the official nail in the coffin of their marriage. Given how much time we had spent talking about this, I was genuinely worried about how he was going to handle the whole thing. But not knowing exactly where his head was at, I decided to remain hands-off and play the evening by ear. I wanted to be available if he needed me, but not hovering if he wanted space.

Around 7 p.m., he called and asked if I would come over. He sounded somber as he explained that he simply did not want to be alone. I immediately threw some things into a bag and made the drive, prepared for a difficult evening. While he was quiet and reserved though, he was not broken down in the way I expected him to be. We laid out his suit for the next morning, talked for a while about how things would likely play out, and then put a movie on to watch before heading off to bed. We did not drink that night. But we did not touch either. We slept on our own sides of his king-size bed with so much distance between us that it would have been comical if it had not been so sad. I was prepared to comfort him, but he never broke. So instead, I followed his cues, keeping my distance while also maintaining my presence.

The next morning, he crawled out of bed and showered at the sound of his alarm. He stood in the bathroom without saying much of anything as he got ready, and I sat on the bed watching him, matching his silence with my own, while still letting him know I was there. I had taken the day off work, wanting to be available if he needed a safe place to land after the hearing. So this morning, the only job I had to worry about was being whatever it was he needed me to be.

As he dressed, I thought about how handsome this man was. With his piercing blue eyes, perfect skin, and a jawline that made me melt, my attraction to him was already undeniable. Now dressed in a suit for his divorce, looking more dapper than I had ever seen him before, I could not tear my eyes away.

In an attempt to ease the tension, I cracked a joke about how nice he looked, asking if he was at all interested in a pre-divorce blow job. I wanted to get him laughing. When he did, I breathed a sigh of relief. We joked back and forth a bit more before he took one last deep, calming breath. Then we each walked down the stairs to his kitchen and out the door to his garage, getting into our separate cars as we said our goodbyes. He promised to call me as soon as everything was said and done.

The appearance before the judge had been set for first thing that morning, so when I still had not heard from him by 10 a.m. I began to worry. I could not imagine divorce proceedings taking that long, especially between two people who did not have any children and who had not even bothered to get lawyers involved. All I could picture was Nick somewhere on his own, hurting and breaking down. I was beginning to crack myself, fearing there was nothing I could do to help.

About an hour later he finally called. He actually sounded as though he was doing alright. He said the judge had been 20 minutes late, but that once they got started the entire thing had lasted only 5 minutes. I knew he was disgusted by this—by how quick and easy it had been to get divorced.

As he relayed to me the events of the morning, it sounded as though he had held it together pretty well. After everything was over, he explained that he decided to see his dogs. He loved those dogs dearly and talked about them all the time but had not seen them in months because the idea of facing her had been too difficult. Now that they had seen each other in court though, he wanted to take the opportunity to see them too.

He told me that was when he finally cried, as he was saying goodbye to his dogs. He called me as he was leaving there. Despite it all, he sounded good.

I was proud of him. Proud of how he had handled everything, proud to know him, and proud to call him mine.

It was official.

He was divorced.

And in my mind, that meant he could finally start healing.

Chapter 51

I relaxed with the knowledge that it was now official. I could finally stop looking over my shoulder fearing what would happen if she changed her mind, if he was faced with a choice between her or me. I was confident in the fact that from here on out things between us would build in a healthy direction. So when he called me that night and asked if he could come over, I did not hesitate. This was the start.

The start of us.

He was leaving for a remote work site again the following day and would be gone for a few weeks. I was anxious to spend this night with him, as a couple, before he left. When he showed up, he seemed fine. Amazing even, considering. He was not distracted or withdrawn or pulled away. He began telling me some stupid story that had me laughing almost to the point of tears, and he was not drinking at all. He seemed to be coping so well.

Allowing myself to believe that was my first mistake, and I was about to make the second.

I reached out to him and made some comment about engaging in a little post-divorce sexual activity. I was half kidding, playing off on the laugh we had shared over a similar joke that morning. I was partially serious too though, wanting to connect with him in that way tonight, before he left, while we were each sober and officially unattached. I *wanted* to be with him. To have him looking in my eyes and to know he was with me.

But immediately he grew serious and said, "I don't want to have sex." Or at least, that was what I *wished* he had said. Because what he really said was, "I don't want to have sex *with you*." There was a venom attached to that "you" I could not define. I was stunned. Shocked into silence and feeling as though my cheek must be red. Because clearly he had just slapped me, hadn't he?

Moments passed like hours before I regained my ability to speak and finally sputtered out, "But … we just had sex two days ago? You couldn't keep your hands off of me?" He unapologetically held my gaze as he replied, "I was drunk."

Paralyzed by how cold he had become, I was confused to my core about what was happening. It was one thing for him to not be in the mood. *That* made sense. In fact, it had been stupid of me to even bring it up on this night. I had just mistakenly trusted in how OK he seemed to be, but the fact that we were even here having this conversation at all was my fault. Clearly my timing had been off.

Still … it was something entirely differently for him to be saying he did not want to have sex *with me*. And suddenly, it felt like a door was flung open. Because he just kept talking.

He told me he would never have any feelings for me beyond friendship. He said he loved spending time with me, but he knew those romantic feelings I wanted him to have just were not there. Then he said there was nothing about me that made him want anything more. It was all I could do not to recoil from the sting of that.

He kept going, saying these things which made no sense at all. We had embarked upon the conversation of "us" more than a few times and it had always been *me* saying we should step back and be just friends and *him* saying that was not what he wanted. He was making it sound like I was stupid to have ever believed he felt anything for me though. And I just kept sitting there, taking it.

Until I could not take anymore. I took a deep breath and proceeded as calmly as I could, but I finally started calling him out. I told him that if what he was saying was true, he had been sending *a lot* of mixed signals. I reminded him of every conversation where he told me the exact opposite of what he was saying now, and I pointed out all the times *he* had initiated intimacy between us, all the times *he* had been unable to go even a single night without talking to me.

He looked at me with a straight face and said that all any of it meant was that he had been lonely. He said he liked my companionship and he liked having someone to be with, but that he wished we had never slept together because he did not want to lose my friendship—and he knew he would never feel anything more for me than that.

I was trying so hard to keep it together—to be calm, cool, and collected. The whole time I had James's words from just a few nights before running through my head. He kept telling me how much Nick cared about me, but how scared he was of whatever that meant. That was all he kept saying—that Nick liked me so much I scared him.

Yet here Nick was now, telling me he did not like me at all. He was using those exact words. "I don't like you." A week before he had been saying he loved me, and now he just kept repeating "I don't like you" over and over again, even when I was not saying anything in return. He kept saying it, like I was a kindergartner on the playground trying to steal kisses from him, rather than the woman he had shared a bed with and been supported by for the past two months.

"I don't like you."

Not even "I don't love you."

Just "I don't like you."

Still, I was holding it together, grasping at straws to keep things from spiraling out of control. My mind was racing but my voice and demeanor were both calm. I kept reminding myself that he had *just* gotten divorced that day, and that this was not a conversation we should be having right now.

I told him that if everything he was saying was true, then the mixed signals needed to stop. I explained that we could be friends, and I could contain my feelings, but that we needed first and foremost to stop sleeping in the same bed. We needed to stop cuddling and I needed to stop being the first number he dialed every time he got drunk and dropped those inhibitions.

But then he started crying. *Really* crying. And suddenly I felt awful. No guy I had ever dated had cried in front of me before. I had no idea how to react. He was *actually* crying, and I felt guilty for that. He had come over in a fairly good mood and now there were tears because of me. Because I had somehow plunged us into this topic of conversation without ever actually meaning to. He was crying because he said he never meant to hurt me, and he was angry at himself for taking my feelings for granted. And he was crying over her, over his divorce.

He was just sitting there crying, and suddenly I was trying to comfort him—even though he had just dumped me in a pretty brutal way. It was ridiculous. I *knew* it was ridiculous. And then it got even more ridiculous.

He said he was leaving. It was almost midnight, and he started getting up to go. I told him that was silly and not to be dramatic. We *did* need to stop sleeping in the same bed, but it was the middle of the night. His office was less than a mile from my house and his place was a 40-minute drive away. I told him not to be crazy, but he was already packing up his stuff, crying the entire time. Which was when I started crying. Or at least, that was when I started *trying* to cry. Because I felt like I should be. I felt like now would be the time for tears.

Except, I couldn't. I sat there as he was packing up thinking to myself that my reaction to all of this should be tears. I was silent, not saying another word, thinking about the fact that I really *should* be crying. Not because I wanted it to have an effect on him, but because ... that was how a normal person would be reacting right now. I could not make the tears come though. And suddenly, that was all I could think about: the fact that I was not normal and that I was not capable of normal human emotions. He was getting ready to leave, and all I could focus on was my inability to cry.

I was hurt. More hurt than I had been in a long time. But I was also numb. Shut down. Emotionally stunted. I had never been great at crying legitimate tears over a broken heart, but especially not in front of the person who was doing the breaking. So I just sat there, pretending to cry, while he packed up everything. It was a bag full of belongings that was supposed to last him the next three weeks. I knew he had not planned on this happening, but now it was. And he was packing and crying, all the while ignoring my own faux tears. Neither one of us was saying a word.

When he got to my bedroom door with his bag in hand, he paused for a second. And then without even looking back at me he said, "The problem is Leah, I'm a guy who had a perfect life. More than anyone else could ever ask for. And now... I don't have any of it."

At which point, he only started crying harder before walking out the door. No goodbye. No hug. No anything. He just left me there, sitting on my bed, pretending to cry.

I remained still for a solid five minutes, trying to determine how things had slipped so quickly out of control. It all felt like it had come out of nowhere. How could I have been so naïve to think for even one second that he was alright? I should have been on the lookout for signs to the contrary. It was so obvious now that he had needed someone to lash out at. I just happened to be the closest person in sight he could hurt. He had been looking for this—for an excuse and a reason to hurt me, to push me away, and to break anything good we had. I recognized it, because it was kind of a signature move of mine. Push the people who care the most away when it feels like the world is spinning out of control. It was how I lost Michael, so I got it. And I knew, in my heart, that we were not over. But I also knew that nothing about what had just happened was OK.

I was still numb and unable to cry. So I got up and walked to the front door to make sure it was locked behind him. Then I went back to my room, turned out the light, and crawled into bed.

Just before I closed my eyes I turned off my phone, making it clear I did not want to speak to him when he called.

Because more than anything else, I knew that he would.

Chapter 52

I woke the next morning still numb. I was hurt, angry, confused, but also profoundly rational. I got ready for work without once crying or veering off course. July was quickly approaching—a year since my first failed IVF cycle. *That* had been an event worthy of tears. This was just a guy.

I grabbed my phone as I walked out the door, keeping it turned off. I could not pinpoint why I was so sure he had already called, but I was, and I knew he would continue calling until I answered. I had no intention of turning my phone back on that day, but I picked it up anyway out of habit.

The events of the night before were playing on repeat in my brain. My logical side kept reminding me that he was hurting. That he had just gotten divorced and had lashed out at me because I was there, because I was close, and because I was someone he could lash out at. Not that I was making excuses for it, because I was not. There was no excuse for how he had spoken to me. It was just that in my need to explain his behavior, I knew this was the most logical explanation.

But my emotional side ... that was a different story. The only thing that kept running through my head was *why*? Why would he *ever* say those things to me? Why would he keep repeating them? He didn't like me. He was using me. He had just been lonely and in need of a rebound. Those words had all come out of his mouth. Why would he say those things after all that had gone on between us in the previous two months?

Why would he say those things, if they were not true?

It was not like I had never been dumped before, because of course I had been. But there was a way to do these things, a tactful way to preserve the dumpee's feelings. No one—whether it was true or not—would *ever* talk to someone who had been good to them in the way that he had talked to me.

So I had these two pictures of him floating around in my brain. The good man, who really did love me and had meant every positive thing he had ever said to me up to this point, but who had lashed out and pushed me away only because he was hurting more deeply than I understood. Or the asshole, who had been full of lies and was using me all along only to finally say to me exactly what had always been on his mind.

I could not figure out how to reconcile those two pictures. Neither one of them seemed to fit completely. I could not wrap my head around how that first guy would ever have used the words he used, regardless of how much he was hurting. And I could not figure out how that second guy could have pretended to care about me so believably, if everything he said the night before was true. Because if it was, he had not just fooled me, he had also fooled everyone who counted themselves as his friends. All the people who had slowly but surely started to become *my* friends. Had they been wrong too? Or were they all in on the act?

I could not figure any of it out, but I knew I had not heard the last of him. And so I left my phone off. Not particularly wanting to deal with *either* guy just yet.

When I arrived at work, I had an e-mail from an old friend I had been close to in San Diego. Blair had just landed herself a gig on a private yacht that was going to be touring the coast of Alaska over the summer. They were pulling into Ketchikan that weekend, and she wanted to know if I could hop on a plane and meet her there.

I had never been to Southeast Alaska. I had heard about how gorgeous it was, but had never taken the time to explore it myself. This was exactly the kind of distraction I needed, and my ticket was booked within minutes of reading her e-mail. I immediately turned my phone on, solely to call her and plan our trip.

Just as the screen came to life, the phone began ringing and flashing Nick's face across the glass. I instantly hit the ignore button, but I knew it was too late. It would have rung on his end. He would know I had declined the call, but he would also know my phone was now back on. Just a few seconds later, I received a text asking me to please call him back. I debated for half an hour (angry at myself for turning the phone on at all), but finally I responded, stating simply that I did not want to talk to him. I had been compassionate and there for him, and he had used me up and tossed me away. I said I needed a breather, from him and the whole mess.

He responded right away:

> **OK. I just wanted to apologize for how I handled the situation last night.**

I did not say anything back, so he texted again:

> **Thanks for treating me so well and being such a good person.**

Again, I did not reply and again he tried once more:

> The truth is, I am still totally in love with her, and until I can move past that I only need friends in my life.

Now I was pissed. Was he really putting this on me? *Really?* My response was about to be one of the most ridiculously long text messages I had ever sent:

> I only ever tried to be your friend. That was my sole intention from the very beginning. You're the one who pushed for it to be more. You're the one who continued to say being friends was not enough. I gave you plenty of outs along the way and have said we could be just friends plenty of times. You're the one who blurred those lines—because you were lonely, or lying to yourself, or lying to me, or whatever. But don't put that on me, because it's not fair. That was all you. It's been all you all along.
>
> The fact of the matter is I'm not even mad about that. I don't like it, but I get it. I'm mad about how you handled it though. About the fact that I have been there for you and been a friend to you and you turned around last night and said a bunch of hurtful things to me without a care at all for how it might make me feel. Like you and what you want/need/feel is all that matters. You broke me down and then you just left. I can honestly say that I don't have too many friends who would make me feel like that and then just walk away.
>
> And obviously this is why we probably shouldn't be talking right now—because clearly I am heated. And I hate feeling like this and putting myself on the line to look like an idiot. I hate letting people know they've hurt me.
>
> Do what you need to do to take care of yourself. I'm going to do the same. I've tried to be there for you, and clearly that was my mistake. I should have known better. I did know better. I just... cared. About you. My heart broke for what you were going through. I wanted to be there for you. But now I'm completely drained. And I just need some space.

It was the kind of text that only a crazy girl would send. But I could not help myself. The words flowed as my anger rose.

At this point I *still* did not for one second believe anything he had said to me the night before, but that did not matter. He said it and then he left. Whether it was true or not was pointless now. He did not deserve a chance to explain himself on this one.

He wrote back pretty quickly.

> **I agree. I fucked up. What's done is done. Thanks for everything, and for whatever it's worth, I'm sorry.**

I hated him. "What's done is done." It was so smug I could have screamed. I hated him, and I turned my phone right back off. Now I was fuming. Finally feeling *something* and going through the rest of my day practically shaking.

I did not turn my phone back on until after five. His plane was supposed to have left at four and I knew his cell phone did not work where he was going. I figured at this point that it was safe for me to reconnect myself to the world, and I had *a lot* of rehashing with friends I needed to do.

But the phone was not back on for two minutes before he called. I sat there, confused and staring at his name. Seconds after it went to voicemail, he texted again asking that I please call him. He should have left at four. So how was he calling me now past five? Had he stayed behind because of me? To fix things?

I am ashamed to admit that was actually the thought running through my head. I waited almost half an hour and battled with myself back and forth before finally deciding that texting was not going to work. Maybe talking was the best option right now. So I called him.

He answered right away, but it was clear he was still at the airport. There were voices all around and I could hear speaker announcements going off in the background. It turned out his flight had been delayed because of engine problems. He was not still in town because of me. He was still in town because he was waiting on a plane. Strike one against me and my master deductive reasoning skills.

At first neither of us said much of anything. Only when I could take the platitudes no more did I blurt out, "What was it you wanted to say?"

I was short with him and obviously frustrated. There was no kindness in my voice. So he took on a similar tone and started off by saying, "I just really need you to know how sorry I am. How things happened last night, that wasn't what I intended. At all. I was hurting, and seeing her really screwed me up, but … it never should have gone down like that."

It would have been fine if he had just stopped there, but he did not. "You just need to know though," he continued. "That everything I said last night was true. I don't have feelings for you beyond friendship. I'm never going to have feelings for you beyond friendship. I was lonely and I needed a rebound, and you were there, but … I don't like you in that way. You need to know that."

Was he serious? Was he *seriously* repeating these same hurtful words to me again? Like I hadn't heard them the night before?

What the hell kind of fucked up apology was this?

I took a breath before responding, and then I said, "I get it. Is there anything else?"

It hit me like a head injury when he started repeating himself once more, a broken record about how little he felt for me. Finally, I cut him off. "I'm not going to argue with you, if that's what you're hoping for," I stated. "I'm not going to sit here trying to convince you that you're wrong. I'm not going to point out all the times you've said something totally contrary to what you're saying now. I'm not going to remind you of every single moment we've shared something beyond friendship. I'm not going to do this with you. If you don't want to be with me, fine. But for the record, I don't need to hear it anymore. So, are you done?"

He seemed surprised. I got the impression he wanted me to fight him on this, like he wanted me to fight for him. But I refused to do it.

He started stammering. Apologizing again. The whole thing was just so ridiculous and I could not for the life of me figure out why he had called at all.

"Listen," I said. "Get on that plane. Go do whatever you have to do. I'm going to Ketchikan this weekend to see a friend. I'm moving past this, and getting on with my life. I don't want to hear from you again. Take care of yourself."

I was done.

Frustrated and angry, yet so calm it almost seemed surreal. He stammered out a few more meek apologies, but none of it meant anything to me. He was all over the place, and I just wanted off the phone.

Chapter 53

I did not expect to hear from him again. Ever. There was this part of me that was still holding on to what I believed we had, this part that deep down thought he would eventually regret this and miss me. Miss what could have been. But then there was that other part of me that was taking everything he said to heart, feeling like he never would have been so cruel if it had not all been true. That part of me truly believed we were done.

So when he called that night from the same remote phone he had used to call me in the past, it caught me a little off guard. He left a message asking that I call him back, but of course I did not. He called again the next night, and the next, and the next. A few nights he called more than once, leaving a message and then trying again five minutes later, almost as if he hoped that after hearing his message I would lose my resolve not to answer. The final message he left that Friday night was borderline desperate. He sounded sober, but also like he was losing confidence in the fact that he would ever speak to me again. All he said was, "Please. Just please call me back. I'm so sorry. Please."

I could not figure out *why* he was calling. Nothing he said on these messages hinted at what he wanted. He just kept asking me to call him back. I did not want to fool myself into believing it was that he missed me or that he wanted to fix what he had broken. I had already made that mistake once, and I was not going to make it again.

I began working on an e-mail I wanted to send him. Editing, tweaking, and playing with it until I felt better about the words on the page and the resolve they stood for. I stayed up for hours writing and rewriting that e-mail, almost up to when it was time for me to leave for the airport. At five in the morning, I finally hit send:

> Nick,
>
> I'm sorry I've been ignoring your calls. It's not my style to blow people off, and for whatever it is worth—it hasn't exactly been easy for me. I do care about you more than I think you know, and there is a very big part of me that does want to talk to you. But I meant it when I said I needed some space.
>
> I need you to know that I'm not mad at you though. I'm not even upset anymore. I can't imagine how hard Monday was for you. I fooled myself into thinking you were OK because you seemed to be taking it all so well. But that was stupid of me. I should have known better. And to an extent, I definitely blame myself for how things went down that night.
>
> The end result was that you pushed me away though. You pushed hard. You drilled a fairly hurtful point home over and over again. Even in calling to apologize, you continued to repeat the same words. You were cold and callous, almost like you were trying to hurt me. Or like you thought maybe I was dense and just wouldn't get it.
>
> Trust me—I got it.
>
> The thing is, I could try to overanalyze the whole thing. I could make myself crazy attempting to reconcile what you said that night with your words and actions over the last two months. I could let my insecurities get the best of me and start wondering what was so very wrong with me that you couldn't even fathom wanting more. I could tell myself that everything was fine between us until the night she texted you. That her popping up to mess with your head one last time made you

question everything. That there really was something there before that. That I couldn't possibly have made it all up.

But... None of that would really serve a purpose. I still don't understand it. I still don't think it all adds up. But it doesn't matter. All I have to go off of at this point are your words. Words that were very clearly, for whatever reason, meant to push me away.

The thing you have to understand is that I spent a decent part of my life being broken down and tossed away like I didn't matter at all by the people who were supposed to care about me. But I'm an adult now. And I have worked too hard to get past my own issues and to be confident and strong and happy for me to allow anyone to make me feel like that again. As much as I know you're in a bad place and probably just needed to lash out at someone, I also know that I have been there for you. I have been a friend to you and I deserve better than that from you.

I think you know that too.

At this point I have to believe that when it all comes down to it, maybe a little space really is the best thing for both of us. Because as much as I have tried to be there for you, I'm not sure I have been doing you any favors by letting you use me. I have been the girl you could call when you were lonely or sad or horny or confused. I have acted as your friend and therapist and faux-girlfriend. I have bent and molded myself into whatever it is you have needed whenever it is you have needed it. And in doing so (in being all of that), I have helped you to avoid your situation. I have helped you to ignore it. Without ever meaning to, I have only added more stress and confusion to your life. And I can't even begin to tell you how sorry I am for that.

I just think that right now, you need to deal with what you're feeling. You need to face it head on and stop pushing it all to the side. I know it hurts. I know it sucks. I know you want to pretend it isn't happening. But until you face it—it is just going to keep popping up and hurting you. Even when you think

> you're over it. Even when you think you're done. It is still going to be there, just waiting to sting you when you least expect it to.
>
> You need to deal with your divorce. You need to work on healing. And you need to figure out how to be on your own for a little while.
>
> I'm afraid that I make it far too easy for you to avoid doing all of those things. And even more— I'm afraid that in all my efforts to help you, I have been making myself and what I need less of a priority. Because let's face it—I still have plenty of heartbreak of my own from the last year that I need to be sifting through and getting over as well. So maybe we both needed someone to take us away from our problems for a little while. But I don't think there is anything beneficial about continuing to do that. Not for either one of us.
>
> I did learn a long time ago that life is a hell of a lot easier if you force yourself to focus on what you do have instead of what you have lost. It took me plenty of missteps to get there, but maybe you will learn that lesson a lot quicker than I ever did. Because you really do have so much Nick. You have two parents who love you, a beautiful home, a good job, and an amazing set of friends in your life who would do just about anything for you. You are intelligent, attractive, witty, and fun to be around. What she did to you was cruel and incomprehensible (and I don't mean to diminish that in any way), but you still have so much. So much more than so many people have. I wish I could help you to see that.

I ended it by saying that maybe one day, we could be friends. After he had healed, and I had gotten over the carelessness with which he had treated me. Maybe he would call me up out of the blue, explaining that he was some guy I met on New Year's Eve at some not-so-distant point in the past, and I would be the girl again pretending to not have any recollection of meeting him. Maybe then, we could just take it from there.

I told him to take care of himself.

I signed it "Love."

I hit send.

And then I grabbed my bag, walked out the door, and put myself on a plane to Ketchikan.

♌

I arrived in Ketchikan a little after noon that day. Blair was not going to be able to meet me until four, so I quickly set out to explore on my own.

I wandered all around town checking out the various shops and restaurants. Eventually I sat down by the marina to read and wait for my friend. I was getting anxious to see her, ready for the distraction I knew she would provide. It was becoming obnoxious how often I checked my phone, refreshing my e-mail over and over again while wondering if he would reply.

I knew I had made it pretty clear that I did not *want* him to, but there was still that piece of my heart desperate for him to fix this. I wanted him to say or do something that would make it suddenly be alright. My mind was on him a lot during those hours I spent alone that day, dissecting the entire situation and trying to untangle the truth from the lies. No matter how hard I tried though, I could not assemble the puzzle he had left me with. I could not pinpoint which man he actually was: the asshole who had lied to me all along or the good guy who was just more broken than I had realized.

I did have one big fear that I could not shake. I started to worry he just was not attracted to me, and that everything else stemmed from that fact. Because on every other level, there was no denying our connection. All I could think was that it was me, *physically*. As self-conscious and pathetic and crazy as it was, that was what I was worrying about now. Thinking it came down to his simply not finding me attractive made me sick to my stomach. But I could not erase the thought from my head either. And so I needed a distraction.

When Blair was finally able to escape the boat, she and I went out to a nice dinner. We ordered a bottle of wine and spent hours catching up like only old friends can. From there we made our way over to a local bar, where some of the guys she worked with were awaiting our arrival. We had a blast that night, with just enough drunken flirting for me to forget how self-conscious I had been feeling. Still, none of these men were him. And the more I drank, the less I could remember why it was that I had not been answering his calls.

We all went back to the yacht a little after 3 a.m. As everyone settled themselves into their respective rooms, I found myself doing something I never would have done sober: dialing the number he had been calling me from while out of town. After taking such a strong stand and proclaiming my need for space, here I was caving. Not even 24 hours after I had built up the courage to hit send on an e-mail that was supposed to sever ties, I was throwing it all away.

He did not answer and I did not leave a message. Common sense somehow prevailing in the end. But of course, I had not counted on caller ID. So when he called me back, almost right away, it was all I could do to keep my heart from pounding out of my chest as I picked up the phone and said, "Hello."

It was obvious I had woken him. He sounded groggy and concerned, but sober. Starkly sober in contrast to my anything but. We spoke for a few minutes as if everything was normal, exchanging pleasantries like this was a conversation we had both been expecting to have at this hour all along. After a few minutes of mindless chatter, he paused and then asked me if I was OK. In all our time together, for all the drunk dials he had made to me, this was a first. I knew that he was worried. Especially because we were hundreds of miles away from each other and there was not a whole lot he could do to help me if something was wrong.

When I assured him I was fine though, tucked safely away on some lavish yacht where I planned to stay until morning, he mentioned the e-mail. I heard myself inhale submissively before questioning, "Are you mad at me?"

I was not sure why this was my concern (why it ever should have been my concern after the way he had treated me), but it was. I was suddenly terrified that maybe *I* had hurt *him*. He was quick to reassure me though. "No," he said. "Not at all. Not even a little bit. It was a really nice e-mail. I just ... I need you to know how sorry I am. I've been sick all week thinking about what I did. I don't know what I was thinking, why I ever would have treated you like that. I'm just so sorry."

I could feel the tears springing to my eyes, but even drunk I was not about to let that happened. I choked them back and simply said, "I know." He asked when I would be heading home, and then if he could call me once I was there.

After all that resolve I had built up, and after putting my foot down so hard and so well, I caved and told him he could. There was not much left to say after that. Not now, with me drunk and him half asleep.

So we said our goodbyes.

And I went to bed telling myself that I had not just made a colossal mistake.

Chapter 54

I recounted the details of that call over and over in my mind the next morning, knowing only that I still had no idea where his head was at. I understood he was sorry and that he felt badly, but I did not know what any of it meant beyond that.

My goodbyes to Blair were a blur as we each battled hangovers while preparing the boat to leave. Before I knew it, she was floating away and I was wandering town by myself again. I did not get home until almost 11 p.m., exhausted from my little adventure and wondering if and when I would hear from him again.

I did not have to wait long. The next night my phone rang just before eight, too early for him to have sounded as drunk as he did. The first words out of his mouth were, "Do you miss me?"

I was sober now and had been granted the time to overanalyze the error in judgment I made in calling him. Second-guessing myself, I gave the answer I wished was true. "No," I said, as boldly as I could manage. "I hate you."

Nick started laughing before replying, "Don't lie. You miss me."

Something about it was contagious. Something about *him* was contagious. I could not help the giggle that leaked out as I told him, "No way! *You* miss me!" He seemed to sober up slightly at this accusation, while replying, "Of course I miss you. I can't even believe how much I miss you."

From there he launched into a whole new slew of apologies and explanations. For the first time he started telling me that the words he said that night (now a week in the past) were not true. He explained that he had been hurting and that everything had spun out of control. Now he was telling me that he could not even figure out why he had said any of it, swearing that of course he had feelings for me beyond friendship and of course he wanted more from me.

He seemed so genuine, so raw. I was having a hard time keeping my walls up.

He just kept going though, finally saying, "I like you. I like you a lot. I don't really know what that means and I feel like I need to take things slowly. But I think about you all the time. You need to know that you're always on my mind. And I would do anything if we could just forget that night. If you could just forgive me, and we could pretend it never happened at all."

I hesitated, unsure of what my response to any of this should be. I knew what my head was telling me to do, but in my heart, I wanted so badly for everything he was saying to be true.

Nick told me he was going to be home for just a few days over the Fourth of July weekend (still almost two weeks away) and asked if he could take me out to dinner once he arrived. He begged for a night to make everything up to me.

I remained quiet. I had not known what to expect when he called, but I had not been prepared for this. So as I struggled with how to respond, he continued on. Nick confessed that he had been battling guilt over our relationship for a while now, saying that part of him still felt as though he had been cheating on her, as illogical as he knew that was. He explained that moving on so quickly and falling for someone else made him begin to question his own integrity in all of this. Being with me made him feel like a bad guy.

He quickly apologized for saying that, not wanting to hurt my feelings in any of these confessions. I had been so silent that he just kept rambling, clearly unsure of whether or not he was making an impact. "I don't know if any of this makes sense," he continued. "But it's what I was feeling. I was never a cheater. I was never that guy. And with you, just because of how fast everything happened ... I guess sometimes it made me feel like I was. And then seeing her that day, even though it was over, and even though it was her choice ... I just felt so guilty. I felt like everything I felt for you was somehow taking away from everything she and I had."

It was here where I finally chose to break my silence. I told Nick that everything he was saying made sense, before confessing to him what *I* had truly feared: that this entire thing boiled down to his not being attracted to me. I was embarrassed saying it, but the words flew out of my mouth before I could stop them. His shock over the fact that I had ever worried about this at all was the only thing that set me at ease. He reassured me profusely that attraction had nothing to do with any of it, repeating over and over again how beautiful he thought I was.

We talked for a bit longer before saying our goodnights. As I was about to hang up the phone, he stopped me and said, "Just please know that I am so sorry for hurting you. I miss you and I really hope you will let me see you when I get home." Then he asked if he could call again the next night. I told him he could.

I had not expected him to so completely switch gears, and because of that, I had not put up the fight I knew I should. In my mind, I still believed that we needed space. But in my heart, I wanted us to be able to do exactly what he had asked. I wanted us to be able to wipe the slate clean.

♌

As promised, he called the next night. Then again the next and the next. He started calling every night without fail. We talked until we were each struggling to keep our eyes open, spending hours at a time doing nothing more than talking.

Every once in a while he was completely sober when I answered. More often than not he had kicked back at least a drink or two with the guys before I heard from him. And on a few occasions, he was absolutely smashed by the time my phone rang.

It was one of *those* nights when he mentioned that he had been talking to his mom about me. He explained that after telling her some story about something I had said or done, she laughed and said, "You are totally going to end up with the whore!" He was poking fun at me when he repeated it, but then his tone shifted a bit and he went on. "I told her she was right," he announced. "We are totally going to end up together. You know that, right? Like happily ever after together. You and me. I'm calling it now."

Hearing those words put me on edge. I wanted so badly to latch on to them, but I still had trouble trusting in anything he said about our future. I grew quiet before replying, "I would be lying if I said that was not the outcome I had been hoping for … " Just as I attempted to finish that thought by expanding on the concerns I still had though, he interrupted and said, "Just wait. It's going to happen." I was not even sure how to begin arguing with him when in this moment he seemed so certain.

A few nights later, when he had not consumed quite so much, I opened up about how guarded I was still feeling. I explained that I did not know how to trust the things he was saying to me now and hesitated before telling him that in the back of my head, all I kept hearing was him saying that none of it was true. He seemed to understand and swore that he was going to do whatever it took to fix this. He said he was committed to helping me trust in him again, in "us." He admitted that he was scared too though, not because of anything I had said or done, but because of his own past.

There was one night in particular when he told me he remembered having the exact same feelings he felt for me, for her. It was such an intense point to make, while he was still healing from the wounds she had left him with. He said he remembered being sure of her and the future they had when their relationship had just been starting out as well. It terrified him to think that he could be trusting in this gut feeling he had found the person he was supposed to be with all over again, only to have me walk away in the end too.

We talked about it. We talked about it all. About how unsure we both were now and how hard it was to trust in something that seemed so unstable, no matter how much either of us wanted it. But as the days passed, we talked less and less about that. We just fell into talking. About our days, our jobs, our lives, and how excited we were to see each other again. We just talked.

That weekend I went to a pig roast thrown by friends of his. It was strange being there without him, but so many of these people were becoming *my* friends as well. Everyone had been quick to make sure I was coming, even in knowing that he was not in town.

Both Kara and Leigh were in attendance. It was the first time I was able to introduce the two of them, even though they were each connected to this group through other people. We spent most of the night huddled in a corner of the yard talking about all things endometriosis and infertility. They were each preparing to embark upon IVF in the month to come—Leigh for her second attempt (after her first round had been canceled mid-cycle due to poor response) and Kara for her first. They would be only a few weeks behind each other if they both achieved pregnancy. I was aware of the sting it would likely cause for me if that were the outcome, but even so, I wanted nothing but success for these new friends of mine. I already could not stand the idea of them experiencing the heartache I had endured.

As the night wore on, Kara mentioned that she had run into Nick's ex-wife that day. I was not surprised when she told me they made plans to get together for lunch the following afternoon. She and I had talked at length about the past Nick and this woman had shared, as well as the friendship I knew Kara was still sad to have seen crumble in the wake of their divorce. It had been months since they had spoken, so I was happy Kara was going to get a chance to catch up with her old friend, because I knew it was something she yearned for.

But there also was a voice in my head telling me there was something more to it. I tried to ignore that voice, to swallow it down and will it away. It was there though, imploring me to be nervous about anything and everything involving this woman I did not know.

When Nick called that night, I told him about the pig and all his friends who had asked how he was doing. I told him about the conversations I had and the people I met. I told him everything, without ever mentioning Kara's run-in with his ex. Maybe I should have, but we had been doing so well. *He* had doing so well. I did not think it would do him any good to know, and I was not in a hurry to put her back in his head.

Right before we got off the phone that night, he told me he could not wait to come home. He reminded me he would be back in Anchorage in a week, saying that all he wanted to do during his short visit was see his mom and spend as much time with me as I would allow.

These nightly calls of his were cracking away at the walls I had built up.

I wanted nothing more than for him to be home, with me, where he belonged.

♌

Two nights later he asked if I wanted to go camping with Kara and Chad when he came home. We had talked about spending time together, but this was different. This would be us, isolated, for days on end over another holiday weekend. We had not seen each other since the night of his divorce. It scared me to think of us jumping right back into this, going too far too fast only to have him push me away again.

I told him I needed to think about it and he said he understood. He was supposed to get back in town on Thursday and said I just needed to make a decision by then, because he was not going at all if I did not go with him. We got off the phone and he promised he would call the following night.

The next day I called Kara to get details on the trip and her opinion on whether or not I should go. She was excited he had invited me and started pushing right away for us to join them, promising that no matter what, she would be there to keep me entertained and happy. She did not think it would be an issue though, as she assured me that Nick would likely be on his best behavior. Not five minutes into our conversation, my decision was made. I went out on my lunch break to pick up boots and other supplies I would need. The more I thought about it, the more excited I became.

That night when my phone rang, I reached for it quickly, sure that it was Nick and eager to tell him my decision. But when I looked at the screen, there was his name. This was not the remote number he had been calling me from for the last two weeks. This was *his* number. Which meant that he was here, in town, two days earlier than expected.

All restraint disappeared. I practically squealed as I answered the phone. Almost immediately though, I knew something was wrong. He was sober, but … his voice. He sounded like something awful had happened, like he was having trouble even just forming whole sentences. He told me that he had just gotten off the plane. He had convinced his boss to let him come home early and had been planning on surprising me. But he said that as soon as he turned his phone on after landing, there was a text from her. It was from only a few days before, asking if they could get together to talk. He was on the other end of the phone, making himself crazy trying to figure out what she could possibly want. And all I could think was … Kara. She had talked to Kara. They had gotten together for lunch the same day she sent this text.

So I told him that was who he needed to call first. I explained what I knew about them getting together and why I had not told him before. He said he understood, but barely even said goodbye before getting off the phone urgently to call her. Or at least, that was what I thought he was doing. In reality, he called *her* first, bypassing Kara completely. He was frustrated, annoyed, and confused, just wanting to get it out of the way. She did not answer though, texting him quickly to say that she was in a movie and asking if she could call him the following day. He did not respond, picking up the phone to call Kara first and then me.

His hurt and confusion was palpable when I answered. She had apparently expressed a lot of regret to Kara, saying that things had happened quickly without her ever really wanting any of it. But once it started ... she had not been able to figure out how to stop it. She mentioned wanting to fix things to Kara, but had never once asked if he was seeing anyone else. Almost like the thought had never occurred to her at all. Kara had not revealed much during their time together. She just sat and listened to her old friend without weighing in one way or another beyond telling her that she had destroyed Nick, perhaps beyond repair. When they said goodbye, she had not given Kara any indication of what she planned to do next. I assumed in hearing all this repeated back that Kara had not wanted to step in the middle either way. It made sense, and it was completely fair.

He was a bundle of emotions as we spoke, initially consumed by anger. He was angry that she would even be thinking these things *now*, two weeks after everything was finalized. And he was angry that she was popping up to mess with his head again. He was so angry that at first he said he had no interest in talking to her.

But everything inside of me was shutting down. This entire time I had been dating a man who I knew was not completely over his ex-wife. *That* had been one thing. It was something entirely different if his ex-wife was not completely over him either. I allowed him to get all the anger out and say everything he needed to say—everything he was thinking and everything he was feeling. And then I built all my walls back up. I could feel myself becoming an emotionless robot about to say all the right things. As if I had no stake in the end result. I told him that I had listened to him over the previous months telling me how much he had loved her and lamenting the end of their relationship, hurting so badly over the pieces of what happened that he did not understand. He still had so many questions about how things had ended. They were questions that some nights were still quite literally tearing him apart. I told him that he owed it to himself to hear her out, to see if they could fix things, and to see if he even really *wanted* to after everything was said and done.

I was calm and rational. There was no anger in my voice. I was speaking to him with nothing but kindness. But I was shut down, resolute if only as a byproduct of being empty.

At first he resisted everything I said, but then he started talking about what his heart wanted versus what his head wanted. They were arguments I had engaged in with myself over *him* 100 times in the previous two weeks, so I recognized exactly where this was going.

The heart always wins.

Always.

I told him that the only way he would ever get the answers to those questions which still plagued him would be to hear her out. In the back of my head I believed that even if they did start talking again, it would not take long before he realized she was not what he wanted anymore. I almost thought that would even be for the best. She had given him no choices in their end. No power. She made a split-second decision to end their marriage and had not looked back. I wanted to believe that maybe if they entered a realm where dating again was a possibility, he would be able to regain some of his power simply in being the one with the choices to make.

And when everything was said and done, I knew that he would never really be able to forgive her. There was a part of him that wanted to go back to the life they had led and pretend the previous months had never happened. But I knew there was a bigger part of him that understood how impossible that would be. If things did start down a path of starting over with them, I knew that eventually he would be the one to realize it could never work. He would be the one to put a stop to it. In that, I hoped there would be healing for him.

I even hoped that in that, he would find himself missing me.

But no matter what the outcome was, I knew he had to close or open this door once and for all. For him, for her, and for me. So as much as it hurt, I encouraged him to walk that path. I shut myself down, as I told him to open himself up. I encouraged him to give her a chance, while also telling him that in doing so he would need to let me go. I could not be there waiting in the background as he tried to decide what it was he wanted. I could not be the one he voiced his concerns and worries to while navigating the way back to her. I told him that I did not want to hear from him again. Not until the point, when and if, he had fully let her go.

Just as he was agreeing to everything I was saying, thanking me for everything I was ... just as he was telling me that he thought he would see what she had to say, and that he would stay away from me until he knew for sure what it was he wanted...

She called.

Beeping in on the other line.

And he managed to rush out only a quick goodbye to me.

Before switching over to her.

Chapter 55

As that weekend I had been looking forward to approached, I began to fall apart. I was hurting over him and the days that passed without my hearing a word, but there was more than that in the rawness I felt. This weekend also marked one year since I had gotten on a plane to Seattle, fully believing that in just a few weeks I would be pregnant.

It seemed crazy to think a year had gone by. In some ways, it felt like I had just been there, trying to get pregnant and build the life I wanted to lead. Instead, I had gotten crushed, forced to build a life that acknowledged the impossibility of that dream.

The days with Nick by my side were among the easier days to do that. So having him gone now—on the cusp of this painful anniversary, knowing only that he had no idea what significance this date held for me, and I had no idea if or when I would hear from him again—made it all sting that much more.

I lamented how hopeful that girl a year ago had been, how much she had trusted in everything working out exactly as she wanted. A year ago, I had believed that every dollar spent and injection endured would be worth it because I would have a baby in the end. Nothing turned out how I had planned. And as the date approached, I mourned that fact. Once more alone, with no one by my side who understood. Grieving, and wondering how long that grieving would last.

Because all I wanted was to be over it.

All I wanted, was to be happy.

♌

I went into autopilot in the days that followed. I still had not cried. Not about any of it. I had not yelled or broken down or gorged myself on Ben & Jerry's. I was just going through the motions, living my life and pretending to be fine.

He kept his promise. I did not hear from him again. I had no idea what the two of them discussed that night and no concept of what was going on between them now. There were no hints into what he may have been thinking as the days passed by. I was completely in the dark.

Kara made it clear that my invite to go camping with them still stood. She said that Nick had decided instead to go fishing with his dad, so I would not have to worry about running into him. I thought about it for a minute, but in the end declined. Over a weekend when I was mourning my own failed cycles, I did not want to bring her down as she prepared for her first round. I was sure I was better off staying home alone rather than exposing anyone else to my sadness.

When Friday night rolled around though, Leigh was having none of it. She and her husband, along with her sister, brother-in-law, and a few friends, were heading to her parent's lake house for the weekend. She convinced me to come along, even if only for one night. She made promises of a campfire, boat rides, and all the food I could eat. After having spent a solid two hours sitting in bed by myself staring at the television, I did not need much convincing.

Once I arrived, Leigh pulled me aside and explained that one of Nick's best friends had called her husband just 15 minutes earlier. They were out on the lake together, planning on stopping in to say "hi" later that night. Playing the role of my hero, her husband apparently told his friend that Leigh had already invited me up for the weekend, and that it was probably best if the two of them kept their distance.

The ties between us all definitely made it difficult for me to know where I did and did not belong if he and I were not a couple. Leigh was *my* friend, but I never would have agreed to come if I thought for even a second he may have wanted to be there. The last I heard though, he was going fishing with his dad.

The last I knew ... he was talking to *her*.

So when I learned instead that he was hopping parties around the lake with his buddy, I did not know what to make of it. I just knew that suddenly—as much as I had been trying to avoid thoughts of him—he was all I could think about. I did my best to play along that night, to slap a smile on my face, drink my beer, and join in on all the fun. But all I kept thinking about was him. Wondering what was going on between the two of them, what had been said, and where his head was at. I was going over everything in my mind as the numbness faded and the sadness started to set in. I smiled and laughed and told stories along with everyone else. I played with Leigh's nephew, ate, and even jumped into the lake on cue. It was all an act though. I was grateful for somewhere to be and the distraction it provided, but there was no combatting the emptiness that now weighed heavily on my heart.

So the next day as soon as I could politely make my exit, I packed up and headed home. I needed time to think.

To process.

And to have my Ben & Jerry's.

Chapter 56

Leigh called Monday to check in on how I was doing. After a few minutes of conversation, she took a deep breath before telling me that Nick had shown up at the house the night before. No one had known he was coming until he was walking down to the campfire where everyone sat.

This was not entirely bizarre. He had been to the house plenty of times and technically he had not been the one who was told two nights before that I was there. His showing up could have been completely innocent, having nothing at all to do with me. Still, Leigh was convinced that I was exactly the reason he had arrived.

I got off the phone only to ask myself all the same questions again. Had they talked? Had they seen each other? Had they ... it hurt to even think about the answer to *that* question. But had he really been looking for me? And if he had been, did that mean he had made a decision?

I did not have to contemplate these questions for long. Only a few hours later he texted me a picture, or rather a picture of a picture. It was a photo I had taken over Memorial Day weekend. He had blown it up to poster size and framed it, hanging it on the wall in his bedroom—a prominent spot for something I knew would always serve, on some level, as a reminder of me. Along with the photo he had written:

Nice pic, huh?

It had been six days since we last spoke. Seeing his name on my phone now, I realized I had been holding my breath all that time. Finally able to exhale, I responded before my brain could catch up with my heart:

Not too shabby. Whoever took it must be pretty awesome.

He called almost as soon as I hit send, as if he had been testing the waters to see if I would welcome contact. Our conversation was awkward though. Stunted. He did not sound like himself, and the words were not flowing on either end as I knew they could. As I knew they should.

He gave me only the briefest of updates. That night (the night he had clicked over from me to her) she expressed to him all the same sentiments she had already unloaded upon Kara. Nick listened, before explaining that he was pretty sure he would never be able to trust her again. He told her it could never be like it had been. They continued to talk though, catching up on each other's lives and exchanging pleasantries that just six months before would have been absurdly cold and out of place between husband and wife.

It sounded like they had talked for a while, maybe even for more than a few nights in a row. Eventually he agreed to meet her for lunch the Friday before the holiday weekend. Just a few hours before they were set to get together though, she sent him a text saying she was sorry but she realized she still did not know what she wanted and it was probably best if they did not meet face-to-face after all.

That was it. He had not chosen me. He had not chosen at all. He was not calling now because he realized I was the one, so much as he realized I was the default. The one left.

For the first time, I felt like the consolation prize.

Of course he did not say that to me, or anything of the sort. In fact, he did not mention anything about "us" at all. It was just how I felt, knowing that in the end no choice had been made—at least, not on his part. I did not blame him for that necessarily, and I was not bitter. I understood that technically he had not even been given a chance to choose. She had taken the choice away from him yet again, and to some extent I knew that was my fault. I had encouraged him to hear her out, and in one fell swoop she had knocked him down once more, checking to see if the door was open before swiftly slamming it in his face.

I knew there were two sides to every story and that if I ever had a chance to get hers it would probably paint a different picture than the one I already had. But in that moment, I hated her. Hated her for what she had done to him and, most of all, hated her for what she had done to *us*. Because even now, I could feel the strain between us. The distance. The cold tension with no point of origin. The walls that had been erected seemingly overnight on both sides.

I thought this call was exactly what I was waiting for. I thought it would leave us both blissed out and planning our futures together. Instead, it simply left me feeling numb again. So when he asked if I would meet him for lunch the following day, I hesitated. I was unsure of whether or not seeing each other could fix this. After all that had happened between us the last time we had been face to face, I was counting on our next meeting to be a happy one. I *needed* for it to be. And this felt like it already was shaping up to be anything but.

I could hear the hurt in his voice though. The pain and frustration and … damage. I could not say "no." No matter how much my head was telling me I should.

The heart always wins.

♌

He called a little before noon the next day and suggested a spot just up the street from me for lunch. Since it was within walking distance, I said I would meet him there. I arrived before he did and sat awkwardly in the lobby, checking my phone and trying not to appear nervous.

When he walked in, there was a moment of discomfort as we both attempted to navigate how we should be greeting each other. We finally settled upon a gracelessly timed hug before asking the hostess to be seated. Something was definitely broken between us. Something that had been there just a week before was now gone.

This was not the man I had spent the previous months falling for. He looked as though he had not slept in days. He barely met my eyes as he spoke. He was distant and emotionless. A pod version of who he had previously been. As I struggled to find a glimpse of that other man somewhere within this shell, I too remained detached.

I kept waiting for him to tell me what I so desperately needed to hear: that when everything was said and done, he never would have chosen her. That he always would have picked to be sitting right where he was sitting now. With me. That admission never came though, and as lunch dragged on we strained to come up with topics of conversation, each of us vagrantly bypassing the subject of "us."

I started to wonder why he had wanted to see me at all. It was obvious what happened with her in the previous week had shaken him, both his pride and his confidence in anything and everything he thought he knew. She was not off his mind now. So why had he called?

As lunch progressed, I began to suspect it was a test. Perhaps it was about seeing if I could fix what she had once again broken. It seemed that he simply wanted to find out if I could swoop in and help him forget. The problem was that even if I could have (and at this point, I really did not believe I possessed that power), I did not *want* to. I was hurt as well. Hurt and angry and untrusting. Even though he had done exactly what I told him to do and even though in my heart I knew it was the thing he had *needed* to do, I could not help it. My walls were up, and they were not coming down any time soon.

So there we sat, with not an ounce of warmth or affection between us. To anyone taking the time to observe, we surely must have appeared to be strangers, perhaps the victims of a setup that clearly was not going well. We pretended that we each were fine, but neither of us pretended very well.

I was counting down the minutes until this lunch could be over, sure only of the fact that I needed to get away from him as quickly and painlessly as possible. So when the check came and he effortlessly put down his card, I thanked him before announcing that I needed to get back to work for a meeting. I pretended not to notice the relief in his eyes as he acknowledged the out I had just provided for us both.

As we each said our goodbyes with an indifference I had not anticipated, neither of us made a further attempt at physical contact. The wall between us had only grown sturdier with this meal. Now it was a tangible barrier I was not sure we would ever again be able to cross.

I was not even sure how to try.

Chapter 57

In the hours that followed, I could not eradicate from my thoughts the picture of him so sullen and broken down. As protective as I was feeling over my own heart, I also ached for what she had once more done to his. I remembered the promise I had made from the start: that I would be a friend to him, regardless of the state of our relationship beyond that friendship. As my compassion returned, I reasoned that it was time to at least temporarily set aside my feelings and be that friend.

Two nights later, I sent him a text. I apologized for my own coldness and explained the fear I had experienced myself the night he clicked over from me to her. I said I had not been sure I would ever hear from him again, and acknowledging that possibility left me feeling wounded. I knew it was what he needed to do and I did not blame him, but my guard was up and I was not sure how to get it back down. I said I was willing to try though, if that was what he needed from me. I ended the text by saying:

> **Just know that I do care about you, and that I'm here if you need a friend.**

He called within minutes. The void between us was not magically erased, but the discomfort we experienced in talking just a few days before *was* eased. We spent the next hour catching up, discussing more intimately the details of the week we had spent apart. We even laughed a time or two, in the facetious way that people sometimes do in the face of regret.

We still never once spoke of "us." But at least we were speaking.

Nick started telling me how he had been feeling since she popped back into and out of his life once more. How it made him begin to evaluate their entire relationship—their courtship and marriage and everything else in between. He said it made him question himself, question her, and question whether or not she had ever really loved him. He was broken. Lost and confused and so incredibly (possibly irreparably) broken.

A few nights later he headed back to remote Alaska for work. He started calling daily again, just as he had the last time he had been gone. Every night my phone would ring from that faraway number. He was drinking with regularity once more, only now it did not seem as though the alcohol was helping. His depression seeped through the phone each time I picked up. Although he was no more than an hour's plane ride away, there were nights he felt completely out of reach.

Gone were the mentions of how much he missed me or the future we could have together. He had not thrown out a drunken "I love you" in what seemed like forever. Instead, night after night, we were talking about her, about what she had done to him and the devastation it caused.

I somehow became his therapist instead of his girlfriend over those nights spent on the phone. Even though I was completely cognizant of what was happening as it unfolded, I could not stop it. I knew this was not the direction we should be heading. I knew this should not be my role. More than anything, I knew he needed to talk to a professional.

And I pushed for that, more than once. The problem was that he was out there in the middle of nowhere. The opportunities for him to get any kind of help were few and far between. He was with a group of guys who were all away from their wives and families and who were all drinking nightly to blow off steam. There were no therapists available for him to visit on his lunch break, so I was all he had when it came to talking about this. I could not cut him off from that. I could not abandon him too. Even though most nights he was irrational and unreachable, so lost and hurt and confused that the words flying out of his mouth sometimes scared me. I still wanted to believe I could pull him back. Instead, I was often left feeling defeated, inadequate, and hopeless.

This was not my fault. I was not responsible for his broken parts. I knew that everything involved in maintaining this relationship no longer held any promise of being in *my* best interest. But I could not help it. I just wanted to fix him. So I put my bachelor's degree in psychology to work, and I went into practice for myself. For him. Something I knew damn well I had no business doing. I just did not know what else to do. I did the only thing I *could* do. I sacrificed pieces of myself to be whatever he needed me to be. I began to let go of any hope for our future. I did not even care about that anymore, about what we were or were not going to become. I just wanted him to be OK. I wanted so badly for him to be OK.

We talked every night, most nights long past when I should have been going to bed. There were more than a few mornings when I reached for the phone as soon as my alarm went off, just to make sure he was getting up for work and to verify he had made it through the night at all. In the deepest, darkest recesses of my brain, that had become a very real fear of mine. That one night,

Nick would do something stupid. And I would lose him. Forever.

It would be my fault. Because I had known how bad off he was and had not been able to fix it.

He would be gone.

And it would be my fault.

♌

I started pushing for him to do whatever it took to come home. He needed to be working in town, where he had his family, his friends, and me. I wanted him surrounded by the people who loved him, and near enough that on the bad nights I could simply get in my car and drive to him if I was worried.

So when he called one night and said he would be home in just a few days, I was ecstatic. I needed him home. I needed him with me, if only so I could know he was alright.

I had a wedding to go to the night he was supposed to get back. I invited him to come with me, mostly because I could not stand the idea of his being in town and us not being together. None of the flights available had him landing in time though, so I was forced to go alone.

I dressed to the nines that night, wasting hours away thinking of him as I got ready. I was anxious just to see his face. The wedding was incredible, but when he called just an hour into the reception to say that he was home, it took zero effort to convince me to sneak away.

He met me at my place minutes after I arrived there myself. My heels had been tossed aside, but I was still in my dress. My hair was still a fancy mess. I was still far more done up than he had ever seen me before. He did not say a word about it though, simply giving me a hug and waiting patiently as I changed into jeans and a sweatshirt. He was quiet, but not cold or distant. Maybe tired and a little sad, but overall much better than I had expected he would be.

On my way to the wedding earlier that night, I had run into friends of his just outside of town. When they heard that he would be coming in, they suggested we all get together for a late dinner. I had been anxiously looking forward to some one-on-one time with him in order to truly assess how he was doing, but I knew he would be happy to see them. So as soon as he and I settled on where we wanted to eat, I gave them a call and the four of us met there. Not long after we were seated, his buddy turned to him and said, "You should have seen her tonight. She really looked incredible." He was gesturing towards me, now sitting at the table with my face absent of even an ounce of makeup. Nick looked at me for a moment, caught my eye, and held it before replying, "I did see her. She looked beautiful."

It had been almost a month since he had gotten off that plane to a text message from her. Almost a month since everything between us had been so effectively pummeled by her uncertainty. For all the sweet words that had flowed out of his mouth in the months before that, this was the first time he had used any since. I had to look away before he did, because I was sure that holding his gaze any longer would have caused me to fall apart. The pressure that had been building up for so long was suddenly releasing, if only a bit.

When we were done with dinner, he and I headed back to my place. We grabbed a movie and crawled into bed. Not touching. Not cuddling. Just two friends, watching a movie. Until the point, when I least expected it to happen, he leaned over and kissed me. After only a few seconds I pulled away and looked at him. I examined his face for any signs of the broken boy I had been counseling in the weeks preceding this moment. "What was that?" I asked. It was a fair question, considering how long it had been since we behaved as a couple.

"I wanted to kiss you," he said. "I just wanted to remember what it felt like." And then he did it again. We had each consumed only a single drink with dinner. This was not a moment borne of a lack of sobriety or inhibitions. Once it started, neither of us made an attempt to stop.

It had been six weeks since we had been together like this, and in some ways the awkwardness that hung between us was reminiscent of that first time. Perhaps our reasons for doing it were as well. He was not entirely with me. He was not completely engaged or attached. But he was trying. And in knowing how hard he was trying, there was no part of me that could say "no." There was no part of me that wanted to.

When it was over he wrapped himself around me, embracing my body so tightly I could hardly remember the distance that had been between us. I fell asleep thinking that maybe I had made the previous weeks up. Maybe it had not been as bad as I allowed myself believe.

And maybe, just maybe …

Everything was going to be OK.

Things seemed right between us the next morning, and when we parted ways he kissed me goodbye and even called later that afternoon to check in. But then I did not hear from him again. Days passed without a call or text. I was feeling vulnerable, so I did not reach out either. If he was going to keep me at arm's length, I was going to do the same.

The following weekend was his 10-year high school reunion. I thought he was going to invite me. We had spent time as a couple with all of his friends and he had invited me to everything else up to this point. Besides, we had been talking about this reunion for weeks. It never occurred to me that he would *not* invite me. Until he didn't.

I spent that night with a friend drinking wine and trying not to let myself grow bitter over the lack of communication between us. While he was gone we had spoken every single day. Now that he was home and we had crossed that line once more, he seemed to have all but forgotten me.

It was not until after midnight that the phone rang. Suddenly, he wanted me there. I was annoyed, not a fan of getting the invite only after he had been drinking. I told him I was already in bed and that I had no intention of getting up and getting ready all over again, but I also told him to be safe and not to drive.

About 15 minutes later he called again to say he would rather just be home with me. He asked if I would come get him. I wanted to say "no," but he was only 10 minutes away and I did not like the idea of him out and drunk. When I arrived, he and one of his best friends walked out to meet me, each needing a ride and place to crash. I had been reduced to his taxi driver and inn keeper, but I tried to be gracious if only for his friend who did not deserve my annoyance.

Nick got in the backseat with his buddy, but spent the drive to my place with his hands massaging my shoulders. He spoke to his friend about how amazing I was, while I remained silent. I wondered internally why I had barely heard from him during the previous week if I was so wonderful. But I kept my mouth shut, not wanting to get into any of it now.

I set his friend up on the couch and Nick and I went to bed, where he tried his hardest to get me naked. I did not budge an inch in terms of keeping my clothes on though. I was still bitter and hurt and angry. We had *just* slept together the week before. He had then disappeared on me until now, when he was drunk and lonely enough to remember I existed. I was not going to let him do that to me again.

Eventually he gave up, wrapping his arms around me and whispering an "I love you" before falling quickly asleep.

I wanted more than anything to believe those words.

But in this moment, I knew better.

Chapter 58

By the next morning, my irritation had subsided. He was still in a good mood and I allowed him to remain wrapped around me as we talked. I told him I felt like he was pulling away, before explaining how difficult it was to not hear from him for days on end, given how frequent our contact had been up to this point. He caressed my arms and kissed my shoulders as he repeated many of the same apologies I had already heard before, giving only his current broken state as the excuse for his distant behavior.

I had started to suspect he was trying to put this space between us. Not because it was what he wanted necessarily, but because he had convinced himself it was what he *should* be doing. Even now, lying in bed together, he seemed so content just to have me in his arms. Yet I feared the walls would be rebuilt as soon as we parted ways.

Once we got out of bed and began preparing to leave the house that morning, I handed him a CD I had made. This was not a first. Sharing music with people was how I spoke to them. I had made him a divorce mix early on as well, full of songs I thought he could relate to during that period. This one was filled with music that reminded me of us. Of what we had and what we could be. I knew he would listen to it. I knew he would put it on in his truck and spend days listening to it. My hope was that it would somehow reconnect us.

Over the next week though, I barely heard from him. I felt like we were going backwards. Suddenly it seemed as if we were in the beginning stages of a relationship where contact was somehow meant to be sporadic, instead of further down the road where I had gotten used to his being a regular part of my life. It was like our relationship was suffering from a case of Benjamin Button syndrome.

I did not like it, but I worried that if I pushed too hard he would only pull away harder. I was afraid of losing him, but I was also afraid that if I continued to allow this, it made me weak, vulnerable for him to take advantage of. And I was not that girl. I *knew* I was not that girl. I never would have let any other man treat me this way. So why was I letting him?

It might have been because I knew it was not just me he was struggling to make a decision about. There were so many other things he could not seem to get himself to commit to. He fought with himself about whether or not to sell his house, the home he had built with her that now held so many memories. He vacillated back and forth on wanting a dog, missing his own but not sure he now had it in him to give another what it would need. There was even a possible trip to New Zealand with one of his best friends that he could not seem to pull the trigger on. It was all up in the air. He didn't trust himself enough to make a decision on any of it.

Including me.

♌

The following weekend turned out much like the previous had. I did not hear from him until almost 11 p.m. on Friday. Now that he was drunk, suddenly he wanted me by his side. I had been sitting at home by myself watching television and had no other plans, but I was not about to go running to him now. I told him I would pass.

A little after 2 a.m. I heard from him again, this time wanting a ride. Angry that he would even ask after another week of distance between us, I put my foot down. I told him I was already asleep in bed and suggested he get himself a cab. Thirty minutes later, he showed up on my doorstep.

When I reluctantly let him in, he initially went straight for the couch, clearly realizing all on his own that I was not happy. But when I did not say anything and instead went back to my room and shut the door, he joined me there less than five minutes later. He sprawled out in my bed without speaking. He knew I was upset, but he did not seem to know what to do about it. My back was turned to him and I pretended to be asleep as I felt him struggling for words. Finally he simply said, "I do love you," before curling up and cuddling behind me. I did not say anything in return.

There was no playful flirting or laughter the next morning. I was finally done, annoyed to the point that I did not *want* to let this slide. He thanked me for giving him a place to sleep, and then cracked what he seemed to think was a joke. "I figure I've only got another few weeks where you'll let me get away with this before just being done with me!" He was smiling when he said it.

It was clear he was trying to tease, attempting to lighten the mood in any way he could. But I paused for only a moment before saying, "Actually … I think we're there."

This launched a conversation that was far too easy in retrospect. I told him I could not do this anymore. I could not continue to be his afterthought. I explained that our relationship was not working for me and that it was time for us to be done with whatever it was we were doing. I told him we could eventually be friends, but that for now I would need a little space, just to clear my head and get to a good place. I asked him not to contact me for a while.

He did not argue. Not with any of it. He said he understood and that he had known all along the point would come when I could not handle him anymore. Hearing him so resigned (as if this had been inevitable from the start), I could not help the next words that came out of my mouth. "I think the saddest part is …" I said, while looking him straight in the eye. "I really did let myself fall in love with you."

It was the first time I said it. The first time those words passed my lips in reference to him. He had said them to me on at least a dozen occasions now. Always drunk, but still … he had said them. And I had always remained silent. Until now, as I was ending this relationship I was no longer sure we even had.

He looked at me for a moment before saying, "I just don't know how to believe you. She said that to me too. I don't know how to believe it coming from anyone else, if I couldn't believe it from her."

I felt like he had punched me. Here I was, opening up and being honest and finally telling him how I felt about him and what his behavior was doing to me—and he tells me he cannot believe me. Not because *I* had ever lied or hurt or betrayed, but because of *she had*. I finally said the words I had been holding back for months, and it meant nothing to him.

There was not a whole lot to say after that. The entire conversation had been incredibly bittersweet, but we were not fighting. We were not arguing at all. It was surreal. Especially when I realized that I still had to drive him home.

By the time we got there, we had been silent for a while. He got out of the car and looked at me for a long time without saying anything. And then he just closed the door. There were no tears. Not from me and not from him. I turned around and drove home, thinking to myself how easy it had been to do something that should have been so hard.

My heart was broken.

But at least I was freed from the suffocation of not knowing where we stood.

Chapter 59

I went to dinner that night with one of my closest friends and, as we both had a few too many glasses of wine, recounted to her the details of the morning. After dinner we found ourselves shopping, mostly just browsing while still talking. Until I spotted sunglasses that resembled a pair Nick had lost just a few weeks before. Without even thinking, I was buying them. I had no plan. No intention of giving them to him anytime soon. But I figured I had them now, for the next time I did see him. It would be a friendly gesture. Or at least that was what I was telling myself. Already though, I was missing him in the most unhealthy way possible. I knew that missing him was crazy and I did not plan on doing anything about it. But then he texted me a picture of a dog. Along with the words:

I think Tatalina would be a cool name for her.

Pieces of my resolve cracked away. Had he finally found something he wanted enough to commit to? I texted back that I loved her and he responded by saying he was at Barnes & Noble, looking at books about New Zealand.

Thoughts whirled through my head at lightning speed. Was this the same guy I had been dealing with for the last few weeks? What had happened to him not contacting me for a while? Was he finally starting to make some decisions? And was *I* one of them?

Having just been dropped off at home, I sat on my bed looking at those sunglasses and the movie that had been waiting in my mailbox. Before I could change my mind, I texted him:

> **Come over when you're done. I just got home and I got you something. There was a movie in the mail too. We can break up tomorrow.**

He was at my door within 15 minutes.

I was not sure what I expected to happen or if I really expected anything to be different at all. He laughed when I gave him the sunglasses and spent a few minutes regaling me with some of what he had learned about New Zealand. We put the movie in and at first cuddled right up. Whether out of habit or circumstance, I was not sure. But when my tipsy hands began to wander, he was quick to pull away. And I was quick to pout.

This was not one of my finer moments in our relationship, but I was feeling rebuffed. I could not figure out why he was here, at my house, after our conversation from earlier that day, if he was not somehow sure that *I* was what he wanted. He said he did not want to go there though. That he was still confused and he did not want to hurt me anymore.

But I was *already* hurt. And with a few glasses of wine in me, I was saying the things I had been holding back on for months. In a moment of exasperation, I finally blurted it all out. "I've spent all this time taking care of you," I said. "Being there for you. Doing whatever it was you needed when you needed it. And whenever you're drunk, you can't keep your hands off of me.

But now, suddenly, you're not interested? I told you this morning we needed to take a break until you could figure out what you wanted, and then you're texting me just a few hours later? What are you doing here if you don't want to be with me? And when does it get to be about me? When do you start worrying about what *I* need? Because what I need is for you to decide. And for you to then stick with the choice you made."

He sat there stunned for a moment. I had never called him out so boldly. Not like this anyway. "I know," he said. "You're right. I'm sorry."

But it was not like anything was resolved. It was not as though we had suddenly broken new ground or he had chosen.

I crawled under the covers and turned my back to him. He did not attempt to hold me. And even though neither one of us got much sleep that night, not another word was spoken.

The next morning Nick got up early, quickly dressing and walking out the door while I was still in bed. I was fairly sure it would be a while before I heard from him again and that we had just experienced our *real* breakup. That night around six though, he called. He left a message, sounding sober and asking if I would call him back when I got the chance. I did not. I did not know what to say or if I even wanted to talk to him, so instead I simply refused to communicate.

A few hours later he sent a text asking if I had gotten his message. I responded that I had and asked if everything was OK. When he asked why I had not called him back, I said I had some things I was trying to figure out. His only response was:

OK. I'll let you be. Goodnight.

It was two nights later before he called again. This time I answered, prepared to talk about all that had been on my mind. I told him how confused I had been lately and how unsure I was of where we stood. I explained that I felt like we were going backwards and as though what I needed was being severely neglected in my quest to support him. Finally I said, "If you can't start being there for me too, I think we need to be just friends. Like, *really* just friends. Not friends who sleep and cuddle in the same bed, or who kiss and get naked every time you're drunk enough to want that. *Just* friends. Without the mixed signals or games. Without the underlying promise of potential for the future. Just ... friends."

At my core I wanted him to tell me that was not what he wanted. That he would try harder. That he would give me what I needed because he loved me. But instead, he said, "That's probably for the best. I think friends is all we really are anyway."

I caught my breath. Not believing him, I questioned, "Do you really mean that?"

"Yeah. I think I do," he responded.

Confused now, I said, "So if I started dating someone else tomorrow, you would be OK with that?"

"Yes," he replied, seemingly without even thinking. "I just know that there's nothing more here between us. I mean, it's weird to me too how often I'm just not interested in sleeping with you. Even I can't figure that out. I think it means something though."

I was trying not to spiral out. I was trying so hard. "What are you talking about?" I asked. "We slept together just two weeks ago. *You* prompted that. And you were completely sober."

"I know," he said. "But… you don't really want to know what I have to think about to sleep with you."

…

The entire world came to a halt. Everything around me stopped. I could not breathe.

What did that even *mean*? Was it a criticism of *me*? Was there something wrong with me? Or was it an observation about *him*? About where *his* mental state was at? About how he would have trouble sleeping with *anyone* right now?

Why would he ever say that?

Why would he ever say it *to me*?

After everything.

Especially in knowing how self-conscious I had already been about his not being attracted to me.

It was just cruel.

So cruel that my stomach had dropped and I felt as though I was going to throw up.

But instead, I cried.

The wall broke down. The emotions won out. For the first time in my entire adult life, I cried tears *as* I was being hurt. With the person doing the hurting right there on the other end of the line bearing witness to it all. They erupted out of me, these tears that had been built up for months, exploding from my eyes before I could contain them. I was shaking and sobbing and hyperventilating.

Finally stripped raw and exposed.

Finally broken down.

Finally beaten.

Immediately it was like a switch flipped for him. As if hearing my tears triggered the realization of what he had just said. What he had just done. He could not stop apologizing. He was calling himself an asshole and telling me how sorry he was. He said he had never meant to hurt me and that he hated himself for this, that he would never forgive himself. He was panicked. He had never heard me like this before, had never known me to be so vulnerable. And there I was, on the other end of the phone, crying so hard I could not respond.

I could tell he felt awful. I knew he had spoken without thought. This was one of the traits he and I shared after all, wasn't it? The lack of a filter. I knew that hurting me like this was the last thing he ever would have done intentionally. But it did not matter. It had happened.

What's done is done.

As soon as I regained my ability to communicate, I told him between sobs to stop apologizing. I said I was not mad and that I understood, but I needed time. Possibly a lot of time. I told him that if he really cared about me like he was saying he did, he needed to stay away. I begged him not to call again. Not to text. Not to show up at my door. I told him that he needed to give me time to heal from this. From all of it. From him.

The remorse in his voice was evident. "I'll stay away," he promised. "I do care about you, more than you know, and I'm so sorry I let this happen. If that's what you need … I'll stay away."

He asked if I was going to be OK. If there was anything he could do. I continued to struggle with getting the words out past the tears, but I told him I would be fine. That it would just take time. And the only thing he could do for me now was leave me alone.

I hung up the phone before curling up in a ball on my bed and finally letting it all out. The tears. The heartbreak. The sadness. The months of buildup, finally releasing. I was crying until I was sure I had nothing left.

And then, I cried some more.

Chapter 60

He said he would stay away. He promised. But not 15 minutes later, he was calling. Still a mess and knowing only that *he* had caused this, I did not answer. So he texted:

> **Please call me back. I'm really sorry. I shouldn't have let this happen.**

I did not respond. He called again, and I did not answer. So once more he texted:

> **Will you please answer so I can explain myself to you.**

I could not figure out what there was to explain. Hadn't he already said it all?

I wiped the tears away for long enough to pen my response:

> **I really can't talk right now. I'm sorry. I'm not mad, I promise. I'm just hurt, and confused, and embarrassed, and sad. You listening to me cry on the phone is not going to help that. I know you never meant to hurt me. I just need some space.**

And then, I turned off my phone. I really was not angry. Not at him anyway. Regardless of what he had meant by that comment, I knew his intentions had never been to cut me so deeply. He likely had not even processed the words himself before they came tumbling out of his mouth. This was who he was after all. I *knew* who he was. So if I had anyone to be angry at, it was me. I knew going into this that it would not be easy. I entered this relationship fully aware of the roller coaster it would become. I made my choices. And I allowed myself to fall in love with him.

In this moment though, I could not quite figure that part out. *How* had I allowed this to happen? How had I allowed myself to believe he felt the same for me as I did for him? I felt so unwanted and discarded that I could not breathe. I was literally having a hard time coming up out of my grief and heartache for air. How had I become so caught up in someone who could so easily take my feelings for granted?

It was because everything else had been right. The way we laughed together and the hours we spent talking about nothing. Or more importantly, the hours we spent talking about everything. The things we had in common. The futures we wanted. The way we had eased right into each other's lives. It all fit. In so many ways, he was the man I had been waiting for.

Wasn't he?

Had I been crazy to imagine he felt the same for me as I did him?

Or just stupid?

It did not matter now. In my heart, I knew that. He had crossed a line. We would not be going back anytime soon. We couldn't.

I woke up the next morning resigned to that fact, and thankful that in just two days I would be getting on a plane and leaving town. My dad was getting remarried and I already had plans to visit Arizona for the wedding. After that, I was going to California to spend time with friends I had not seen in ages. The timing could not have been more perfect. I would regroup in a way I knew I could only do there.

But before I left, I had to put a final nail in the coffin of our relationship. I had to close the door. So I broke my silence about Nick on the blog and I shared the story of our demise. It was the abbreviated version, of course, but still ... I accepted defeat. I declared our relationship over.

And then I left Alaska, determined to leave him behind as well.

♌

I spent my trip intentionally submerged in anything that could serve as a distraction from him. I surrounded myself with family and friends, laughing and drinking and fighting to forget. By the time I arrived in San Diego, I almost believed I would be able to move on.

I was with some of my oldest girlfriends while there, one of whom happened to be dealing with a brutal and unexpected breakup herself. We spent our nights doing nothing more than drinking wine and bashing men. It was not until my second-to-last night that I started to miss him. We were in the car driving when out of nowhere I realized I was fighting back the tears. I tried to explain to my friends what I was feeling, but I could not put it into words. I knew he did not deserve these tears of mine. I knew he did not deserve anything from me. But I was having a hard time letting go of what I believed could be, and I was beginning to dread going home. After spending more than a week with the people I loved, distracted entirely from his absence in my life, I was suddenly afraid of being back in Alaska. Without him.

I had not heard from him since that night. Ten days, the longest we had ever gone without speaking. I was glad he kept his promise, but there was also a part of me that hated it. I had gone through our first weekend apart on edge, sure that a drunk dial from him was imminent. But it had not come. And despite my best efforts not to, I felt slighted. Even though he was only doing exactly what I had asked: staying away. I was not proud of my feelings. I knew I should not be missing him or secretly wishing he would call, but that was the reality. His lack of contact had me beginning to wonder if maybe I had made up everything we shared.

So of course it was that very night, as I had just allowed these thoughts to seep back in, that I heard from him. He sent a text a little after 11 p.m. asking about my trip. I was with two of my best friends, and their presence helped me to ignore it—even though I probably would have anyway. I did not hear from him again.

Not until the next night that is, when at 2:30 a.m. my phone beeped once more. My plane was leaving in a few hours and my friends and I were in the living room, spending the last of our time together laughing and talking. When I looked down at the text that interrupted us, all it said was:

>**Are you alive? Yes or No?**

It seemed unfair. He knew I was alive, and he also knew I had a near impossible time ignoring people. Why wasn't he just leaving me alone? Like he had promised? Annoyed, I responded:

>**Of course I'm alive. Pretty sure you would probably hear about it if I wasn't.**

As soon as I hit send, he called. And I hit the ignore button. Why was he doing this? I knew he was drunk. That much was assured simply by the hour. But was that really all this was about?

He sent another text:

> **You just screened me!**

And I responded:

> **Yes I did. I'm in San Diego with friends. And you're giving me space. Remember?**

I should not have responded, but I felt like he was due that reminder. He replied right away:

> **Yes, sorry. I miss you. Goodnight.**

Now I was pissed. *Finally* I was angry. Not at myself, but at him. He made me a promise, and now he was breaking it. As much as I had secretly wished I would hear from him (if only so that I could know he cared), it was not acceptable for him to be telling me he missed me now. I lost my temper in response:

> **That's not fair. After a conversation where you said to me 'you don't really want to know what I have to think about to sleep with you,' you don't get to miss me. You have no idea how much you hurt me. How stupid and embarrassed and naïve I felt for letting myself believe anything you ever said about wanting to be with me. I care about you, I want you to be OK, and I want to be your friend. But not at the expense of me getting trampled on. And not if it means only hearing from you when you're drunk enough to realize you miss me. I need that space. And you said you cared enough to give it to me. So ... do it.**

He responded with a simple "OK." But five minutes later, he responded again:

> I love you, either way. Take care.

Why was he doing this to me? Why was he using that word now, after basically telling me he had never meant it before? I waited to respond until over an hour later, as we were driving to the airport:

> They're only words Nick. They don't mean a whole lot coming from you anymore.

I felt justified in that. It was true. *I* did not throw those words around. *I* did not use them haphazardly and without care. So why did he get to?

I got on my return flight to Alaska feeling much the same as I had felt in leaving.

Hurt. Confused. Toyed with.

And still completely brokenhearted.

Chapter 61

Upon returning to Alaska, I forced my focus to shift away from Nick and toward Kara and Leigh, each on the cusp of their own IVF cycles. These were women I knew I would have been friends with even if not for this shared disease. They were genuine, hilarious, intelligent, and strong. They had each also been incredible friends to me. I was grateful to have them in my life, and anxious to support them as they fought for motherhood.

Still, there was a sinking feeling in my stomach that came with witnessing them walking this path I had walked not too long before. It was an impending dread, the knowledge that no matter how their cycles went, I was going to be hurt.

The last thing I wanted was to see either of these women fail. I cared about them and hated the idea of their experiencing even a fraction of the pain I had felt. But I also feared that witnessing them face a failure would thrust me right back into the memories of my own heartbreaking cycles. I did not want to go there. I did not want *them* to hurt like that, and I did not want *me* to hurt like that. Not again.

Of course, I was also anxious to see them succeed where I had failed. It scared me to be the odd man out. Obviously that was the option I preferred, but I knew their success would once again leave me pondering my own failure. Wondering what I had done wrong and why I did not deserve the same happiness. I worried it would be difficult for me to partake in their joy, if only because my own sadness would be in such stark contrast.

Nick had served as a distraction from all of this. He needed so much from me that I was able to ignore these past hurts of mine while they slowly scabbed over. In a way, it had been a good thing. Now that he was not around to distract me though, I was returning to a place of grieving—a feeling I almost embraced, because it now served as a distraction from him.

There was no distraction great enough to help me ignore what came next though. It was a Thursday night at a reasonable hour, less than a week since I had gotten home, when my phone beeped alerting me to his text:

> **For whatever it's worth, I'm sober and I still really miss you. You are a wonderful person and a great friend. You have stood beside me and supported me through one of the toughest times in my life and I don't take that for granted. Take care.**
>
> **PS I decided not to get Tatalina.**

It caught me off guard. Technically, it had been exactly what I needed. It was confirmation that he did care about me and that I had not made it all up. But it still was not enough.

I thought for a while before finally texting back:

> **It is worth something. Thank you. And I miss you too. But ... I can't keep letting myself get hurt. It's not good for you or me. You need to deal with everything and get your head back on straight. I think it's obvious I wasn't helping you to do that. If anything, I was just confusing you more. Or putting too much**

> pressure on you to be something you couldn't be. I can't be your friend. Not right now. Not when we both know I want more. Not when every time you're drunk, you suddenly want more too. It just hurts too much. It was breaking me. And I'll never understand how you could have said something so hurtful to me—even if it was true. I just ... I don't get it. But I do miss you. Even if I wish I didn't.
>
> I'm sorry you didn't get Tatalina. I really wanted her for you.

It was more than I had meant to say, but epic text messages were expected from me, especially with so much still hanging in the air. I assumed that would be the end of that, at least for a while. Until his response came through:

> I am so sorry for hurting you. You didn't deserve any of this. The truth is I am very confused and don't know how to handle things with you, so as a defense mechanism I push you away. The sad part is, I always regret it later and feel like a jackass. I am thankful for the support you have given me, but wish we could have met later when I wasn't so fucked in the head. This is a shitty situation and it breaks my heart not having you in my life. You have been so there for me; there is no way I can ever repay you for that. I only wish I was half as good of a friend as you have been to me.
>
> There are so many things I would like to say to you in person, so if you would consider meeting me let me know. I am terrified to lose you and it is unfortunate (in some ways) we met at such a shitty time. As a matter of fact, the timing fucking sucked, but the last five months of my life would have been miserable without you. Meeting you has been the best thing that's happened to me since the divorce. I miss you. Dammit I wish we could just start over. I hope to see you again. Love always, Nick.
>
> P.S. I have been listening to your CD every day.

He had just out-texted me. And all I could think, after reading all of that, was:

Crap.

♌

I was in disbelief. I had anticipated him coming around eventually, but assumed it would be *months* before that happened. Not weeks.

Crap.

I was not over this. My hurt had not yet been dispelled. I did not trust him. Not to protect me, and not even to have healed enough himself to be able to stand by those words. But what he was saying was *exactly* what I had been hoping to hear.

Crap.

And the length? What *was* that? It was not like I had ever before questioned his ability to communicate (I hadn't). And he had always fared pretty well when it came to me and my own verbosity. But seriously ... had he just *out-texted* me?

Crap.

My head was spinning. He just *had* to add in that last bit, didn't he? The part about his listening to my CD every day. The one I made very intentionally, picking every song with care. The one that had been created *specifically* to remind him of us. He had picked up on that, without my ever saying a word. And he was listening to it every day.

CRAP!

When I did not respond right away, he followed up by saying the conversation had just taken far too serious a turn. He made some quick quip clearly meant to make me laugh. He then ended it by simply saying "goodnight."

So rather than attempt to form a response to the words I knew he was waiting for me to reply to, I instead wrote back, "Get some sleep…" I could not figure out how else to respond. So I pretended as though all the rest had not been said at all. I only knew I was not ready for this yet, and I was pretty sure he was not either. So the next morning, I wrote him an e-mail:

> I need some time to wrap my head around some of what you said last night. I appreciated it, and I do miss you. More than I really care to own up to. But I can't meet up with you right now. I'm still hurt and confused. I swear that when you and I started hanging out, I was this strong, confident girl who was great about knowing what she wanted and what she deserved. Somehow over the last few months though, all of the back and forth with you has left me insecure, confused, and unsure of myself. That's not who I want to be.
>
> I think we both still need space. I need you to know what you want from me. From her. From all of it. I need you to be in a place where you're secure in whatever that is. I think it's obvious you need time to figure that out. And I need time to let go of how badly so much of this has hurt me.
>
> Just know that I am still here though. Worrying about you, wondering what you're up to, and hoping that you're OK.

That was it. No long-winded diatribes this time around. It was quite possibly the first time in my life I had said what I needed to say without saying too much.

I did not expect to hear back from him after that. Not right away anyway. He had said his piece and I said mine. The door was still open. I had not slammed it shut. But I had been clear: I needed time. We *both* needed time. I just hoped he would be able to see that, because the truth of the matter was that I knew already I was not strong enough to resist if he started putting in the hard sell. As much as I hated admitting that to myself, I knew I would not be able to hold my ground if he pushed.

I already missed him too much.

♌

When I did not hear back from him that day, I let myself believe that he *did* get it. It was a realization that filled me with a strange mix of relief and sadness, but mostly relief.

I missed him, and I did not like his absence from my life, but I truly believed this was for the best. We needed this time away from each other. If we were going to stand any chance, we both needed to heal first. I knew myself well enough to know that as much as I wanted him fighting for my forgiveness right now, I would not be able to stand my ground for long if he did. No matter what my head was telling me.

The heart always wins.

So when he texted me a few nights later, I again was filled with that strange mix of relief and sadness. But mostly relief—

although for entirely different reasons. It was a little after 10 on a Sunday night. All he said was:

> **When you told me you loved me, I believed you. I don't know why I acted like I didn't.**

I was not sure what to do with that or how to respond. So I just didn't, holding my ground as best I knew how. An hour later though, he texted again:

> **I want to take you to my parents' house and reintroduce you to them. Let me know if you would ever be up for that.**

What. The. Hell. That was all I could think: *What the hell?!?*

I had met both of his parents that very first night at his BBQ, and I had bonded with them immediately—especially his mother. Ever since then though, Nick had managed to keep the two of us apart, almost intentionally so, as if that was his way of drawing the line between friends and something more. Yet he talked to her about me and to me about her with regularity. Whenever he was on the phone with her and I was around, she would tell him to say "hi to the whore" for her. It was a joke that had continued from the very start. Even with that though, he still made an effort to keep distance between us.

I never once pushed, or even asked, for an opportunity to spend time with his parents again. I knew why he had not mentioned it himself, and I assumed that he would open that door again when he was ready. Had he really just opened it all on his own though? Without my ever having said that it was something I was waiting on?

I could not take it anymore. Realizing even in the moment how weak of me this was, I picked up the phone and called him. As soon as he answered, the first words out of my mouth were,

"You have got to stop this. I asked for space. I need you to give it to me."

I was trying so hard to be strong, to *sound* strong. But he instantly saw right through me, letting out a laugh before saying, "I am so glad you called."

In a perfect world, I would have gotten off the phone immediately after that. I would have held my ground and kept my distance. This was not a perfect world though, and I was not as strong as I had always believed myself to be. We spent the next two hours talking about us, where we stood, what he wanted, what I wanted, and what we both needed. We talked about *everything*.

In the end, Nick asked me to give him another chance. He swore he was ready and that he had spent the last few weeks thinking about nothing more than me. He said that as soon as we had each hung up the phone that night more than two weeks before, he realized what an idiot he was, but he could not figure out how to fix it. He said he had been listening to my CD nonstop ever since I had given it to him, and I could hear it playing in the background now even as we spoke. He told me that he had been thinking about everything and realizing how well we fit together and how much he missed not being able to share even the stupidest pieces of his day with me. And then he said that in comparing me to her, he was starting to see the ways in which I filled up holes for him that she never had. He said it all. When I continued my push for space, he countered by asking me to give him a chance. He *begged* me to let him prove it. He swore he was ready and that *I* was what he wanted. That we could make this work out exactly the way it was supposed to.

"I can't make you any promises," he said, "because I know I've already lost your trust. But please, just let me show you. Let me spend the next however long it takes making it up to you. I will never do that to you again. Just please, let me prove to you how much I care."

He did not know it, but once upon a time I had spoken almost the exact same words to Michael, aching for the opportunity to fix what I had broken. All I had wanted was a chance to prove to him I was ready for what we could have. In a way, I still lamented the fact that he had not been willing to try, knowing that I would have given just about anything for the opportunity to spend the rest of our lives making it up to him.

My resolve was softening if only because I felt as though I knew exactly where Nick was standing now. And when I had been in his shoes, I had known with everything inside of me that if given that chance, I would have gotten it right.

I told him that he needed to be sure. That all I knew for certain was that we did not have many chances left, and if he hurt me again I did not think I would ever be able to forgive him. I believed that. I knew it to be true. If he said these things now and then could not live up to them in the end, I did not see how there would be any going back from that. My pride had already taken too many hits. I was already embarrassed that I was even *considering* this. Embarrassed and terrified.

He promised he was sure though.

And my head once more lost the battle against my heart.

Chapter 62

We talked for so long that night, eventually I was laughing. My walls came crumbling down with so much less effort than expected, even as I remained firm on the fact that I did not want to see him face-to-face. I knew I would cave completely if he said these things while standing directly in front of me, and I could not allow that to happen. Not yet anyway.

When it was time for us both to head off to bed, he asked if he could call again the following night. He could not wait until then though, texting a little after 8 a.m., only hours after we had said goodnight. He maintained communication throughout the day, and as I was walking out of work that night Nick asked if I would meet him for dinner. I reminded him that I was not yet ready for that, and he responded with, "Fair enough." He still called just a few hours later, as promised. And again, we talked the night away.

The next evening he tried once more, sending a text a little before five asking if I would go to dinner with him. I responded:

> I can't figure out if you're being charmingly persistent, or just willfully determined to get your way.

He replied simply with:

> **Neither, I just want to see you.**

I surrendered, but not before being clear on the fact that he would not be spending the night once dinner was over. He agreed to those terms and picked me up at seven.

I was incredibly nervous, more nervous than I had ever been around him. My head and my heart were involved in such an epic battle, I could not tell which end was up anymore. He caught on to that fact not long after we were seated, interrupting an uncommon lull in conversation between us to say, "You look sad tonight." I took a deep breath before responding, thinking through my words carefully. I wanted to be true to myself without ruining an otherwise promising evening.

"I am kind of sad," I said. "It scares me to be here. To be with you. And I feel like at this point, if you hurt me again, I have no one to blame but myself. That makes me a little sad. I don't want to get hurt. And I don't want to be the stupid girl who fell for lines she shouldn't have."

"I'm not going to do it again," he promised, before grabbing my hand. "I'm not going to hurt you. And you're not stupid."

That was the extent of discussing "us" that night. We both almost immediately agreed that we did not want to focus on the past. Right now, in this moment, we just wanted to have fun. And we did. We talked and laughed all throughout dinner, and when it was over, I was not ready to say goodbye. So I was the one to suggest we get frozen yogurt to take back to my place. We ate our dessert and laughed over mindless reality television before I began teasing him over something silly. He looked at me for a moment with a grin on his face and then tackled me, pinning my arms down with one hand and tickling me with the other. I squirmed and wrestled while we both laughed until we were out of breath. Everything about this felt right.

When he stopped tickling and I stopped struggling, we each grew quiet and did not move. For a moment, I was sure he was going to kiss me. But at the last second possible, he stood up instead. I was glad he had, if only because I was not sure I would be able to contain myself if we started kissing now.

I walked him to the door, where he hugged me and said goodbye. I went to bed thinking to myself that if we could just take this slow, it might be alright. It might not end with my heart broken in pieces. It might not end at all. I wanted to believe that maybe, just maybe, my head had it all wrong.

The heart always wins.

But even then I knew, the heart was not always right.

♌

I was instantly nervous when I woke the next morning. It had been too easy. We had fallen too seamlessly into having fun with each other once more. I was waiting for the other shoe to drop, terrified that once he got what he wanted, he would not want it anymore. He texted me mid-day though, just to check in and see how I was doing. Then he called again that night, just to talk. It was too soon to let myself breathe, but ... I was beginning to exhale.

Labor Day—the last big summer weekend in Alaska—was coming up. Things between us were still too fresh and raw for me to feel comfortable planning an excursion with him, and I was honest about that. So he made plans to go fishing for a day while I made plans to spend time with friends. We went more than 24 hours without speaking while he was out of cell range. When he sent a text Saturday night saying he was back in town and asking if I wanted to meet him and some friends for dinner, I rapid fired back with three different messages all addressing three different subjects. My excitement at hearing from him was apparent.

Nick immediately called, laughing before saying, "You must have missed me, huh?" We talked for a few minutes and came up with a plan. He was just getting home and wanted to take a shower and check off a few quick chores before dinner. I had just gotten out of the shower myself and still needed to get ready. We agreed it would be easier if we both met there.

We had dinner with Nick's buddy Brian and his girlfriend, the four of us talking nonstop as we caught up on each other's lives. When the bill came, we all decided to head back to Nick's house and continue the evening sitting by his fire pit. Brian's girlfriend was already proposing we pick up a bottle of wine, and I was sure this was going to end with me spending the night. I knew that was not a good idea. Not yet, not so soon, and not with both of us drinking.

But I was having fun. I liked spending time with these people. I liked being with Nick. I did not want to be the stick in the mud that started interjecting "rules" upon what otherwise would have been a completely normal evening for the four of us. I could not bring myself to say "no"—most likely because I did not *want* to. No matter what my head was saying.

So we went to his house and sat around the fire. We laughed over horror stories from our collective dating pasts and discussed our plans for the following day. After hours of drinking and amusement, we all said goodnight before Nick and I headed upstairs to bed. I became frustrated when I remembered I had not been planning to stay over, and therefore hadn't packed a toothbrush. Nick was quick to pull a new one out just for me. I had spent the night without a toothbrush on more than a few occasions in the past, but this was the first time he had supplied one for me. The first time he had ever pointed out where I should keep it for the future. It was a simple gesture, but somehow it still meant so much.

Still, when we crawled into bed I had every intention of keeping things PG. We had not kissed or shared any physical contact in over a month. I was not ready to jump off the bridge back into too much too soon, but I also knew how difficult it could be to draw a line that had never really been drawn before. When he leaned over to kiss me, it suddenly became all the more difficult. Still, I resisted. Despite the wine I had consumed. Despite how passionately he was kissing me now. And despite the many attempts he made over the next several hours to get me to go further. I resisted.

I knew I was not ready for this, that *we* were not ready for this. I also knew that more than anything, when and if we did cross that line, I did not want it to be something he could later blame on alcohol. So I held firm, strong in my stance that we were not going to go there.

For once, my head was in the lead.

At least, it was until the next morning, when he was sober yet still so sweet. So attentive, so cuddled up, and so ... Before I knew it, there we were, on his bathroom sink, doing something I had promised myself we would not do again for a long time to come.

My heart won out.

Or maybe it's fair to say the situation had far more to do with parts of me other than my heart. Because the truth is, even as it was happening, I could not get into it. I was terrified. My head was screaming, calling me stupid, naïve, and a masochist.

And when it was done, even my heart was scolding.

Chapter 63

Once it was over, Nick showered and I sat silently on his bed trying to calm myself. When he walked out of the bathroom with only a towel wrapped around his waist, he looked over and must have sensed my panic. "Do you regret it?" he asked.

"Do you?" I countered.

He sat next to me and promised he did not, swearing that for what had likely been the first time, this was exactly what he wanted. He smiled and reassured me that the guilt he felt in the past was no longer there. I wanted so badly to believe him. But that voice in my own head just kept getting louder, telling me this had all been a monumental mistake. I was waiting for him to turn on me as he had already done so many times in the past. And I knew that this time I would never be able to forgive myself for giving him another chance.

He convinced me to get ready, saying we were going with Brian and his girlfriend to find Kara and Chad. They were camping an hour away, and Nick thought it would be a good opportunity for me to see some of Alaska. It was sweet, and I was excited to talk with Kara. The drive was gorgeous and we spent over an hour with them before heading to Brian's family cabin later in the day.

We were all sitting around the fire that afternoon when Brian's mom mentioned the collection of firewood that needed to be moved across their property. Nick immediately volunteered for the job, even as his buddy was shooting him death glares from across the fire. But they went right to work and kept at it until all of the wood was moved almost two hours later.

There was a point there, in watching him work, when I finally told my head to shut the hell up. This was the man I had fallen for. A man who was sweet and good and kind. A man who would jump up to help his buddy's mom with hard labor even as he was tired and hungover. For all the fears that had been running through my head, *this* was a glimpse of the man I wanted. The man I loved.

When they finished, I had a hard time keeping my hands off of him. I wanted to be touching his knee or holding his hand. After feeling so held back with my affection toward him over not just the last week but also the last few months, I suddenly wanted to shower him with it. I had always been someone who showed (and felt) love through physical affection, and this change signaled the trust I was allowing myself to feel for him again. Even though it was probably still too soon to trust in anything, I was seeing the man beneath the hurt once more. I was starting to relax into this.

Into us.

♌

As we headed home that night, I mentioned wanting to stop by Leigh's family lake house. It was not far from where we were and I knew that she and her husband were there with friends.

They had just arrived back in town from her IVF cycle a few days before. I wanted to see her and assess for myself how she was doing near the end of her two-week wait.

For some reason though, Nick did not seem interested. I had broached the subject that morning as well and he quickly shut it down, saying he did not want us there all night when we were each running on so little sleep already. It was a valid point, but still … I brought it up again as we started the drive home, wanting desperately to see my friend in the midst of what I knew was a mind-wrecking journey. Again though, he shut it down, saying he just wanted to get home.

I let it go, figuring I would drive there myself in the morning. I was not upset exactly. I was tired too, and I understood (to an extent) *why* he was resisting. Besides, we still had Brian and his girlfriend with us, and I knew they were anxious to get home as well. But I also felt a little sad that he had not agreed to go simply because he knew I wanted to.

It was just as I was thinking this that he suddenly pulled down the road heading in their direction. Without a word, without ever saying he had changed his mind, he drove the four of us there.

I lit up. It was again something so small that meant so much to me, forcing those voices in my head to quiet down even more. I found out later Brian told his girlfriend that Nick must really love me, because he had never before seen him do *anything* he had not wanted to. It was true. He could be stubborn and set in his ways and sometimes even incredibly selfish. He never meant to be, and I had always assumed it was just part of his being an only child, but it was a facet of his personality that wasn't lost on me. It was one of the reasons I had not argued with him further about making this one last stop. I knew it would not make a difference. If he did not want to go, he was not going to.

Yet he had turned down that street solely because he knew that I did. I did not realize his friends caught on to the significance of that act at the time, but I had. My head shut up entirely, and my heart was doing a victory dance.

When we walked into the house, I noticed immediately Leigh's euphoric glow. I had been anxious to see her, worried that perhaps the two-week wait would wear her down. But I should have known better. I should have remembered the unquestionable hope I had been filled with during my own first two-week wait, before I really knew what it was like to fail. I could see it in her eyes now, as I attempted to combat my own fear for her. My attention was immediately drawn away from Nick as I realized how much I wanted this for Leigh and how scared I was that she would face the same fate I had.

Within minutes of our arrival, she grabbed my arm and pulled me into a side room. I assumed initially that she wanted to discuss my dating status, but as soon as we were in the room I noticed her pulling something out from behind a set of blankets. I knew it was a pregnancy test. I also knew by the look on her face that it held two lines. Leigh was not floating around euphoric with hope. She was euphoric with *knowing*.

The mix of emotions that instantaneously hit me were more than I had properly prepared myself for. The feelings of pure elation and anguished jealousy were overwhelming. I felt the tears spring to my eyes like acid, and I fought to force them back. I plastered a smile on my face and hugged my friend with everything I had. She was pregnant, and I was not. I had been so focused on Nick and our relationship lately, that I had all but entirely pushed infertility out of my mind. Now though, looking at those two lines, I was confronted once more with the realization that it would likely never be me. In feeling that, all I wanted to do was crawl into a bed and cry.

That was not an option in this moment though. My friend deserved nothing more than to see me happy for her, and after Nick had come along for this ride without even wanting to, I was not going to let him see me break now either. So I put on my best happy face and walked back out to the living room with Leigh. I spent the next few hours socializing as though nothing was amiss, alternating between a need to ensure that Nick was enjoying himself and that Leigh did not see my pain. I sacrificed pieces of myself in those hours for each of them, because it seemed like the only thing I had any real right to do.

By the time we left, I was exhausted.

♌

I had to fight off sleep on the drive back to Nick's house. I could not remember the last time I had been this tired. Between the emotional roller coaster I had been riding with him and the concentrated effort I had just made to show Leigh only my happiness, I was now completely drained.

I wanted to talk to him about it. Leigh was still feeling protective of her news and had told only me that night. We had each headed back into the living room pretending as though she was not carrying a miracle beneath her heart. But now, I wanted to talk to him about it. I wanted to describe the complex mix of emotions I was feeling. I wanted him to comfort me. To hold me. To tell me that everything I was feeling was OK. For once, I wanted to be able to lean on him.

Instead, when we arrived at Nick's house, Brian got out of the car and the two of them made plans to throw a movie in. I was too tired to contemplate driving home, and still hopeful that I would be able to curl up into him in the morning and describe what I was feeling. So while they decided what movie to watch, I jumped in the shower and threw on one of his old t-shirts before going to bed. They were not even 15 minutes into Rambo when I passed out, and I did not wake when he wrapped his arms around me later that night.

When I opened my eyes the next morning, he was in the shower. Even though I felt like I could still sleep for hours, I forced myself up and into the bathroom. I popped my head in to tell him good morning, but he barely looked up as he said it back. I asked a few questions, and he responded with only one-word answers, still avoiding eye contact with me at all costs. Something was up, and my heart sunk.

My first instinct was to get out of there. I had overstayed my welcome or he was freaking out or … All I knew was that I needed to leave before he had a chance to overthink it any more. I quickly packed my things and changed before shouting into the bathroom that I was leaving. All he said in response was "OK." I was in my car before he was even out of his towel. My head was formulating an argument once more, telling my heart it had celebrated too soon. But my heart believed he would come around and that I would hear from him in a few hours, as soon as whatever this was passed.

Only I didn't. He never called.

The next day passed slowly. I kept waiting for him to reach out, to text, to call … anything. As I worked throughout the day, I told myself I would hear from him soon. Only, I didn't. My head and my heart began battling once more, my heart saying I should not be playing games, while my head reminded me it had only been a week since he had been fighting so hard just to see me. If he was blowing me off already, this was not a good sign of things to come.

The heart always wins though, and I sent him a text a little before six asking if he wanted to come over. He responded almost immediately:

> I'm going to stay here tonight. I got really depressed yesterday and didn't sleep at all.

I was not sure what to do with that. Was he asking me to comfort him or telling me to keep my distance? I put far too much thought into my response:

> Yeah... I noticed a shift yesterday. I wasn't sure if I should stick around and try to get you to talk to me or take off fast in case it was me you were annoyed with. If it's any consolation—I had a rough day yesterday too. Try to get some sleep tonight. I'm sorry you're hurting...

I did not hear from him again. I thought for sure he would call that night, but he didn't. Not that night, and not the next day either.

By Thursday I was starting to fall apart. Had I jinxed this by letting myself believe, even if only for a second, that it could work? *He had promised* me, begging for another chance to prove he could do this and would not hurt me again. He knew how scared I was and how hard it had been for me to put any trust in him. *He had promised.* Sworn, begged, and pleaded. Saying everything I needed to hear and more. *He. Had. Promised.*

And it had only lasted a week.

He was pushing me away again, shutting me out, putting up walls, and closing the door. I was tempted to call him. To tell him he was not allowed to do this to me again and to hold him accountable for his actions, to hold him accountable for me. But my pride would not allow it.

My head was finally winning, telling me that if he really cared he would call. If he was really worth all this heartache, he would try to make it right. He would reach out, even if just to tell me he needed time.

Only, he didn't.

The next morning I got up and showered. I put on my makeup and made a breakfast smoothie like it was any other morning. I followed my routine to a 'T', without ever once faltering in my steps. And then, as soon as I got a chance, I called my cell phone company. I blocked his number so he couldn't call or text me again. His cell, his home, and his office. It was the only way I could think of to say goodbye and make it stick.

My head was finally winning.

And my heart was accepting defeat.

Chapter 64

I had not expected it to be so easy to block him. The woman on the other end of the line explained that if he called he would receive a message saying I was not accepting calls from his number. The result would be similar if he texted. It was perfect. The best part about the whole thing was that it blocked me from being able to contact him as well. Not that I thought I was going to make that mistake again, but it was nice knowing that if I tried, it would take a whole other level of steps before I would be able to follow through. Steps that I was fairly sure would slow me down and stop me if I found myself suffering from a bout of momentary insanity.

At this point, I *still* was not convinced we were completely over. But I told myself this was the best way to enforce that space I had been saying we needed for months. This was the best way to keep him from getting in touch with me when he was drunk and lonely, and the best way to keep me from caving when he came crawling back full of excuses. Because I was sure he would. By this point, I recognized the pattern.

In so many ways, this had become far too similar to the cycle of abuse for comfort. I had a degree in psychology. I knew how this worked. He would hurt me, turn on the charm and beg for forgiveness, and then he would hurt me again. Wash, rinse, repeat. All I knew for sure was that we were cycling faster and faster as time went on. The good periods became more abbreviated as the bad increased. He had never physically harmed me, nor did I believe for even a second that he ever would. But I knew enough to know that this was not healthy.

Never in my life had anyone given me the runaround like he had. Never in my life had anyone put me on such a roller coaster. And never in my life had I believed anyone to be so capable of completing me and breaking me all at once. I was not ready to say we were done. In the back of my mind, I still believed that eventually he would make this up to me. But I knew we needed time, and this was the only way I could think of to make that point crystal clear.

♌

The weeks passed, and we did not speak. No contact at all. I remained confident in my belief that this was for the best, that it was something I needed to do and something he needed to realize I was capable of doing.

But as time went on, the guilt started to creep in. I envisioned him calling, night after night, trying to see if I had unblocked him yet. I pictured him hurt and alone, knowing of course that he had caused this, but still … suddenly feeling even more lost and abandoned in not having me to reach out to. I started to feel guilty, both for having severed those ties and for having done so with no explanation at all.

I knew he would understand. That as soon as he realized what I had done, he would know it was because he had broken those promises to me. But the over-communicative side of me still lamented the fact that I had not given him an explanation before I shut the door. I began to wonder if how I had dealt with things had really been the right way, or if it was instead the coward's way.

With each passing day, I grew stronger in my resolve that we could not be together. Right now, I knew nothing good would come from us crossing those lines. As I felt more confident in that, I began to wonder if maybe I *could* be his friend. I cared about him. I found myself worrying about him more, wondering how he was doing and hating that I was not there to support him. But I did not do anything about it. I did not act on those worries. I just worried about him—and less and less about myself every day.

Three weeks after I blocked Nick, Amanda sent me an e-mail saying she and James were going out the following night after an event they had purchased tickets to weeks before. She said they wanted to see me and asked if I would be up for meeting them downtown.

I immediately responded with a resounding "yes." I loved hanging out with these two but had not been sure where my place was now that Nick and I were not speaking. Her inviting me out eliminated some of those conflicting feelings I felt about continuing the friendship. Not long after I responded though, she sent me a text.

> **Just a heads up, Nick will be with us too.**

My stomach flew up into my chest. It had been almost a month since we had last seen each other. Almost a month since we had spoken. While I was feeling stronger in my resolve every day, I still was not sure this was a good idea. On the other hand, I also kind of wanted to see him, to know how he was doing for myself.

I responded back that I would have to think about it. If anyone understood, it was Amanda. She had been through this mess with James years before. She got it. She even offered to ditch Nick once they got downtown, just so that she and James could see me. I told her she did not have to do that, and to just call me when they were heading out. I promised I would think about it.

And I did think about it. I thought about it *a lot*. I thought about it so much that for some reason that night, I decided to unblock his number. I was feeling so much guilt over having blocked him in the first place, and I no longer believed I needed that barrier between us. Even at the prospect of seeing him, I was strong in my resolve to keep the distance.

I did not call or text after unblocking him. I had no intention of doing either, and I assumed that even if he had been calling to see if I had removed the block, he had probably given up by now. I did not anticipate hearing from him any time soon. It was a fairly meaningless act. I was not sure what I expected to get out of it.

But I felt better, just in knowing that those lines were open once more.

It was a little before nine the next night when Amanda sent a text saying they were heading out to the bars. I was at dinner with a friend, but told her I would text as soon as I was done. Then I asked if they were still with him. She said they had actually gotten separated and she was not sure where he was, but explained he might pop back up at any time. Something about that made me more comfortable. I could go see them for a bit and then if he showed, make up some excuse and head home. I did not have to invest too much of myself into it.

As I was walking out of the restaurant, I sent her a text saying I was on my way. She immediately responded by telling me Nick had arrived. I started to question myself. I asked if she thought this was a horrible idea, but I knew the answer as soon as I hit "send." So I replied again that I was thinking I should probably just head home.

She sent me a series of texts after that. First asking if she should ask him, then saying that James wanted me to come, and finally replying that Nick was fine with it, he just did not want to give me any false impressions. She wrapped it all up by saying that she wanted me to come so that she could see my beautiful face.

Hold up.

Wait a minute.

Back the fuck up.

I couldn't breathe. He had said *what*? He did not want to give me any *false impressions*? *That* was what he was telling them? Like I was some sad little puppy who had been following him around and just could not get the hint? I almost threw up.

But I maintained my cool. James started in on the texting now, saying that they really wanted to see me and promising it would be a fun night for all. Meanwhile, I was fuming.

I responded with grace though. All smiley faces and exclamation points saying I just thought it was a bad idea, but I would love to see them if they wanted to grab breakfast in the morning. I was keeping the peace.

James replied again to say that Nick was totally good with my coming and that it would be fun, but before I could reply back ... I got a text from Nick himself:

Come out and meet us! I won't bite!

He did not know when he sent that text what it would signify, but for me it was the breaking point. Because in that moment, with that text, I realized he had no idea I had blocked his number. Which meant he had not tried to contact me at all over the last month. Not even once.

It had been almost four weeks since the night he had declined coming over to my house, citing depression. Four weeks. He had not called, texted, or e-mailed since. He had never shown up at my doorstep wanting to talk. So, presumably, he had not been thinking of me at all—even after fighting so hard to get another chance and after never before being able to go more than a week without contacting me, even when I had *asked* him to. After all the promises, all the "I love you's" and all the assurances that *I* was what he wanted. After he had sworn to me that he was ready. He had not attempted to contact me even once in four weeks to explain that he had been wrong.

And now he was telling James and Amanda that he did not want to give me any false impressions. Making me look (and feel) like an idiot, even though he had never bothered to give me the *right* impression in the first place.

Suddenly, the barrier broke. I texted both Amanda and James saying that while Nick may have been totally cool with my coming, I now realized that I was not. I let all maturity fall away when I wrote:

> I kind of want to punch him in his stupid asshole face.

I knew it probably made no sense to them. Up to this point, I had at least been *entertaining* the idea. I knew my dramatic shift would likely catch them both off guard. But I did not care. I was finally pissed. Really pissed.

Not 10 minutes later, I received another text from Nick:

> Thanks for calling me an asshole.

I could not contain myself as I replied:

> You are a fucking asshole. If you don't know that already, you're a fucking idiot too.

It was so unlike me, so out of the realm of normal for how I would typically have reacted. But I suddenly felt more clarity than I had in months.

He responded with:

> Wow!! Not the girl I know. Take care.

It only pissed me off more. It felt so manipulative. So contrived. So calculating. It felt like him telling me I was not allowed to have feelings about this. Like just because I had treated him with compassion and sympathy up to this point, he believed I should not be angry that he had so royally screwed me now. Not without tainting the image he had of me in his head.

I did not respond. I had no intention of responding. I just sat there in my car shaking, trying to calm down enough to drive home. As I was pulling into my garage, he called. I did not answer. Parking without crashing took all of my concentration. I was literally having a difficult time seeing straight. But he texted immediately after that:

Answer your phone.

It felt like an order now, coming from him, and I was in no mood for orders. But I also had more than a few things I was bursting at the seams to say. So when he called again, I answered.

"What the hell is going on?" he asked. He sounded genuinely confused, which I did not get. At all. Was he fucking kidding me? Was he delusional? Did he really have no idea what it was he had done to me?

I launched into an expletive-filled account of "what the hell" was going on. The main point being ... "You disappeared. You sucked me back in when I was doing just fine without you. You made all kinds of promises, and then you *disappeared*. What kind of a soulless fuck would do that?"

His argument against this rant was simply, "Well ... it's not like you called me either." At this point, he still had no idea I had blocked his number. No clue, because he had never bothered to call. All those weeks I had spent worrying about him, feeling guilty, and questioning my own moves. All those weeks .... And he had never once thought to pick up the phone.

But he was right. The phone lines worked both ways. As I explained to him though, what the hell was I supposed to do? I mean, really? When he pulled away, seemingly without explanation, it had only been a week since he had begged for my forgiveness, pleaded for another chance, and sworn that he was ready and would not hurt me again. A week. Was I really supposed to chase him down at that point? To call him when he was not calling me? Was I really supposed to be that sad little puppy dog who could not get a hint? The sad little puppy dog he was already apparently portraying me to be.

It had never in a million years occurred to me that he would not have called in all that time. That he would not have tried, even once, to make contact. But the fact that he hadn't, made it pretty clear no good ever would have come from my contacting him. I was suddenly infinitely grateful that I had been oblivious to this. Blocking his number had kept me from waiting night after night for a call that would never have come. Because I was sure that had I been waiting for that call, I eventually would have caved and called him myself. The absence of communication would have made me crazy enough to reach out, if only to ask what was going on. It turned out that blocking his number had been the best thing I ever could have done for myself. Even if he never realized I had done it.

But that did not stop me from yelling now. From calling him out on every misstep he made and from seething with a rage he had never before witnessed rising out of me. He had been right. In this moment, I *was not* the girl he knew. But that was his fault. He had broken that girl. And I was intent upon making him see that, intent upon using my words to show him *exactly* what he had done.

This was not who I was. Not anymore. Once upon a time, I had been an angry girl. As a teenager I had possessed a gift for spewing venom in every direction, including toward those I cared for the most. I had been skilled at conjuring up the words that could cut the deepest. But as an adult, I had worked hard to suppress that side of myself. To put people and their feelings ahead of my need to make others hurt as much as I did. Here I was now though, that girl fighting to get through, begging for just 30 seconds with Nick. Just 30 seconds to make him bleed the way he had made me.

There were so many things I could have said, so many words on the tip of my tongue that could have pummeled him. But I held back that assassin inside of me. I succumbed only to the yelling. There was a fierce coldness with which I addressed him and his excuses. The assassin was there, just at the edge, but I never fully allowed her to break through.

It had been years since she had come so close to the surface. I had worked to send her away, to let go of my anger and hurt. Even in the deepest darkest depths of infertility, I had fought to live my life with compassion and understanding, to live my life *without* her. And after years of thinking she was gone, he had managed to bring her back to the surface in only a matter of months.

For that, I almost hated him the most.

He began throwing out the now tired line that he was just "so messed up" right now and had no idea what it was he wanted. In fact, at one point he even shouted that back at me. "Do you really think I know what I want? Do you really think I know what I need?"

I did not care anymore. I no longer felt sorry for him. Not in the slightest.

"Do you think you're the only person in the world who has ever been hurt?" I screamed. "Do you think you're the only one who has ever felt this pain? Who has ever had to sit helplessly back as they watched the life they always believed they would have ripped away from them? Because you're wrong. You're dead wrong! *I've* been hurt! I've been hurt by the people in my life who were supposed to protect me! I've been hurt by life! I've been hurt by **you**! And I've lost the one thing I always believed I would have. The one thing I always truly wanted. But you don't see me using that as an excuse to hurt other people! You don't see me using my past as a reason to take others down!"

I was so angry I had almost stopped thinking before speaking. I was now just unleashing upon him so much pent up hurt from the past few months. I was shaking with my own disgust.

One of the things I had always admired about Nick was that while he could be selfish and insensitive, he was also almost always open to what I had to say when I called him on it. He was always quick to apologize and attempt to rectify the situation, typically something he had not even been aware he had done or said until I pointed it out. He was good about this. Good about dropping all defenses and looking himself in the mirror when directly confronted with his own misdeeds.

Not now though. Now he was fighting back, defensive right out the gate and barely listening to a word I was saying, even as I shouted those words for all to hear.

I could not really blame him. Gone were the days of my being rational and sensitive to his feelings. Gone were the times when I had carefully picked my words before approaching him. Now, with *her* fighting in the background to be released, I was attacking. With almost everything I had. It made sense that this would push him into defense mode.

So when I finished telling him that he was not the lone survivor of heartache, his immediate response was to yell back. "You have no idea what I've been through!" he hissed it, almost as if through his teeth. "You have no idea how it's made me feel! You may have been through plenty yourself, but that doesn't mean you understand what this is! What it means to love someone and to plan on spending the rest of your life with them, only to have them walk out on you! You have no idea!"

I knew I was not getting through to him, that I would need to tone it down, even just a little, if I was going to make the impression I needed to make. So, I took a deep breath and dialed back.

"I never said you didn't have a right to feel the way you feel," I continued, locking my jaw as I spoke in an attempt to keep the words from coming out as daggers. "I never said I was judging what you were going through. You're right—I have no idea what it is she really did to you. But I have been compassionate and understanding and *there* for you every step of the way. I have spent entire nights listening to you. I have never once blocked you out or told you that you didn't have a right to feel what you were feeling. I have worried about you, cared about you, and supported you with everything I've got. I know you're hurting, and I get that. I hate her for what she did to you. All I'm saying is that *nothing* she did gives you an excuse to turn around and do the same to me."

Suddenly, it was like a light bulb went off for him—a moment of clarity against the madness. "You're right," he said. "I'm so sorry. You're right."

Another moment passed before he continued, "I … I don't know what I'm supposed to do now."

I did not even have to think about my response. I had made my point. I had forced him to see. And that was all I cared about in this moment.

"You just keep doing whatever it is you've been doing," I replied. "It's obvious you haven't been wasting a whole lot of time thinking about me, so you might as well keep that up. I really don't care *what* you do anymore though … I'm done."

I told him goodbye, before promptly hanging up. Still shaking. Still seething. Still boiling red with hatred. I focused only on my last words to him.

"I'm done."

And for the first time, I knew …

I meant it.

Chapter 65

When we got off the phone that night, I was sure once more it was the last I would hear from him. So of course it was only a few hours before I received a text. Or rather, a series of texts which only served to show how truly drunk he was.

>Text 1: **You're right. I am an a**

>Text 2: **I am truly sorry for treating u like shit. U were really good to me and I took that for granite. Yes, I am a fucking asshole.**

>Text 3: **You didn't deserve this. I am really really sorry.**

>Text 4: **Goodbye Leah.**

They came in one right after another, at a little past two in the morning when the bars must have only just kicked him out. It was the last one that irked me the most. "Goodbye Leah." It just felt so dramatic.

I did not respond. I knew he was drunk. I figured if he really wanted to apologize—if he cared enough to give me what I actually deserved—he would call sober at some point over the next few days. But I was not counting these text messages sent in the middle of the night, when he was too intoxicated to properly spell, as apology enough for what he had done.

Not long after he sent those texts, he also sent an e-mail. It was full of pictures from a wedding he had just attended in Texas. We had discussed his going when he booked the ticket a few months before, so it was not something I was unaware of. But the only words he had written in this e-mail were, "Thought you might like to see these."

I could not figure it out. Why was he sending me these photos now? And what on earth made him suddenly think I wanted to see them?

OK, so I did, but that was not the point. The point was, it made no sense for him to send them to me while also apparently saying goodbye.

A snippet from the night before popped into my mind as I looked at those photos. It was a moment when—at the height of his defensiveness—he had said to me, "You're the one who chose to get involved with someone who was mentally unstable." It was one of those times when I would have laughed, if I had not already been so angry. Was he seriously blaming me? For *caring* about him? And had he honestly just called himself mentally unstable?

I could not argue though. The roller coaster he had put me on was a clear indication that things were not all right in his head. And he was correct. I *had* entered into this knowing full well that he was broken and that I may not be enough to heal him. No matter how many times it felt like he was depending on me to do just that.

But still, I cared about him. I tried to be a friend and support him as best I knew how. Yet he was turning around now and basically saying I *deserved* to get hurt because I had made the stupid choice to trust him in the first place. It reminded me a bit of that old fable. The one about the farmer who helps the snake, only to have the snake turn around and bite him as soon as it has gotten what it needs. The moral of the story? A snake is always a snake in the end.

I had never before seen Nick as a snake though. I had seen him as broken, wounded, and in need of time and patience, but never as a snake. I had never believed (even for a second) that he would take me or my feelings so monumentally for granted.

Or "for granite."

Over the next few weeks, I agonized over what had happened between us. I sifted through the details like an excavator, searching for what went wrong. Not because I wanted to fix things, but because I needed to understand. I needed to know how it was possible that after everything, he could so casually discard me and walk away. As if I were some whore he had met in a bar for a one-night stand, rather than the woman who had been there for him during the darkest period of his life.

I was determined to find the answers. To figure out which man he had been. The one I had loved and believed loved me back, or the one who had pummeled me with almost no concern for my well-being at all. I rationalized and defended. I grew angry and indignant. I turned it all into a joke, poking fun at myself and embracing the fact that I really had only ever been a rebound in the end. But I still could not figure it out.

And as hard as I tried, I still was not over it. Over what he had done, how callously he had treated me, and how easily he had walked away.

♌

In spite of my broken heart, time kept moving forward. Kara and Chad came to the end of their IVF cycle, and I was just as on edge for them as I had been for Leigh. The day before her transfer she was told that of the nine eggs which had originally been retrieved, only three had become embryos. Hearing her tears and the fear in her voice as she fretted over the outcome nearly broke me. I remembered being there. I remembered feeling the loss and fear that accompanied such a drastic drop in numbers. I also remembered how going through a cycle and coming out empty handed had hurt worse than anything else ever would.

I knew then beyond a shadow of a doubt that I never wanted to see anyone I cared about go through that, even if the alternative meant feeling that pang of jealousy when they succeeded where I had failed. I lost sleep as she went through her two-week wait, worrying more about her than I even remembered worrying about myself. So when she received those two pink lines, I was better prepared this time. The jealousy was still there, but the joy won out.

Of course, when Stephanie told me a few days later that she and her husband had just found out they were pregnant with their third, I was not quite as prepared. With Kara and Leigh, I had known they were trying and had been able to plan for the happy news. But Stephanie caught me off guard. So much so, that I was ashamed to admit I was a little angry at her in the days following the announcement. I could not even explain why. I knew I was being irrational, but the anger lingered even as I fought to will it away.

Eventually though, it did pass. I embraced this pregnancy just as I had the other two. This was an infertile woman's nightmare: three of my best friends pregnant at the same time, due within weeks of each other. But I was determined to make the best of it and to shower these important women in my life with love. No matter how much their happiness stood in stark contrast to my own sadness.

Still, I could not shake the voice in my head telling me that I was the only failure. Like somehow I had done something wrong which kept my own cycles from working. Or maybe I had not deserved it enough. Or was not careful enough. Or just plain had not tried hard enough. Even though I knew I had.

I understood that their being pregnant had nothing to do with my inability to accomplish the same, but it still brought to the surface all those old wounds once more. Physically, I had been doing amazingly well since surgery. I continued to improve month after month and had even started running—a hobby I had loved years before, but had never been able to fully embrace while dealing with the chronic pain of endometriosis. I was growing stronger and healthier by the day. I knew I should be rejoicing in that. But confronted with three pregnancies at once, I was forced once more to acknowledge the emptiness beneath my heart.

Now that Nick was gone, I had no choice but to turn my attention back to recovering from the scars of infertility; starting with a return to the therapist's chair. It was hard. It hurt. But I was surprised to find it was easier now than it had been — almost as if the reprieve from sadness had given me the strength to take it on once more. Because of that, I was able to be part of my friends' pregnancies alongside them without breaking. I knew that a year before, I never would have been able to say the same.

And as much as I hated to admit it, I knew I had Nick and the distance from infertility he had provided to thank for that.

Even if he had now left me with a whole new set of hurts to heal from.

Chapter 66

In the end, stepping back from the world of trying to conceive turned out to be exactly what I needed. I had been up against a wall I could not climb before Nick came along. The only choice had been to accept defeat—something I had never done before, and likely could not have done at all without him serving as the distraction he had been. It wound up being my saving grace, the piece that helped me to refocus and then rebuild.

I had always heard that people struggling to find love needed to first learn to love themselves. I started to realize the same could be said for women struggling to bring a child into this world. I had gotten lost first in infertility, and then in him. I now needed to learn to love my single and child-free life again. I had no idea what the future held, and even after everything, there was still a flicker of hope burning in the back of my head that I would one day see my dreams fulfilled. But there was no running away now. This was my life to live. Starting over meant embracing all the things I enjoyed about being on my own. I had to learn to love the life I was given, instead of mourning all that had been taken away.

I went through the normal stages after he disappeared from my life. Wishing we had never met or praying that I could change him. Questioning why he had done the things he did and why it was that he had not cared about me enough. Enough not to lie to me. Enough not to string me along. Or simply enough to attempt in some way to respect the friendship we had formed.

But when I was truly honest with myself, I knew he hadn't meant to hurt me. He had been careless with my feelings, but it had not been his intention. The timing was wrong. He was wrong. I was wrong. I could not control any of it. All I could do was forgive him. Even if he was not asking me to.

He had left me more wounded and unsure of myself than any man before him, but he entered into our relationship broken and confused from the start. I had known that. I did not want to spend the rest of my life hating him. I wanted him to heal—to find love and happiness. Even if the person he found it with was not me.

I wanted to be able to move on, knowing that he was alright.

I wanted to be able to move on.

He did what I had asked him (begged him) to do so many times before. He left me alone. He stayed away. And I never did find out if that was because he cared about me enough to do so, or if it was because he had never cared at all. I would never know if any of it had been real. But it did not matter. He was gone. We were over. It was one more lesson in learning to let go.

So I let go, and in doing so I made a list of all the things I wanted from my freedom. Unlike my friends who were married with children, I realized I was at the stage in my life where I could do anything. I had no one to answer to.

In embracing that freedom, I dated. A lot. A parade of boys and men who I had no interest in pursuing anything serious with – practicing with my training wheels once more, in the hopes of learning not to crash and burn the next time around. I also focused on myself and goals I had always wanted to complete, training first for a triathlon and then a half marathon. I booked a boudoir photo session, re-teaching myself to love the body that had so epically let me down. I traveled. I wrote a book, pursuing a dream I had always been too scared to chase. I welcomed my friends' babies into the world, loving on them as any doting auntie would. I threw myself into the friendships I was blessed to have. And I healed. Sometimes in fits and bursts, but I grew more whole every day.

It was a marathon rather than a sprint, but I truly was learning to be happy again. First with Nick by my side to help me ignore all the rest, and now without him – facing everything head on and alone. As a year went by and the healing commenced, I was able to acknowledge all the other paths to motherhood available to me. I was not sure which I would eventually take, but I knew my story was not over. And in the meantime, I was remembering what it meant to simply be in the moment.

I was finding my way once more.

Healing from infertility, and from him.

Months went by. Nick and I had no contact. Then as spring arrived, I started seeing him everywhere. Three or four times a week I would drive past him on the road. I could not take a lunch break anymore without being accosted by his face. Eventually we were thrust together by mutual friends, a group invite neither of us had declined. We smiled and were polite. We pretended we had no shared history, as if we had never been anything more to each other than passing acquaintances. It was the most closure I would ever get. He was not the man I had believed him to be. The one who would have given me more of an explanation or apology, simply because it was the right thing to do. I would never know if any of it had been real, but I was not going to spend the rest of my life lamenting this relationship, any more than I was going to spend it mourning my infertility.

I would move on. I would find the man who was right for me, the one who was capable of giving me as much as I could give him. Together we would map out the next steps. Whether it be adoption, or foster care, or taking the leap and trying again. We would face the rest as a team, me and this man who would be strong enough to deserve me.

Because as I healed, I finally realized:

There was so much more to my future than just being a single infertile female.

And my happy ending was waiting. I just needed to go out and find it.

Made in the USA
Lexington, KY
01 May 2019